PATERNOSTER BIBLICAL MONOGRAPHS

Theological Antinomy

A Biblical Theology of Paradox

Joel Arnold

To Sarah
with unquenched awe at the incomprehensible privilege
of spending our sojourn together.

καὶ ἔσονται οἱ δύο εἰς σάρκα μίαν.
τὸ μυστήριον τοῦτο μέγα ἐστίν·
ἐγὼ δὲ λέγω εἰς Χριστὸν καὶ εἰς τὴν ἐκκλησίαν.

Ephesians 5:31-32

'It takes logic to get from the biblical statements about Father, Son, and Spirit to a full-orbed doctrine of the Trinity—a doctrine that would appear to defy logic. In Theological Antinomy: A Biblical Theology of Paradox, Joel Arnold asks, "How can one defensibly set logic aside only moments after relying on it?" This is a question requiring a careful and biblical epistemology, and a willingness to stop answering a question where divine revelation does—and not to stop until it does. As with many thorny theological questions, you can reason in two directions: from the Bible to someone's views, or from someone's views back to their view of the Bible. Arnold is a guide I trust to take me in either direction. Even his clear posing of the relevant questions was a significant step forward for me.'

Mark Ward, Academic Editor, Lexham Press

'This impressive work by Joel Arnold breaks new ground on the issue of paradox in theological prolegomena, helpfully integrating exegetical, historical, and methodological perspectives. I consider it an excellent complement to my own work on paradox in Christian theology, since it addresses some of the very questions I had posed for further exploration. In addition, the application of Arnold's "complementarian analysis" to the ongoing debate over open theism brings a fresh perspective to the issues at stake.'

James Anderson, Associate Professor of Theology and Philosophy at Reformed Theological Seminary in Charlotte, NC

'Joel Arnold tackles one of the most challenging of theological phenomena—the presence of paradox in biblical revelation—with insight, finesse, and, at the same time, a firm adherence to the reliability and authority of that revelation . . . Arnold proposes a working model for accurately identifying and working through theological paradox as objectively as possible. Along the way, he demonstrates that the presence of paradox in Christian theology is not an embarrassment devoutly to be wished away, nor a dilemma demanding resolution, but a revelatory reality to be humbly received by faith and embraced with confidence in the Revealer's wisdom even—and especially—when we don't fully understand.'

Layton Talbert, Professor of Theology, Bob Jones University & Seminary (Greenville, SC)

Copyright © Joel Arnold 2020

26 25 24 23 22 21 20   7 6 5 4 3 2 1

First published 2019 by Paternoster

Paternoster is an imprint of Authentic Media
PO Box 6326, Bletchley, Milton Keynes MK1 9GG
authenticmedia.co.uk

The right of Joel Arnold to be identified as the Editor of this Work has been asserted by him in accordance with the Copyright, Designs and Patents Act 1988.

All rights reserved. No part of this publication may be reproduced, stored in a retrieval system, or transmitted, in any form or by any means, electronic, mechanical, photocopying, recording or otherwise, without the prior permission of the publisher or a license permitting restricted copying. In the UK such licenses are issued by the Copyright Licensing Agency, Barnards Inn, 86 Fetter Ln, London EC4A 1EN

British Library Cataloguing in Publication Data
A catalogue record for this book is available from the
British Library

ISBN 978-1-78893-030-7
978-1-78893-031-4 (e-book)

Unless otherwise noted, Scripture quotations are taken from: NIV (New International Version) © 1984, Anglicized

Typeset by Joel Arnold

ACKNOWLEDGEMENTS

If some things are best not understood beforehand, the scale of this project would be an excellent candidate. Entering into the process, I saw only the outlines of a distant horizon and failed to appreciate the terrain I would traverse to get there. Thankfully, I did not have to find my way alone. Dr. Gary Reimers, my committee chairman, provided encouragement and direction while Dr. Brian Hand patiently and unwaveringly challenged me to write more clearly. Dr. Bob Bell and Dr. Dan Olinger also gave of their time and expertise to improve the quality of the final result. Dr. Layton Talbert, my mentor, was the genesis of my topic, and the influence of his thought pervades this work as well as all of my theological reflections.

I also enjoyed the help of family and friends through this process. My parents, Bruce and Virginia Arnold, and my in-laws, Dan and Janice MacAvoy, were always quick to show interest and ever ready with encouragement. I could not be more blessed with parents and in-laws that love me, love God, and earnestly desire my faithful service to Him. Others gave their time to read the finished work and provided helpful feedback: Rose Mary Kelly, Rebecca Goernandt, David Lowry, Dan MacAvoy, Sarah Arnold, and Dani Carter. Brian Collins, a fellow-traveler on the same road, assisted me with helpful recommendations and stimulating conversations as we worked side by side.

Sarah Arnold, my wife, life's companion, and best friend, never complained or doubted God's leading in this endeavor, though it also required her constant personal sacrifice. It is one of my personal mysteries that God blessed me with such a perfect עֵזֶר כְּנֶגְדִּי—a helper fitting for me. I am so thankful that we walked this path together, and even more thankful that in God's gracious disposal we can anticipate many joyful miles ahead.

Finally, I can only offer overwhelmed praise to the one who rescued me when I hated Him, chastens me when I stray from Him, and will love me without end. Two years of reflection on the incomprehensible God leave me more aware of my childish understanding and more astounded at the preciousness of what He has revealed. *"To the One who is able to do immeasurably more than all which we are asking or understanding according to the power energizing us, to Him be the glory in the church and in Christ Jesus to all generations forever and ever, amen"* (Eph. 3:20-21).

CONTENTS

Acknowledgements	v
Introduction	1
Chapter 1: Understanding and Accounting for Paradox: Past and Present Views	6
Chapter 2: Understanding and Accounting for Paradox: Biblical Evaluation	18
Chapter 3: Encountering Paradox: Past Views	34
Chapter 4: Understanding and Accounting for Paradox: Theological Examples	58
Chapter 5: Understanding and Accounting for Paradox: Systematic Analysis	91
Chapter 6: Coexisting with Paradox: A Way Forward	113
Chapter 7: General Application	138
Chapter 8: Specific Application to Open Theism	153
Conclusion	170
Bibliography	182

Introduction

Whatever other components the *imago Dei* may entail, humanity's ability to know truth and reason from it to other truths certainly reflects at least one aspect of the divine nature. In fact, our knowledge as an analogue of the divine offers the best foundation for a truly Christian epistemology. Human beings innately assume the logical structure of truth, but this structure is a function of God's nature and his own thinking. Most remarkable in this respect is our capacity to reason about the character and works of God—systematic theology. In some way, then, the assumed thought patterns of created humanity manifest the structure and interrelationship of God's own being.

Yet just as clearly, humanity's ability to know is limited in at least two ways—by his natural, constitutional limitations and by his fallenness. The ontological divide between Creator and creature necessarily limits our ability to comprehend the nature of God. When sin marred the *imago Dei* at the fall, it exacerbated our noetic limitations. Throughout the history of human thought subsequent to the fall, humankind has continually co-opted reasoning to suppress revealed truth. These dual limitations of human knowledge conspire so that in their depravity humankind forgets that they are creatures and seeks to build an intellectual tower to heaven itself.[1]

Theologians and biblical exegetes are far from immune to natural human limitations or the noetic effects of the fall. On the contrary, there could hardly be an area of human discourse more vulnerable to fallen reasoning than theology and interpretation. This fact leaves theologians in a quandary—when should they trust their reasoning, and when must they limit it in deference to revelation? By necessity and biblical example, theologians must reason about God's nature, but on the same bases, they must limit their reasoning and accept the paradoxical. How can theological reasoning and theological paradox coexist? How can theologians and biblical exegetes confidently discriminate between valid deduction and true but irreconcilable propositions? How can theology proceed in a way that reflects the renewed *imago Dei* rather than the fall?

---

[1] 1 Corinthians 1:18-25 and Romans 1:18-20 demonstrate both sides of humanity's intellectual nature. On the one hand, "what is known of God is evident within them," but on the other hand, people "suppress the truth in unrighteousness." Unless otherwise noted, all translations are the author's own.

Need for this Study

Most questions of hermeneutics or prolegomena are unavoidable—even those who ignore the problem still assume a position by default. Similarly, apart from completely denying either the existence of paradox or any role for logic, it is impossible to avoid relying on some type of discriminating criteria between the two. The problem is that though every theologian relies on these criteria, most do so by assumption and without self-critical analysis, resulting in subjectivity and inconsistency. The same problems are paradoxical for some and logically correlated by others because theologians use contrary definitions of biblical paradox, and naturally, such differences result in polemical conflict. As writers attack one another regarding what should be properly understood as paradoxical, they appeal to no set of explicit, objective criteria; rather, their definitions of paradox seem to be controlled by their polemical agendas and theological conclusions.[2]

These difficulties are evident even in established orthodoxy. With the doctrine of the Trinity, for example, orthodox theologians rightly demonstrate that God is one (Deut. 6:4-5), that he exists in three persons (i.e., that each of the three is distinct and personal—Matt. 5:16-17), and that each of the three persons is fully God (John 1:1-2; Acts 5:3-4). Though the reasoning is clear, Scripture never states most of these propositions in this form, and therefore the conclusion does involve some amount of reasoning. Most theologians suggest that the seemingly contradictory truths must be held in tension as a paradox. This conclusion is exactly as it should be. Nevertheless, how can theologians correlate the doctrine of the Trinity with logic but depend on paradox to defend it? How is reasoning used in

---

[2] In *Evangelism and the Sovereignty of God*, J.I. Packer defines antinomy as an apparent contradiction or incompatibility between two truths (Downers Grove: InterVarsity, 2008), 25-29. Robert Peterson and Michael Williams, *Why I Am Not an Arminian* (Downers Grove: InterVarsity, 2004), 159-60, similarly argue for compatibilism because it allows for mystery and they attack Arminianism for its rationalism. R.C. Sproul, *Chosen by God* (Wheaton: Tyndale, 1986), 43-47, seeks to demonstrate that there is no real conflict between sovereignty and freedom. His discussion distinguishes contradiction, paradox, and mystery, and faults Packer for his use of antinomy. Paul Helm, *The Providence of God* (Downers Grove: InterVarsity, 1994), 65-66, also finds fault with Packer's appeal to antinomy, since this position provides no criteria for distinguishing apparent contradictions from genuine logical inconsistencies. From an Arminian standpoint, Jerry Walls sharply attacks Packer for his definition of antinomy and offers his own definition—see Jerry L. Walls and Joseph R. Dongell, *Why I Am Not a Calvinist* (Downers Grove: InterVarsity, 2004), 154-59. Each position differs sharply in its presentation of mystery, but none appeals to any objective and consistent basis.

one step but set aside in the next, and why is logic useful in the approach to a paradox and not after? How can one defensibly set logic aside only moments after relying on it? The doctrine of the Trinity is certainly a necessary foundation of orthodoxy, but while believing it, one struggles to give a methodological account for it.

Given that both logic and paradox necessarily exist within theology and that they are mutually exclusive by definition, it is necessary to find some method for limiting them. Methodological controls must discriminate the legitimate role of logic from theological paradox, and these controls must be both objective and grounded on legitimate bases. This study posits that it is both possible and necessary to do so.

Building on these guidelines, the need is much more pragmatic—a method for working with paradox in theology. This method must be able to identify paradox, distinguishing it from harmonizable propositions on the one hand and full contradiction on the other. In the words of Michael Goulder, it is "important to recognize that some paradoxes are apparent contradictions, while others are apparent nonsense".[3] This model must be practicable, eliminating illegitimate formulations while accurately maintaining biblical truth. Since every proposition is part of a broader epistemic context, this model must also handle logical inferences— objectively controlling what conclusions theologians can draw from propositions on either side of the tension.

Definition of Terms

In much of the theological literature, three terms are used synonymously—*mystery*, *paradox*, and *antinomy*.[4] *Mystery* is the standard translation for musth/rion in the NT, where it refers to that which was or is unknown rather than that which appears to be contradictory. Throughout this study musth/rion will designate the NT or Pauline sense of mystery, and *mystery* will be used synonymously with the other two terms. *Paradox* often refers to the literary technique of stating truths in an apparently contradictory format, such as "whoever should lose his life for my sake will find it" (Matt. 16:25).[5] But *paradox* can also refer to an

---

[3] Michael Goulder, "Paradox and Mystification," in *Is the Doctrine of the Incarnation Logically Coherent?* (Grand Rapids: Eerdmans, 1979), 53.

[4] Mark A. Snoberger, "Engaging the Enemy . . . But on Whose Terms? An Assessment of Responses to the Charge of Anti-Intellectualism," *DBSJ* 8 (Fall 2003): 78. Also, David Basinger, "Biblical Paradox: Does Revelation Challenge Logic?," *JETS* 30.2 (June 1987): 205; Kenneth Boa, *God, I Don't Understand* (Colorado Springs: Victor, 2007), 23-24.

[5] J.I. Packer, *Evangelism*, 25-29, distinguishes between paradox and antinomy, describing the former in this literary sense. R.C. Sproul, *The Mystery of the Holy*

epistemological category—two tenets that are separately true but also appear to contradict one another.[6] *Antinomy* has a more complex history because of its history in the philosophy of Immanuel Kant. In keeping with his ambition to describe the limits of science and philosophy, Kant used *antinomy* for logical conundrums reached by invalidly applying phenomenal categories to noumenal realities. Still, *antinomy* has been broadly used for "a contradiction between conclusions which seem equally logical, reasonable, or necessary; a paradox; intellectual contradictoriness".[7] Therefore, this work will use all three terms synonymously to refer to theological truths that appear to be contradictory and for which no resolution is presently possible.[8]

The law of non-contradiction states that no statement can be both true and false at the same time and in the same way. A *contradiction* is any proposition that violates this rule, typically by proposing two truths that are directly irresolvable. Most theologians regard *contradiction* as an impossible and theologically unacceptable epistemological status and on this basis typically distinguish it from *paradox*. This distinction must be substantiated, but for now, *contradiction* will not be used synonymously with *paradox* or its related terms. Instead, it will be used in its more standard meaning—two propositions which are incommensurable and therefore cannot both be true within the normal constraints of logic. Many writers also distinguish between *apparent contradictions* and *full* or *genuine contradictions*. When not otherwise qualified, *contradiction* will refer to the latter category—truths that are contradictory even in the mind of God.

Spirit (Wheaton: Tyndale, 1994), 55-59, also distinguishes paradox, mystery, and atinomy, content to call the Incarnation and Trinity only "mysteries," and strongly qualifying that they do not have any contradictory content.

[6] Grudem, *Systematic Theology*, 256. William H. Austin, "Complementarity and Theological Paradox," *Zygon* (December 1967): 367.

[7] D.A. Carson, "How Can We Reconcile the Love and the Transcendent Sovereignty of God?" in *God Under Fire: Modern Scholarship Reinvents God* (Grand Rapids: Zondervan, 2002), 295-97, clarifies Kant's use of the term in comparison to the concept of biblical tensions—*theological antinomy* is "an apparent contradiction that is not in fact real."

[8] Some have drawn various distinctions among these terms—particularly between mystery and paradox, though there has been no emerging agreement about the terms. For instance, John Sanders, *The God Who Risks: A Theology of Providence* (Downers Grove: InterVarsity, 1998), 35, defines a paradox as literary—something which goes against our normal method of expression. For him, mystery is an unknown, or something that we cannot fully comprehend; antinomies are logical conflicts. Because a number of writers and complementarians in particular use the terms interchangeably, it is legitimate to do so here.

Introduction

Finally, *biblical theology* and *systematic theology* are more challenging to define. *Biblical theology* has become an exceedingly flexible term in the 200 years of its usage, but will be used in this study more specifically of the attempt to derive correlated propositions from the interpreted text with a minimum of inter-propositional analysis. *Systematic theology*, on the other hand, gives much greater concern to logical relationships between propositions. *Systematic theology* also extrapolates from known propositions to questions Scripture does not directly discuss.[9]

The Structure of this Study

How then to move forward? Chapter 1 describes and analyzes the major views of paradox, giving particular attention to the three that fall within orthodoxy. The following three chapters seek to evaluate these views on the basis of the biblical data (chapter 2), church history (chapter 3) and systematic theology (chapter 4) in order to gain perspective on the present theological milieu. Chapter 4 also identifies five major examples of paradox in Christian theology and briefly discusses the major attempts to resolve them. The examples discussed are the Trinity, the hypostatic union, the problem of evil, the sovereignty of God with human responsibility, and the infinity of God (God in time; God and dimensional space). Chapter 5 analyzes the concept of paradox itself, offering conceptual tools for how it relates to logic. These concepts are foundational for the analytical model central to a theology of paradox. Chapter 6 builds that model, suggesting a theological process for distinguishing between paradox and contradiction, and outlining how the model is useful. This chapter also discusses the issue of implications drawn from paradox. Chapter 7 returns to the five major examples of paradox and applies this new model to each while chapter 8 illustrates the process with a specific example—open theism. Together, these chapters seek to demonstrate that the proposed model is practicable and offers real analytical value over other possible models for paradox. The final chapter points out areas for further study and suggests practical implications from a biblical theology of paradox.

---

[9] Since some amount of reasoning is necessary for both, it is evident that the difference between *biblical* and *systematic theology* is not in absolute epistemological categories. Rather, the distinction involves the degree of methodological emphasis on logic.

CHAPTER 2

Understanding and Accounting for Paradox: Biblical Evaluation

As wheels in a complicated machine may move in opposite directions and yet subserve one common end, so may truths *apparently opposite* be perfectly reconcilable with each other, and equally subserve the purposes of God. . . . The author feels it impossible to repeat too often, or avow too distinctly, that it is an invariable rule with him to endeavour to give to every portion of the Word of God its full and proper force, without considering one moment what scheme it favours, or whose system it is likely to advance. Of this he is sure, that there is not a decided Calvinist or Arminian in the world, who equally approves of the whole of Scripture . . . who, if he had been in the company of St. Paul whilst he was writing his different Epistles, would not have recommended him to alter one or other of his expressions.[1]

With such widely varying perspectives on paradox, what is the best way to evaluate them? Scripture does not explicitly address the finer points of distinction between views, but biblical data exists in two categories: (1) biblical statements that relate in some way to paradox itself, and (2) instances or examples of paradox that arise from biblical statements.[2] The second category appears in chapter 4. This chapter will discuss the first (biblical statements about epistemology), highlighting points of continuity and discontinuity between God's thinking and our own. All of these observations can then be used to assess the three conservative perspectives on paradox.

Continuity between Divine and Human Thinking

Scripture's teaching about paradox begins with the nature of God, particularly in comparison to the nature of human beings. God's thinking contains logic in a form

---

[1] Charles Simeon, *Expository Outlines on the Whole Bible* (Grand Rapids: Baker, 1988), 1:xxiii.

[2] Another way of describing these categories might be the distinction between biblical and systematic theology. Using biblical theology, it is possible to correlate a number of statements about God's knowledge and how it relates to human understanding. Systematic theology, on the other hand, exposes logical tensions in the process of correlating those doctrinal propositions with each other.

that shares certain characteristics with human reasoning.[3] Since Scripture is divine revelation and self-attesting through the witness of the Spirit, God could have simply made raw assertions without logical connections.[4] But the fact that he chose to communicate so much of his revelation through reasoning emphasizes the continuity between his reasoning and our own. In Romans, Paul uses prepositions or inferential conjunctions to draw explicitly logical conclusions at least 37 times.[5] For instance, Romans 4:9-12 moves through a series of logical inferences: (1) Abraham was justified when he believed; (2) Abraham believed while uncircumcised; (3) Therefore, justification cannot be dependent on circumcision; (4) Abraham's justification is paradigmatic for all believers; (5) therefore, all believers are justified by faith, independent of circumcision. Besides the fourth proposition, which could almost have been assumed, this entire progression of thought derives from the timing of Abraham's faith. Similarly, Isaiah argues from the lesser to the greater (49:14-15), moves from God's creative act to his rights of ownership over all (45:8-12), and proves that Yahweh is the true God because he alone can predict the future (41:21-26).

There could be no more authoritative teaching ministry than that of Jesus, but though he made strong assertions based on his own authority, he also supported his teachings with reasoning. Jesus assured his listeners of God's care with an argument from the lesser to the greater: (1) God cares for the ravens; (2) people are more important than birds; (3) therefore, God will take care of his people (Luke 12:24). Jesus also used much more complex logical sequences with categorical and disjunctive syllogisms. His reasoning in John 8:39-47 is structured cyclically but can be stated in linear form: (1) Those who are from God listen to the truth (v. 47), and those who do not listen to the truth are of the devil (v. 44). (2) I am speaking

---

[3] Gordon H. Clark, *Logic* (Unicoi, Tenn.: The Trinity Foundation, 1998), 119, identifies Romans 4:2 as an enthymematic hypothetical destructive syllogism, Romans 5:13 as a hypothetical constructive syllogism, and 1 Corinthians 15:15-18 as a sorites. John M. Frame offers a helpful survey of logic's critical role in Scripture in both "Logic," in *Dictionary for Theological Interpretation of Scripture*, ed. Kevin J. Vanhoozer, 462-64 (Grand Rapids: Baker, 2005), and *The Doctrine of the Knowledge of God* (Phillipsburg, N.J.: P&R, 1987), 251-54.

[4] One could aver that reasoning adds apologetic credibility to biblical arguments, and that is certainly the case. But Scripture either assumes the most foundational components of the biblical worldview or grounds them on minimal reasoning. The superstructure of biblical revelation is the area that contains the most logical deductions. This is natural, since all human discourse necessarily rests on a foundation of presupposition. Since the most foundational components of Christian theology are simply asserted or assumed, the rest of biblical truth could have been given in a similar way. In any case, the point is not why God chose to use reasoning so much as the fact that Scripture could still be a legitimate revelation of truth with or without reasoning. The ultimate ground of biblical veracity is the authority of God.

[5] These include ou]n (18x), a1ra ou]n (5x), dio/ (6x), w3ste (3x), dia\ tou=to (3x), dio/ti (1x), and a1ra (1x).

the truth from God (v. 40). (3) You are not hearing my words (v. 43). (4) Therefore, you are not from God (v. 47) and are of the devil (v. 44).[6]

Clearly, God speaks to us using logical constructions, and therefore it is fully acceptable for us to derive logical inferences from God's revelation. In other words, God's logic has enough continuity with ours that reasoning works in reverse—we can draw logical inferences about God. In Genesis 22, Abraham reasons that Isaac must remain alive since God promised that there would be a continuing seed through Isaac (Heb. 11:17-19). Later, Abraham reasons from God's promise of descendants that God will provide a wife for Isaac (Gen. 24:7). In fact, this continuity is so strong that people can appeal to God and make arguments based on the logic they share. In Genesis 18:25, Abraham appeals to the angel of the Lord with the assumption that the Judge of all the earth will act justly.[7] Moses' reasoning with God in Exodus 32:11-14 is shocking. Moses responds to God's intention to destroy the nation of Israel with several arguments: (1) if the people are destroyed, the Egyptians will dishonor Yahweh's name (v. 12). (2) Yahweh promised the patriarchs that their seed would multiply and possess the land (v. 13). Moses' logical appeal is effective, and Yahweh turns from what he intended to do as a result.[8]

Scripture takes this one step further when God rebukes people for failing to draw logical conclusions from revelation. In Mark 12:24-27, Jesus criticized religious leaders for failing to infer the resurrection from Exodus 3:6—"I am the God of Abraham and the God of Isaac and the God of Jacob." In fact, their failure showed that they did "not know the Scriptures nor the power of God" (Mark 12:24) and was tantamount to not having read Exodus 3:6 at all (Mark 12:26).[9] Within the framework of a parable, the lazy slave is rebuked and punished for inferring a wrong conclusion from what he assumed about his master's character (Luke 19:20-27). In this case the servant's logic was wrong in both its premises and deduction,

---

[6] An additional disjunctive enthymeme (an unstated premise) gives a redundant way of inferring the same conclusions: "an individual is either from God or from the devil". Jesus' argument is logically complex in that there are multiple ways for the logic to proceed. Furthermore, there is a sense in which the logic can also flow backwards: the fact that the religious leaders will not listen to Jesus' words proves that he is speaking the truth. Ultimately the whole chain holds together as an explanation for how Jesus can be speaking the truth while the religious leaders are rejecting his words.

[7] The reasoning could be simplified as follows:
(1) The judge of all the earth will do right.
(2) To slay the righteous with the wicked would not be right.
(3) Therefore, the judge of all the earth will not slay the righteous with the wicked.

[8] None of Moses' reasons were new considerations to God, since he is omniscient. Even aggressive attempts to limit God's knowledge (such as open theism) grant that he has enough wisdom to think of these considerations. Therefore, this response is anthropomorphic on some level. But still, the text indicates that God responds to human appeals and even to the force of logic within those appeals.

[9] William L. Lane offers a helpful explanation of the difficult problem surrounding the verb in Exodus 3:6 in *The Gospel of Mark* (Grand Rapids: Eerdmans, 1974), 428-30; or see R.T. France, *The Gospel of Mark* (Grand Rapids: Eerdmans, 2002), 471-72.

but his flawed reasoning still manifests the underlying problem in his heart. Scripture expects people to reason appropriately, and failures to do so often represent underlying unbelief.

Discontinuity between Divine and Human Thinking

As much as Scripture assumes continuity between God's logic and our own, it never directly points out this fact. Scripture does, however, repeatedly emphasize the opposing truth: though in many points God's thinking is continuous with man's, there are others where it is not.[10] This appears in a number of passages.

Musth/rion

The NT word for "mystery," musth/rion, occurs 28 times, of which 21 are in Paul's epistles.[11] The meaning of musth/rion differs from paradox as it has been used in this dissertation: while paradox involves theological truths that appear to be contradictory and for which no resolution is presently possible, Paul uses musth/rion for truths that could not be known in the OT era but that have since been revealed. This has clear precedent in Jesus' usage, where the disciples have been given "the mystery of the kingdom of God, but to those who are without everything is in parables" (Mark 4:11; Luke 8:10). Paul develops this much more, "telling" (1 Cor. 15:51), "speaking" (1 Cor. 2:7; Col. 4:3), "making known" (Col. 1:27), and "manifesting" OT musth/ria (Col. 1:26). Often, a musth/rion is an extension of truths that had already been revealed: a further step in progressive revelation (Rom. 16:25-26).[12] In either case a musth/rion always imparts

---

[10] This follows the broader theological pattern of God's immanence and transcendence. Though it is disastrous to forget the fact that people are created in God's image (Gen. 9:6), it is equally disastrous to assume that God is the same as humanity in every respect (Ps. 50:21). Regarding the intellect, Scripture assumes both significant similarity and dissimilarity between our minds and God's.

[11] The literature on this subject is vast and the most thorough treatment is certainly G.K. Beale, Benjamin Glad, *Hidden But Now Revealed* (Downers Grove: Intervarsity, 2014). Other useful articles and monographs include C.F.D. Moule, "Mystery," in *Interpreter's Dictionary of the Bible*, ed. George A. Buttrick (Nashville: Abingdon, 1962), 3:479–81; G. Bornkamm, "Musth=rion, mue/w," in *Theological Dictionary of the New Testament*, vol. 4 (1967), 802–28; Raymond E. Brown, *The Semitic Background of the Term "Mystery" in the New Testament* (Philadelphia: Fortress, 1968); Chrys C. Caragounis, *The Ephesian Mysterion: Meaning and Content* (Lund, Sweden: Gleerup, 1977); A.E. Harvey, "The Use of Mystery Language in the Bible," *Journal of Theological Studies* 31 (1980): 320–26; Markus N.A. Bockmuehl, *Revelation and Mystery* (Tübingen: Mohr, 1990), H. Krämer, "musth-rion," in *Exegetical Dictionary of the New Testament*, 2:446–49; and Peter T. O'Brien, "Mystery," in *Dictionary of Paul and His Letters*, 621–23.

[12] In Romans 16:25-26, the musth/rion that has now been revealed is the gospel and the preaching of Jesus Christ. Clearly both of these truths are present in the OT (Isa. 11:1-10; 53; c.f. Luke 24:27). In fact, though this mystery was kept secret (v. 25), it is "now being manifested through the writings of the prophets" (v. 26).

information that was previously unknown to men or hidden by God (Rom. 16:25; 1 Cor. 2:7; Eph. 3:3-5, 9; Col. 1:26).[13]

Does musth/rion bear any significance for the subject of paradox? Clearly musth/rion is not the same as paradox, but perhaps paradox for NT believers might be analogous to musth/rion for believers in the OT? Perhaps musth/rion provides a window into how believers in the past regarded propositions they could not understand—propositions we now understand more fully.[14] For instance, would Isaiah have struggled to answer how a child could be born who would be the Mighty God (Isa. 9:6), or how the Messiah could die (Isa. 53:7-9) and yet reign eternally (Isa. 9:7)?[15] NT believers have much more sufficient answers to these and other questions that even the writers of the OT could not explain (1 Pet. 1:10-11). Still, the NT does not answer every question exhaustively. In fact, some of the confusions that the OT never answered were only carried a step further. For instance, the NT is much clearer in its revelation about the Incarnation, but at the core the logical conflict is as troubling as it would have been to Isaiah. We can describe Isaiah 9:6 with the doctrine of the theanthropic person, but we still cannot fully explain how one person can be both human and divine or how these natures can coexist without contradiction.

The direct connection between musth/rion and paradox is inconclusive, but a proper understanding of the NT musth/rion might provide real and significant insight on paradox. NT believers can extrapolate from their received knowledge of

---

[13] 1 Corinthians 2:7, Ephesians 3:9, and Colossians 1:26 use the perfect passive of a0pokru/ptw, "to keep secret" (BDAG—c.f. Luke 10:21), which could almost imply that the information would have been accessible to human investigation had God not hidden it. But this presses the lexical meaning too far (2 Kgs. 4:27). It is even clearer that humanity could not have reasoned to these truths by itself from several other considerations: (1) the context of the passages (1 Cor. 2:9-16; Eph. 3:5), (2) other NT passages that further describe these truths (Rom. 11:25 with 33-34; Eph. 3:8), and (3) passages describing more specifics of how God has veiled his truth (Eccl. 3:11; Isa. 6:9-10; Matt. 13:12-15; Rom. 1:18-22).

Romans 16:25 uses siga/w (Louw and Nida 33.121: "to keep quiet, with the implication of preserving something which is secret") which may carry a connotation of maintaining silence against one's desire (AV: "hold one's peace" in Luke 19:39 or "hold one's tongue" in Sir. 13:23). Note also 1 Maccabees 11:5; Sirach 20:7; Psalm 32:3; 39:2; 50:21; Acts 15:12 and the only other Pauline instances in 1 Corinthians 14:28, 30, 34. If this is correct, it would imply that God desired to reveal these truths at the proper time.

[14] Naturally, paradox is not what Paul has in mind when he refers to musth/ria. The question is whether these topics of progressive revelation may have included some theological tensions in previous, limited revelation. For many instances of musth/rion, it is quite evident that paradoxical content was never involved in the OT revelation (Rom. 16:25-27; 1 Cor. 15:51; Eph. 6:19). In other cases it seems much more plausible that these dynamics may have been at work. 1 Timothy 3:17 is the clearest example, where Paul identifies the Incarnation as a musth/rion. This passage even specifies the truth that God was revealed in the flesh—a point which OT believers would have naturally struggled to integrate logically.

[15] Jesus used one of these OT paradoxes to humiliate and silence his questioners in Matthew 22:41-46.

OT musth/ria and remember that just as God had plans that OT believers knew nothing of, he has other purposes that are still unrevealed. This yields several conclusions for paradox: (1) The questions that are paradoxical in the present could be the subject of future, progressive revelation.[16] (2) Even if progressive revelation does give further explanation, there is no guarantee that all problems will be resolved and all questions answered. In fact, God's infinity and the doctrine of his incomprehensibility suggest the opposite. (3) Like the writers of the OT, NT believers should recognize that investigative effort will not unlock the truths that God has not yet revealed (1 Pet. 1:10).

Romans 11:33-34

Romans 11:25-36 explains a musth/rion (v. 25) that had been unknown for OT believers. Specifically, Paul explains the counter-intuitive truth that the hardening of the Jews is part of God's plan for universal salvation (v. 25, 32). Jewish unbelief resulted in Gentile salvation for the ultimate purpose of bringing Jews and Gentiles within God's salvific plan. Paul teaches that because of the depth of God's wisdom and knowledge, no one has known his mind, his judgments are unsearchable and his ways are unfathomable (Rom. 11:33-34). Each of these descriptions implies a knower or investigator that is external to God and denies the possibility that such a knower could comprehensively apprehend God's thoughts. *Depth* (ba/qoj) refers to something "so remote that it is difficult to assess".[17] *Unsearchable* (a0nexerau/nhtoj) negates a verb that speaks of making "a careful or thorough effort to learn something" (BDAG). Unfathomable (a0necixni/astoj) negates a verb meaning to track out or thoroughly investigate (c. f. Job 5:27; 10:6).[18] No one "has known the mind of the Lord."[19] In other words, every attempt to know God

---

[16] Though the canon of Scripture is a completed whole, believers have every expectation of learning about God in a glorified state for all eternity.

[17] BDAG. Of course, this is a somewhat metaphorical extension of ba/qoj, which can refer to a literal pit or unattainable depth (Jonah 2:4; Rom. 8:39). The point is that God's thoughts are unattainable (1 Cor. 2:10).

[18] According to Newman and Nida, "the first of these terms [a0nexerau/nhtoj] describes something that cannot be found by searching for it, while the other [a0necixni/astoj] suggests footprints that cannot be tracked down." Barklay M. Newman and Eugene A. Nida, *A Translator's Handbook on Paul's Letter to the Romans* (New York: United Bible Societies, 1973), 230. "Unfathomable" (a0necixni/astoj) also occurs in Ephesians 3:8 regarding Paul's commission "to preach to the Gentiles the good news of the unfathomable riches of Christ." In a similar construction he prays for believers "to know the love of Christ that exceeds knowledge" (Eph. 3:19). In both cases the fact that believers know something of these truths cannot negate the lexical meaning of "unfathomable" or "exceeding knowledge." An accurate interpretation of these passages must maintain both the doctrine of God's knowability and his incomprehensibility.

[19] The reference is to knowing God's mind exhaustively or as he himself knows his own thoughts. As such, this passage shares much in common with 1 Corinthians 2:10-16—the other quotation of Isaiah 40:13. (The same emphasis appears with ba/qoj in Rom. 11:33

exhaustively will be a failure.[20] In fact, the exclamation of vv. 33-36 arises from Paul's teaching about the musth/rion God has recently revealed. Paul wants to insure that NT believers are no longer ignorant of a fact that OT believers could not know (v. 25). How does Paul's exposition of a recently unknown truth lead him to revel in God's inscrutability? As discussed with the Pauline musth/rion, the fact that God had purposes that OT believers knew nothing of should remind us of his immensity and incomprehensibility. But Romans 11:33-34 also teaches that even as believers receive new and clearer revelation, there are still elements that remain mysterious.[21]

In summary, this passage teaches that (1) any attempt to understand God exhaustively is futile. (2) Truths that were previously unknown are now revealed for all believers to understand. (3) Even though additional truths have been revealed, elements remain that are inscrutable for human minds.

Deuteronomy 29:29

Moses' charge to Israel posits a clear distinction between the revealed and the unrevealed—a distinction that dictates the recipient's response.[22] Moses places responsibility on the nation for how they respond to both. Structurally, the verse could be broken into two contrasting clauses.

Table 2.1 The Structure of Deuteronomy 29:29

Theological Reality	Applied Result	Human Response
God has hidden certain truths. →	These truths are his. →	(Leave them to him.)
God has revealed certain truths. →	These truths are ours. →	Do all the words of this law.

The hortatory force of the passage is certainly in the second clause. The fact that some things have not been revealed serves to highlight the importance of obeying the instructions that have been given. But this also works in reverse: there is much to obey that has been revealed; therefore God's people should not concern

---

and 1 Cor. 2:10.) In both passages there are truths that have been revealed, but internal, comprehensive knowledge of God's thoughts belongs to him alone.

[20] It is clear from other texts that God is knowable (Jer. 9:23-24; John 17:3; 1 John 5:20). Therefore, one must understand these statements in the sense that God cannot be known *comprehensively* or *exhaustively*.

[21] Illustratively, we might think of God's immensity as a mountain peak that disappears into the clouds. Even when one layer of clouds clears, exposing a greater portion of the peak, more of the mountain is still shrouded—in this case, infinitely more.

[22] The niphal participle of rts refers simply to things that have been hidden. As a passive, it does not specify the semantic subject, but the only meaningful subject would be Yahweh. As such, it is legitimate to conclude that God has intentionally hidden certain truths from people (c.f. Rev. 10:4).

themselves with what is unrevealed. It would be unbiblical to say that God's people must never ask questions or ponder information beyond revelation (1 Pet. 1:10-11), but at a minimum, Deuteronomy 29:29 warns against any preoccupation with questions beyond the scope of revelation, distracting from commands that have been revealed (c.f. 1 Tim. 6:4, 20; Titus 3:9).

This response is necessary because the boundaries of revelation are intentional. The hidden things are not merely the limitations of a finite revelation, as though an infinite book would have been better if it could only be manageable in a limited world. Rather, certain things are hidden in keeping with God's purposes. Like the rests in music or the empty space in a painting, the undisclosed things are a part of God's revelation right along with the truths that are disclosed. Given the profitability, perspicuity and sufficiency of Scripture, if God did not reveal an aspect of doctrine, he had a reason for doing so. Human attempts to help God finish the job are doomed to failure before they start.

In summary, this passage teaches that (1) there are hidden matters that are not humanity's rightful preoccupation. (2) God's intentions for revelation include the things that he has chosen not to reveal. (3) That which is unrevealed highlights our responsibility to obey what has been revealed.

Job 11:7-9; 26:14; 42:3-4

The book of Job details the crisis of one man's faith as he wrestles from a simple to a much more accurate understanding of his relationship with God. From the onset of his suffering, Job is confused by what appear to be galling contradictions in God's dealings with him. Without answers, Job can only take refuge in the limitations of his own understanding and the immensity of God. Even in the words of Job's interlocutor, the book reminds readers that no one can "thoroughly find out God's depths or thoroughly find out the Almighty's limits" because "they are as high as the heavens: what can you do? Deeper than Sheol: what can you know? Its measure is longer than the earth and broader than the sea" (Job 11:7-9). Here, "depths" (rqx) refers to the inner essence of something and "limits" (ṃik:ta@) speaks of the furthest boundary.[23] The comparison to heaven, earth, and sea highlights the fact that God's knowledge extends beyond the furthest realities that Job could know and experience. In fact, the wording poetically describes the limits of Job's knowledge in every dimension. People can know God, but not exhaustively or to the fullest extent.

Throughout the book of Job, God's works in creation illustrate his incomprehensibility. The weather is just one example of something "which we cannot understand" (Job 37:5).[24] Likewise, we cannot understand how God created

---

[23] John E. Hartley, *The Book of Job* (Grand Rapids: Eerdmans, 1988), 197. Like the span between "height" and "depth," these terms metaphorically stretch from God's essential being to his outermost limit. Humanity is limited in every dimension in which he approaches God.

[24] The hubris of the modern mind might dismiss Elihu's reflections as "pre-scientific," but while modern science has accumulated remarkable information, it still cannot claim a

and sustains the universe. Yet "these are the outskirts of his ways, and what a whisper is the word we hear of him! But the thunderings of his power, who can understand?" (Job 26:14).[25] Though the context is primarily concerned with God's work in nature, the natural understanding of the expression, "the word we hear of him," subsumes everything we know of God, including revelation. This passage describes not only the fact that our knowledge is limited, but some relative measure of how limited it is. The word "outskirts" (hcfqf) refers to the outside extremity of something, such as the end of a rod (Judg. 6:21), the bank of a body of water (Num. 34:3), or the border of a region (Exod. 13:20; Ezek. 25:9).[26] Likewise, our knowledge of God lies only at the extremes, the borders and the margins. Or in another comparison, our knowledge of God compares to what he is, just as a whisper might compare to the sound of thunder. Neither comparison is intended as an objective measure; Scripture is clear that God is infinite and our knowledge is limited. Still, these descriptions give some relative sense of the orders of magnitude we should imagine.

One other passage occurs at the conclusion of the book. Job was confused about why he was suffering and asked to be weighed justly (Job 31:6, 35). In response God confronted Job with the myriad things he never can understand. In the end Job can only bow in quiet trust before the immensity of God: "Who is this concealing counsel without knowledge? Therefore I declared what I did not understand: things too difficult for me which I do not know. Hear, now, and I will speak; I will ask

---

comprehensive knowledge of these phenomena. The fact that science has made so much progress without coming close to exhausting the truth still to be known illustrates that Elihu's words were accurate. Even more critically, no one can explain the mechanics of God's agency through these phenomena—the core of Elihu's argument.

[25] This passage, together with a number of others, is not concerned with the extent of God's knowledge or understanding so much as the complexity of what is true about him. But God's knowledge extends to everything that is true, and one epistemological strategy is to ground truth in God's mind: truth is defined as that which corresponds to God's knowledge. It is, therefore, completely legitimate to move between God's infinite knowledge and the infinite extent of the truth about him, since these are two ways of expressing the same reality.

[26] Layton Talbert, *Beyond Suffering* (Greenville, S.C.: Bob Jones University Press, 2007), 146, illustrates this expression: "What we can discern of the infinite God from his works in nature and history are the mere coastlines of the continent of the mind and character of God. Imagine landing for the first time on the seventeenth-century American continent. You have no idea that the sand onto which you step is the fringe of a continuous landmass over 3,000 miles wide and 9,500 miles long. Imagine formulating views of what this whole continent is like based on what you can see from the bay where you drop anchor. Suppose you forge your way five miles inland, or even fifty miles, to get a better idea of what this new country is like. As tangible and verifiable as what you see is, you are experiencing a minuscule fraction of an unimaginable stretch of vast and varied terrain yet to be explored—massive and multiple mountain ranges, trackless prairies, impenetrable forests, mammoth lakes and mighty rivers with deafening waterfalls, swamps and deserts, flora and fauna yet unknown. How much more is there to know about our magnificently infinite God than what we can see from where we are, only eternity can tell."

you and you teach me" (Job 42:3-4).[27] The immensity of God limits the questions that people should ask and requires an attitude of quiet trust.[28]

The book of Job reveals several conclusions: (1) Our understanding of God in nature and revelation is limited—in fact, relatively speaking it is only a tiny fraction of what is true about him. (2) It is possible for us to presumptuously reason to questions that we should not ask. (3) The biblical response to God's immensity is an attitude of quiet trust.

Other passages

Several other strands of biblical data offer direction regarding paradox. In Ecclesiastes Solomon's attempt to understand life ends with his discovery that mankind cannot answer the deepest questions of existence (Eccl. 3:11; 5:2; 7:23-24; 8:7, 17-9:1; 11:5). In fact, this is intentional—God has purposefully kept the ability to discern these things from human beings (Eccl. 3:11; 7:14).

Psalm 131 describes the same trusting response that Job learned before the truth of God's incomprehensibility: "I do not tread in great matters or too difficult for me to understand. Truly I have calmed and quieted my soul like a weaned child against his mother" (vv. 1-2). In Psalm 139:6, David confesses that the doctrine of God's universal, sovereign care is "knowledge that is too wonderful for me; it is high—I cannot reach it" (Ps. 139:6).[29] That is to say, any understanding of this doctrine that blithely makes it simple enough to reach ignores essential components that David had in mind. Likewise, Psalm 147:5 praises God because "His understanding is infinite."[30]

John records a fascinating insight into the limits of revelation when God forbids him to record the seven peals of thunder (Rev. 10:4). John recorded other events he witnessed, and he apparently comprehended the seven peals of thunder enough to assume they should be written. But God considered it best that future believers not

---

[27] This response contains verbatim parallels with God's earlier speech to Job (Job 38:2 with 42:3 and 38:3; 40:7 with 42:4). Job heard Yahweh's response to him and so assimilated it that these words became his evaluation of himself.

[28] D.A. Carson, *How Long, O Lord?* (Grand Rapids: Baker, 1990), 172-74, comments that "God does not here 'answer' Job's questions about the problem of evil and suffering, *but he makes it unambiguously clear what answers are not acceptable in God's universe."* The problem with many approaches to the book is that "they assume that everything that takes place in God's universe *ought* to be explained to us." The point of God's speech to Job is that "if there are so many things that Job does not understand, why should he so petulantly and persistently demand that he understand his own sufferings? *There are some things you will not understand, for you are not God"* [emphasis not added]. There is a real sense in which Job's honesty in expressing the struggles of his heart is laudable. The problem is when logical problems or deductions violate what Scripture reveals to be true about God's nature.

[29] "Too wonderful" (y)l:p,i) speaks of limitations in human comprehension. It shares roots with one of the OT words for miracles ()lepe,), speaking of events that are extraordinary or beyond normal expectations.

[30] *Infinite* translates rp,s:mi N), more literally "without number."

have that information. Once again, God's providence in revelation extends both to what he has given and what he conceals.

Many of these passages confirm ideas that are evident in the preceding exegesis. God has intentionally withheld or even concealed certain information from humanity (Eccl. 3:11; 7:14; Rev. 10:4); we must quietly trust in the face of things beyond our understanding (Ps. 131:1-2); and God's truth is above human understanding (Ps. 139:6; 147:5). But these passages add new insights as well. Ecclesiastes broadens the truths we cannot know from questions of progressive revelation alone to the philosophical givens of our existence. Psalm 147:5 is the clearest biblical passage teaching that God's understanding is infinite. Revelation 10:4 indicates that information exists that humans could hypothetically understand but that God has intentionally withheld from us.[31]

Summarizing the biblical data in Table 2.1, Scripture uses a number of expressions to affirm that God's thoughts are beyond human understanding, and he intends for it to be that way. The knowledge we do possess is tiny compared to what there is to know. Wayne Grudem boldly comments that *"we can never fully understand any single thing about God.* His greatness (Ps. 145:3), his understanding (Ps. 147:5), his knowledge (Ps. 139:6), his riches, wisdom, judgments, and ways (Rom. 11:33) are *all* beyond our ability to understand fully."[32] As a result of our human limitations, we should not be preoccupied with what we cannot know or draw conclusions that conflict with revelation.

Table 2.2. Summary of Biblical Data

Passage	Descriptive Terms	Propositions
Romans 11:33-34	*depth, unsearchable, unfathomable*	(1) Any attempt to understand God exhaustively is futile. (2) Progressive revelation still leaves unanswered questions.
Deuteronomy 29:29	*secret* vs. *revealed*	(1) There are hidden matters that are not our rightful preoccupation.

---

[31] 1 Corinthians 2:6-14 also contains significant statements about our inability to know God's truth apart from revelation. But Paul's concern in this passage is to demonstrate that unregenerate thinking about God is empty while believers have received genuine knowledge through the testimony of the Spirit. A careful understanding of this passage reveals that it does not address the limitations of human knowledge except to say that the Spirit knows God perfectly (v. 11), and this is the very Spirit we have received (v. 12). Based on other biblical texts (including the other passages surveyed here), we must conclude that the Spirit communicates this information to us partially (though with complete accuracy). This is confirmed by Paul's closing quotation in v. 16: "who has known the mind of the Lord?"

[32] Emphasis original. Grudem *Systematic Theology* (Grand Rapids: Zondervan, 1994), 150, further supports his statement with the fact that "in order to know any single thing about God exhaustively . . . we would have to know it in its relationship to everything else about God and in its relationship to everything else about creation throughout all eternity!"

		(2) God's intentions for revelation include the things he has chosen not to reveal.
Musth/rion	*hidden*	(1) Theological difficulties may be the subject of future, progressive revelation. (2) Still, not all questions will be answered. (3) No efforts can reveal what God has hidden.
Job 11:7-9; 26:14; 42:3	*depths, limits, outskirts, whisper, too difficult for me*	(1) Our understanding of God is a tiny fraction of what is true. (2) There are questions people should not ask. (3) The right response to mystery is quiet trust.
Ecclesiastes 3:11; 7:23-24; 8:17-9:1; 11:5	*remote, exceeding mysterious, man cannot discover, you do not know*	(1) People cannot answer the deepest questions of their existence. (2) God has limited humanity's knowledge intentionally.
Psalm 139:6	*too wonderful for me, I cannot reach it*	Rightly understood, doctrines such as omniscience are beyond human understanding.

The Nature of epistemological discontinuity

The biblical data considered here is only foundational to a theology of paradox. Most of the passages relate rather to fundamental questions about epistemology—particularly how human and divine knowledge differ. Almost any aspect of human discourse contains both information (premises) and reasoning that moves between these premises. For example, we cannot identify Paul's thorn in the flesh—we simply have no way of filling the informational gap. The difference between our thinking and Paul's, therefore, would be informational. But much more would be involved if Paul flatly contradicted himself and this were an acceptable form of reasoning. At that point, our thinking would differ from Paul's in the structure of logic itself. The question is whether our thinking differs from God's in the extent of information we know or also in the fundamentals of our reasoning. Is the discontinuity informational, logical, or both?

The paradox-minimizing view emphasizes the idea that no paradox is a logical conflict. Any paradox can be resolved; we only lack the information for *how* it should be resolved. Scripture certainly supports this assertion that our understanding differs from God's in the information we know. At a minimum the major passages considered above require that God's knowledge is above ours (Ps. 40:5). Scripture clearly teaches that the information God knows is infinite and ours is limited. Isaiah cites this fact repeatedly as proof for Yahweh's deity and sovereignty (41:22-23, 26; 42:9; 43:9-12; 44:7-8; 45:21; 46:9-11; 48:5-8, 14). Only the true God can proclaim events before they happen, because he possesses unique knowledge of everything.³³ But can the exegetical data be completely satisfied with an informational discontinuity between God and ourselves, or do some of the passages require logical discontinuity as well?

Most of these passages highlight only God's knowledge or the vastness of the truth about him. In every case the passages can be understood as speaking of information alone or of both information and logic, but the most natural reading is of both without distinction. Romans 11:33-34 is ambiguous, though there is no reason to limit the statements to information alone. Job 26:14 also pertains to this question because it grows out of Job's concern to resolve logically how his suffering coheres with his innocence. As a result, the verse seems to imply that we cannot resolve such galling contradictions with simple pat answers, because we can see only the outskirts of God's ways and there is much more beyond our understanding.³⁴

The multiple passages in Ecclesiastes emphasize humanity's constitutional inability to answer the deepest questions of life. This seems to indicate that human beings' limitations extend to the deepest levels of their intellect, rooted in their very constitution. On the other hand, however, humanity is also fundamentally limited by the information it lacks. Apart from the revelation God chooses to give, humanity is constitutionally incapable of discovering further knowledge about God, and perhaps this is the limitation Solomon had in mind. Psalm 131:1 has a similar meaning, where the psalmist refuses to "tread in great matters or too difficult for me to understand". Once again, the limitation is constitutional and seems to involve one's ability to process information rather than only the information itself. But here also, the limitation could be humanity's constitutional inability to acquire information about God beyond revelation.

Psalm 139:6 is slightly clearer, since the "knowledge that is too wonderful" for David and beyond his reach is information that he himself communicated (Ps. 139:1-5). The idea seems to be that though David knows the information, he cannot comprehend these truths—a focus on the logical inter-relationships rather than the information alone. Nevertheless, perhaps he would have understood had God given him the necessary explanation.

Scripture's clearest statement of God's infinity in Psalm 147:5 designates God's *understanding* rather than his knowledge. *Understanding* (hnfw@bt@: from Nyb@i)

---

[33] The fact that God's knowledge is infinitely above ours follows naturally from God's holiness of majesty—another major theme in Isaiah (40:18; 46:5,9). Isaiah also connects God's knowledge to his sovereignty. In other words, God knows what events will take place because he is the causal agent behind those events, causing them to take place according to his plan (46:10-11; 48:14; 55:8-9). The point is that God's intellectual transcendence is deeply interrelated to his other attributes. We should anticipate that God's knowledge is unique, since he is unique in every aspect of his being (holiness of majesty). Likewise, we should expect him to possess information that is unavailable to us since he is the ultimate cause behind every event (sovereignty).

[34] Of course, if paradox is an absence of information and not a genuinely logical conflict, then this statement tells us that the information we do not know is only "the outskirts of his ways" and there is infinitely more information to know about him.

emphasizes "the insight that comes from knowing" more than (δγ (knowing) but not specifically enough to identify the content as logical versus informational.[35] One can legitimately conclude that God's capacity to process the information he knows is also infinite, but this passage falls short of saying that God operates above human logic or with a different kind of logic altogether.

Ultimately, the biblical data is not conclusive on this question. Some passages teach not only that God's knowledge is infinitely higher than ours, but also that his understanding of that knowledge is infinitely higher. On this basis it seems questionable to assert that the structure of the logic God uses must be identical with our own. But none of the passages clearly eliminate this possibility. We could summarize this evidence with several propositions. (1) At a minimum, God's informational knowledge is infinitely above our own. (2) The explicit biblical statements about paradox say nothing contradicting the notion that God's thoughts also differ from ours in logical or analytical relationships. (3) A few passages might even imply that God's transcendence extends to logical relationships, though no passages are clear or conclusive.

Evaluation of the Five Perspectives on Paradox

The biblical data affirms that God's thinking is both continuous and discontinuous with our own. From the viewpoint of human beings, some elements are logical and others are paradoxical. But how do these observations relate to the major perspectives on paradox?

Biblical data clearly excludes the two unorthodox views at either extreme. Theologians who overemphasize logic neglect Scripture's clear teaching that God's truth is not limited to human understanding; those who overemphasize mystery neglect the deeply rooted logical foundation of Scripture and God's expectation that believers should reason according to his Word. Both approaches use their method to deny clear statements of Scripture.

The three conservative approaches fare much better by allowing logic and paradox to coexist. Among the three, the *sui generis* view suffers most before the biblical data, because this view places theology or special categories within theology beyond the control of logic. Yet Scripture expects us to reason based on biblical data. Nor does biblical data support any pattern of special categories for reason or mystery. Logic applies to the practical (Heb. 11:17-19) and the abstract (Isa. 41:21-26); the specific (Luke 19:20-27) and the general (Isa. 45:8-12); the human (Rom. 4:9-12) and the divine (Gen. 18:25). Likewise, it is difficult to bracket paradox to a single category or department because antinomy occurs throughout theology. A number of biblical statements broadly describe the fact that humanity's knowledge of God's truth is incomplete, but none distinguishes any separate categories (Job 11:7; Ps. 131:1; 147:5; Isa. 55:8-9; Rom. 11:33-34).

---

[35] Terence E. Fretheim, "Nyb" in *New International Dictionary of Old Testament Theology and Exegesis*, ed. Willem A. VanGemeren (Grand Rapids: Zondervan, 1997), 1:652.

If Scripture teaches that our thinking differs from God's in the fundamentals of our reasoning and not only in the extent of our information, the paradox-minimizing view cannot stand. Nothing in the data eliminates this possibility, and a few passages seem to suggest it, but the data is inconclusive. In reality, the paradox-minimizing view suffers its greatest problems from the biblical data in subjective ways. For example, the paradox-minimizing view attempts to avoid paradox as much as possible and minimize it where it does occur. Scripture, on the other hand, exalts the fact that God's thinking is above our own. Where the paradox-minimizing view jealously guards the idea that God's thinking must operate within the same logical constraints as our own, the biblical text freely exults in his unlimited wisdom and complexity that is utterly above our own. This leads to a final subjective point of friction. According to the paradox-minimizing view, theologians should make every effort to resolve apparent contradictions, most often through theological or verbal distinctions. But biblical texts recommend a different solution to the problem—quiet trust (Job 42:3-4; Ps. 131:1-2; Eccl. 5:2). Ultimately, however, this is a subjective matter of emphasis in how the paradox-minimizing view regards paradox.

Conclusion

Biblical data supports radical discontinuity between human thinking and God's. Even the extensive revelation of Scripture is only a tiny fraction—merely the fringes—of God's infinite complexity. At a minimum, God's thinking differs from our own in the amount of information he knows, and his wisdom and capacity to process that information are clearly superior to humanity's. But using only exegetical data, it is impossible to answer definitively whether God's use of logic is different from our own. Answering that question requires specific examples of paradox in Scripture: the subject of chapter 4. But first it will be helpful to consider the historical viewpoints on paradox.

CHAPTER 3

Encountering Paradox: Past Views

> These are the back parts of God, which he leaves behind him as tokens of himself, like the shadows and reflections of the sun in the water which show the sun to our weak eyes because we cannot look at the sun himself for by his unmixed light he is too strong for our power of perception.[1]

Church history is always relevant to any theological inquiry. How has the church historically handled propositions that appeared to be paradoxical, and how has it evaluated this phenomenon? Are the three orthodox views (*sui generis*, complementarity, and the paradox-minimizing view) recognizable throughout church history?

But first, there are several challenges. One is to transcend the context-specific issues that generated the conflict. Generally, the questions surrounding paradox arise only in connection with a specific theological concern or controversy. As a result, only rarely have theologians discussed and analyzed paradox as an independent topic in church history. Another challenge is that because there has been very little consensus on terms or even the central questions involved with paradox it is hard to translate the positions of thinkers in separate time periods into equivalent forms.[2]

Nevertheless, church history contains many helpful insights for discussing paradox. Specifically, a recurring pattern appears in the conflicts between complementarity and the paradox-minimizing view, and this historic trend holds clarifying observations about theological paradox.

The Church Fathers

The Fathers generally assumed the existence of mystery but rarely discussed it directly. What they did emphasize was the principle that divine realities are beyond complete human understanding—particularly when it comes to God's metaphysical essence and the doctrine of the Trinity.

---

[1] Gregory of Nazianzus, *Oration* 28, section 3. *A Select Library of Nicene and Post-Nicene Fathers of the Christian Church*, ed. Philip Schaff and Henry Wace, trans. by Charles Gordon Browne and James Edward Swallow (Grand Rapids: Eerdmans, 1956), 7:289.

[2] Yet another challenge is brevity. Space constraints here prevent a thorough study of mystery in church history, but for a more in-depth study, see Stephen D. Boyer and Christopher A. Hall, *The Mystery of God* (Grand Rapids: Baker Academic, 2012), 39-68.

In general, the Fathers use musth/rion to refer to the Pauline concept of truths that were not previously revealed, or as a term for what later became the sacraments.³ The philosophical sense of mystery appears in Clement of Alexandria but continues in successive thinkers.⁴ Gregory of Nyssa developed the concept much further, seeing much of his theology through this lens. For him, "mystery no longer meant just the secret doctrine, but the ineffable truth of God, knowable in some way only through God's gratuitous revelation."⁵

Gregory of Nazianzus is also concerned to speak only of that which is attainable and not press on to knowledge in the realm of mystery.⁶ One example that is beyond comprehension, requiring the silence of faith, is the ontological relationships of the Trinitarian persons.⁷ Regarding the essence of God, he comments,

> It is impossible to express Him, and yet more impossible to conceive Him. . . . To comprehend the whole of so great a Subject as this is quite impossible and impracticable, not merely to the utterly careless and ignorant, but even to those who are highly exalted, and who love God, and in like manner to every created nature; seeing that the darkness of this world and the thick covering of the flesh is an obstacle to the full understanding of the truth.⁸

Gregory most emphasized the limits of human understanding in his debate with the Eunomians, who argued that our knowledge of God must be complete in order to be authentic.⁹ A fragment from Eunomius boldy states that "God does not know anything more about his own essence than we do, nor is that essence better known to him and less to us. Rather, whatever we know about it is exactly what he knows, and conversely, what he knows is what you will find without change in us."¹⁰

---

³ Cyril of Jerusalem, "Five Catechetical Lectures to the Newly Baptized," Lecture I, section 1. *A Select Library*, trans. Edwin Hamilton Gifford, 7:144. Gregory of Nazianzus even extended musth/rion to refer to festival days such as Easter (7:203).

⁴ Basilio Studer, "Mystery," Vol. 1, in *Encyclopedia of the Early Church*, ed. Angelo Di Berardino, trans. Adrian Walford (New York: Oxford University Press, 1992).

⁵ Studer in *Encyclopedia of the Early Church*.

⁶ *Oration* 2, section 20-21. *A Select Library*, 7:295-296. Also, *On the Theophany*, section 7-8. Ibid., 7:346-347.

⁷ *A Select Library*, 7:303. Gregory goes on to compare this to the paradox of time, the liar's paradox, and another paradoxical question regarding the self (7:304).

⁸ *Oration* 28, section 3. *A Select Library*, 7:289-290.

⁹ This is the context of the passage in the heading of this chapter (*Oration*, 28.3). Christopher A. Beeley, *Gregory of Nazianzus on the Trinity and the Knowledge of God* (New York: Oxford University Press, 2008), 91-93.

¹⁰ Quoted in Beeley, *Gregory of Nazianzus*, 92. Gregory's attack on Eunomius in some ways anticipates the debate between Gordon Clark and Cornelius Van Til on the nature of humanity's knowledge. Of course, Eunomius's position was far more extreme than Gordon Clark's. The most significant point of commonality is that like Clark, Eunomius seems to have argued that in order for authentic knowledge of God to be possible, our knowledge must be equivalent to God's rather than comparable.

Gregory responded with strong comparisons between God's knowledge and our own: God is like the entire ocean compared to a small living creature; God is the reality in itself as opposed to a picture; God is as incomprehensible as the light of a lightning bolt is blinding to our weak eyes. Our understanding of God is quantitatively partial, and even the part we know is ultimately incomprehensible.[11] Nor does limitation apply to the information alone; human logic is also limited. Gregory enjoins believers to "let faith lead you rather than reason, that is if you have learned the weakness of reason in matters close at hand, and have acquired enough knowledge of reason to know things that are beyond reason".[12] Applying this to specific theological questions, Gregory was satisfied to let tensions stand and limit speculations. Grappling with the Trinity, he comments, "I am satisfied with the declaration that he is Son and that he is from Father, and that the one is Father and the other Son; and I refuse to engage in meaningless speculation beyond this point."[13]

As doctrine developed further and ecclesiastical debates became more complex, discussions of paradox also became more sophisticated. The early struggles with Trinitarian and Christological heresies only increased the need for more critical discussion of logic and paradox.[14] Dealing with the eternal generation of the Son, Ambrose comments, "For me the knowledge of the mystery of His generation is more than I can attain to—the mind fails, the voice is dumb—ay, and not mine alone, but the angels' also."[15] Discussing the same subject, Hilary of Poitiers comments,

> If any one lays upon his personal incapacity his failure to solve the mystery . . ., he will be still more pained at the ignorance to which I confess. I too am in the dark, yet I ask no questions. I look for comfort to the fact that Archangels share my ignorance. . . . Let such pitiful complaints cease. Whoever you are that search into these mysteries, I do not bid you resume your exploration of height and breadth and depth; I ask you

---

[11] *Oration* 38.7-8. Beeley, *Gregory of Nazianzus*, 96. This distinction also mirrors Cornelius Van Til's argument for knowledge that both quantitatively *and* qualitatively differs from God's. Some interpreters have misunderstood Gregory's statements about incomprehensibility, thinking that he denied knowledge of God altogether. It is true that he sometimes overstated his position—particularly where knowledge of God related to his ontology. Still, Gregory's strong statements should be interpreted in light of the rest of his theology, where he clearly affirms that genuine knowledge of God is possible, though exhaustive knowledge is not. We know the edges of God's being (peri\ au0to/n) though we cannot know it comprehensively (kat' au0to/n—*Oration* 28.3). Beeley offers a balanced interpretation by observing the number of times Gregory speaks of human knowledge, even as he qualifies it. Ibid., 98-99, 101-104.

[12] *Oration* 28.28. Beeley, *Gregory of Nazianzus*, 111.

[13] *Oration* 20.10. Beeley, *Gregory of Nazianzus*, 224.

[14] This also explains why almost all of the extended discussions of paradox are written after the middle of the 4th century.

[15] *Of the Christian Faith*, book 1, chapter 10. *A Select Library*, trans. by H. De Romestin, 10:212.

rather to acquiesce patiently in your ignorance of the mode of Divine generation, seeing that you know not how His creatures come into existence.[16]

Discussing the incarnate Word, Leo of Rome confidently asserts that

> He is at once both eternal from His Father and temporal from His mother, inviolable in His strength, passible in our weakness: in the Triune Godhead, of one and the same substance with the Father and the Holy Spirit, but in taking Manhood on Himself, not of one substance but of one and the same person [so that He was at once rich in poverty, almighty in submission, impassible in punishment, immortal in death.][17]

Of all the theologians in the patristic era, Augustine certainly discussed the problem of paradox the most. He referred to the Trinity as an enigma that we cannot now know with clarity, because we see as through a glass darkly.[18] Anyone who believes the doctrine will be faced with challenging philosophical problems and conundrums.[19] He comments that "when the question is asked, What three? human language labors altogether under great poverty of speech. The answer, however, is given, three 'persons,' not that it might be [completely] spoken, but that it might not be left [wholly] unspoken."[20] Discussing the difference in terminology between the Greek and Latin churches, Augustine argues that it is not possible to assign a clear content of meaning to 'person' and 'essence.' Rather, he argues that these terms have been coined simply so that theologians have a way to speak of God's threeness or His oneness.[21] Still, Augustine commends the ambition to understand as much as possible and compares the Trinity to a large number of analogies in human experience.[22] Augustine also laboriously analyzes the divine attributes and the Trinity according to the metaphysical categories of his time.[23]

---

[16] *On The Trinity*, book 2, section 9. *A Select Library*, trans. by E.W. Watson and L. Pullan, 9:55.

[17] Letter 35: to Julian, Bishop of Cos, section II. The editors regard the bracketed portion as textually uncertain. *A Select Library*, trans. Charles Lett Feltoe, 12:49. Leo goes on to compare Christ's two natures in one person with the fact that every complete human being also possesses body and soul in one person.

[18] Augustine, *On The Trinity*, book 15. *A Select Library*, trans. A.W. Haddan, 3:199-228.

[19] This theme is especially repeated in *On The Trinity*, books 5-7. *A Select Library*, 3:87-114.

[20] *On the Trinity*, Book 5, chapter 9. *A Select Library*, 3:92.

[21] *Trinity*, book 7, chapter 7-9. *A Select Library*, 3:109-111. It is especially interesting that Augustine goes on to suggest that these terms are essentially apophatic. In other words, "three persons" is intended not so much to affirm plurality as to deny simple singularity; likewise "one essence" is intended not as much to affirm singularity as to deny polytheism.

[22] *On The Trinity*, Book 15. *A Select Library*, 3:199ff.

[23] This itself is an insight for current discussions of the Trinity and other antinomies. No theologian is ever free from subjectivity, but where theologians move far beyond the text in their analysis, they are particularly exposed to the philosophical biases of their era—many of which later theologians will dismiss out of hand.

In summary, it is difficult to state the perspective of the Fathers because they gave little extended analysis about the relationship between logic and mystery. Leo typifies the attitude in which the Fathers are completely willing to tolerate propositions in tension and even highlight the tension by juxtaposing difficult ideas. Several of the Fathers repeatedly emphasize the fact that human understanding cannot attain to the divine. At the same time, the apologetic thrust in the Fathers drives them to explain theological tensions as much as possible—often through analogies. Extended theological reasoning plays a key role in patristic literature—often concerning the very subjects they regard as ultimately inscrutable. One point of difference between the Fathers is in the attitude towards these inscrutable areas. Some regard such topics as sealed from human understanding so that we have an ethical responsibility not to pursue knowledge beyond revelation. Others commend further inquiry, confident that valid reasoning will lead to sound conclusions. In general, the differences were probably polemical and situational. A writer's attitude seems to differ based on whether he faces challenges from a rationalist or feels confident to polemically reason against heresy. Thus the patristic perspective on the question ultimately awaited further clarification from later thinkers.

This leaves two observations from the patristic era: (1) Even from early times, most of the church has maintained that there are some theological issues and problems that cannot be completely resolved. In fact, the majority of heresies in the early church arose from thinkers who sought to resolve these problems completely. (2) Many theologians have made the connection between the existence of paradox and the biblical teaching that God's thinking transcends our own. For them, in other words, these logical conflicts illustrate God's intellectual transcendence.

Medieval Thinkers

Discussion about a proper theological method became somewhat more clear and self-critical during the medieval era. In this period the issue of paradox often arose in discussions about the proper limits of human knowledge and especially in connection to the Trinity. As with many medieval questions, these controversies stemmed from the debate between the nominalists and realists. Theologians almost never discussed paradox independently or for its own sake. For the most part the Church used the concept polemically—as a defense against baseless speculation. Medieval views on logic and paradox varied quite widely, ranging beyond the orthodox views presented in this study, as well as in almost every possible combination of the three views.

As an early developer of conceptualism, Peter Abelard faced censure and condemnation from the Church for his confidence that logic could resolve the mysteries of the faith.[24] Developing his thought into a rigorous rationalism, Abelard seems to have anticipated the more modern concern for articulating propositions in

---

[24] There was no lack of other issues involved in Abelard's conflict with the church and his eventual condemnation. Still, the issue of how much can be known or logically comprehended was definitely central to the conflict.

a way that is meaningful and unambiguous.[25] Abelard's controversial book on the Trinity probed into questions that were previously regarded as mysterious. He intended the book for his students,

> because they were always seeking for rational and philosophical explanations, asking rather for reasons they could understand than for mere words, saying that it was futile to utter words which the intellect could not possibly follow, that nothing could be believed unless it could first be understood, and that it was absurd for any one to preach to others a thing which neither he himself nor those whom he sought to teach could comprehend.[26]

Abelard was eventually condemned based largely on the testimony of St. Bernard of Clairvaux, who commented that "inasmuch as he thinks that he is able to comprehend the whole that God is by his unaided human reason, he is ascending to the skies, he is descending to the depths. There is nothing which can escape him."[27] For his part, Bernard's mystical epistemology probably shared the most in common with the *sui generis* view. He seems to suggest that there are certain doctrines and questions that are beyond the rightful inquiry of human beings and that the proper knowledge of God in these areas is only mystical rather than logical. On this basis Bernard contended that Abelard erred by making it his ambition to understand as much as possible about the Trinity or matters of salvation. Bernard commented that his opponent

> endeavors to scrutinize by the light of his reason alone, the mysteries which are apprehended by the pious mind only by the intuition of faith: the faith of the pious, which believes and does not discuss. But that man holds even God in suspicion, nor is willing to believe anything unless he shall have first considered it by reason.[28]

Bernard also confronted another aberrant view of the Trinity in Gilbert de la Porrée, but this time at an opposite extreme. Porrée so emphasized the limitations of human understanding that all predication about God was only by analogy. Gilbert also overemphasized the unity of the Trinity but clouded most of his teaching in

---

[25] Abelard might seem to argue the opposite view in the prologue to his *Sic et Non*, where he comments, "In such a multitude of words, it is not surprising that some sayings even of the saints seem not only to differ from one another but indeed even to contradict one another." He recommends that readers assume they have erred rather than the saints or the church. He attributes the conflicts either to the unfamiliar way the saints spoke or to the fact that the same word might sometimes refer to different things. More likely, however, Abelard simply recognized the significant political and personal dangers of writing such a direct assault on the church's veracity and sought to hedge against the censure.

[26] Peter Abelard, *Historia Calamitatum*, trans. Henry Adams Bellows (New York: William Edwin Rudge, 1922), 36.

[27] Letter 191 to Pope Innocent, *Life and Works of Saint Bernard*, ed. John Mabillon, trans. Samuel J. Eales (New York: Burns and Oates, 1889), 2:592.

[28] Letter 338 to Haimeric in *Life and Works of Saint Bernard*, 2:872.

mystical terms.[29] Here Bernard again argued that human comprehension of the Trinity is ultimately only partial, but he attacked Gilbert for denying biblically necessary propositions. In short, for all of his mysticism, Bernard did demonstrate an objective standard for theological truth coupled with a strong emphasis on the limitations of human comprehension.

Thomas Aquinas also maintained an interesting hybrid view. On the one hand he was so confident in the utility of reason that he suggested human knowers might access truth about God apart from revelation. Yet on the other hand Thomas carefully placed certain mysteries of the faith beyond human reason. Such truths dwell in a realm of knowledge that is not accessible apart from revelation, and this truth is never fully comprehensible.[30] For instance, reason alone cannot derive the doctrine of the Trinity, nor can it confirm it as the most reasonable viewpoint. We are dependent on revelation and faith for such points of doctrine, and ultimately the Trinity must remain an unexplained and incomprehensible mystery. This stems from the simple principle that a finite mind cannot ever understand an infinite reality.[31] Likewise, Aquinas comments concerning the theanthropic person of Christ that "to explain this union perfectly is beyond man's strength".[32]

Aquinas spoke of human knowledge as neither univocal with God's nor entirely distinct, but analogically related.[33] Our knowledge, therefore, is a partial representation of the divine. For Aquinas the epistemological foundation for human

---

[29] Reginald Lane Poole, *Illustrations of the History of Medieval Thought* (London: Williams and Norgate, 1884), 181-182.

[30] Thomas Aquinas, *Summa Theologica*, trans. Fathers of the English Dominican Province (New York: Benziger Bros., 1947-1948), 54-55 (Part 1, Question 12, Article 7).

[31] Aquinas, 441-443 (Part 1, Question 86, Article 2).

[32] Stephen T. Davis, "John Hick on Incarnation and Trinity," in *The Trinity*, ed. Stephen T. Davis, Daniel Kendall and Gerald O'Collins (Oxford: Oxford University Press, 1999), 258.

[33] Aquinas adapted Aristotelian epistemology in his analysis of divine, angelic, and human knowledge. For him each type of intellect belonged on a different level of an epistemological hierarchy. As the pinnacle of the hierarchy, God's knowledge is the ultimate ideal because he possesses direct knowledge of the thing in itself, rather than being dependent on abstracts derived from sensory experiences. Aquinas's model suggests that divine knowledge differs in the quality of the knowledge itself and not merely in the volume of truth known. See John I. Jenkins, *Knowledge and Faith in Thomas Aquinas* (Cambridge: Cambridge University Press, 1997), 56-66. Aquinas probably regarded analogical knowledge as a mediating position between two problematic extremes. On the one hand, if descriptive terms are completely equivalent between God and human beings, it limits God's perfections. But if these terms are completely equivocal, it makes meaningful communication impossible. See Alexander Broadie, "Duns Scotus and William Ockam," in *The Medieval Theologians*, ed. G.R. Evans (Malden, Mass.: Blackwell, 2001), 251. This concept is not unlike Van Til's qualification about human knowledge, though the other aspects of their epistemology are completely different. Van Til never acknowledged this commonality because he was so strongly averse to Thomas's idea of a natural theology based on empiricism—knowledge independent of revelation. See Cornelius Van Til, *A Christian Theory of Knowledge* (Grand Rapids: Baker, 1969), 16-17, 170-173.

knowledge is a combination of reason and faith. These two means of knowledge have a supplementary, mutually confirming relationship. Ultimately, however, faith is the only proper foundation at the kernel of knowledge, though reason also plays a crucial role in Aquinas's theology.[34]

Duns Scotus did not directly discuss the rationality of theology or the existence of mystery, but he maintained a strong confidence in the role of reason and proposed distinctions intended to explain the Trinity. His concern seems to have been that theology should always be philosophically coherent.[35] He also took issue with Thomas's distinction regarding analogical knowledge, averring that there must also be some component of univocal agreement for two things to be analogically related and for knowledge to be possible—an argument that reappeared in a similar modern context.[36]

William of Ockham took issue with Aquinas's confidence in reason and relegated faith and reason to separate spheres. In fact, for him these two epistemological principles may lead to contradictory conclusions, and at such points faith is primary. Ockham based his argument on a strongly voluntarist understanding of God's omnipotence. If God can do whatever he chooses, it is just as logically possible that the Incarnation be in the form of an ox or a pig rather than a human body. He is capable even of completely misleading people's sense perceptions or distorting their knowledge. Therefore, religious truths should be accepted by faith, and reason has no foundation as a basis for truth.[37]

Gabriel Biel probably held to a middle way between confidence and doubt in logic. He maintained the universal validity and consistency of logical laws and tried to penetrate the mystery of the Trinity as far as human reason can allow. At the same time, he also suggested that the doctrine belongs to the realm of pure faith and is not fully accessible to human reason.[38]

In sum, the medieval theologians represent the full range of perspectives, from overemphasis on paradox to excessive confidence in logic. On the rationalistic extreme, Peter Abelard dispensed with mystery almost entirely, and Duns Scotus sought to explain problems that were traditionally regarded as mysterious.[39] Gilbert de la Porrée moved to the opposite extreme with excessive emphasis on paradox.

---

[34] Aquinas, 168-170 (Part 1, Question 32, Article 1). C. Stephen Evans offers a more extended discussion of Aquinas and the role of reason in *Faith Beyond Reason* (Grand Rapids: Eerdmans, 1998), 55-64.

[35] Richard Cross, *Duns Scotus* (New York: Oxford University Press, 1999), 10.

[36] Broadie, "Duns Scotus and William Ockam," 251-56.

[37] W.T. Jones, *A History of Western Philosophy* (New York: Harcourt, Brace, 1952), 517.

[38] Heiko A. Oberman, *The Harvest of Medieval Theology* (Grand Rapids: Baker, 1963), 85-86, 88.

[39] G.R. Evans, *Language and Logic of the Bible,* 140-63, demonstrates that integrating apparent contradictions was a significant concern for many medieval writers and that the most common strategy was linguistic—distinguishing different meanings in ambiguous propositions.

Most thinkers, however, mediated the two extremes. Bernard of Clairvaux was moderate in some ways, though he apparently regarded reason with suspicion, and his epistemology left much to be desired. Similarly, William of Ockam granted the existence of paradox and gave faith preeminence in such points but also came to conclusions with problematic implications for logic and epistemology. Both thinkers fall somewhere between complementarity and the *sui generis* view, seeing a limited role for logic and granting a great deal to mystery.

On the other side of the moderate views, Aquinas's and Biel's views are probably a hybrid of complementarity and the paradox-minimizing view, acknowledging mystery but granting a great deal to reason.[40] Thus, while most of the medieval thinkers acknowledged paradox on some level, other imbalances and extremes also accompanied their thought in every case, and their views on paradox demanded further clarification.

Three observations emerge from the medieval era: (1) The problem of paradox is inseparably tied up with the problem of faith and reason. (2) A thinker's view on paradox is often dictated by his broader philosophical and epistemological pre-commitments. Specifically, anyone who enters the theological process with a strong commitment to logical rigor as a methodological ideal will be more inclined towards the paradox-minimizing view. (3) It is not a given that all theological questions should be explored as much as possible or that logical solutions should be proposed wherever possible. In fact, this has been one of the central points of debate in some discussions of paradox.

The Reformers and Post-Reformation

Following the medieval era, the Protestant Reformation reestablished the limitations of human knowledge in a clearer way. Luther and Calvin are relatively explicit in their confidence that some theological propositions cannot be logically harmonized, though the terminology they use is not always unambiguous.[41] In addition, the reformers' perspective on paradox was often clearer and more exegetically based than that of the medieval scholastics before them.[42]

---

[40] The fundamental problem with Aquinas's epistemology is with his confidence in human reason apart from revelation. This leaves open the logical conclusion that human knowers could derive unrevealed answers to theological paradoxes by working up the logical chain of known propositions. As a result, the epistemological category he assigns for paradox (which is mostly complementarian) is inconsistent with the rest of his epistemology.

[41] Fairly consistently the Reformers referred to the sacraments with "mystery"—an equivocation that had ancient basis in ecclesiastical literature. However, the sense intended is not paradox, and in fact Luther resisted equating the Pauline musth/rion with the sacraments. See Martin Luther, *Luther's Works*, ed. Jaroslav Pelikan and Helmut T. Lehmann, 55 vols. (Philadelphia: Muhlenberg Press, 1959), 36:93.

[42] Richard A. Muller, *Post-Reformation Reformed Dogmatics* (Grand Rapids: Baker, 1987), 1:227: "The Reformed debate echoes the debate over the Scotist distinction between the infinite and perfect *theologia in se* and the various forms of finite theology typical of the fourteenth and fifteenth centuries. On the one hand, this debate moved toward a clearer statement of the paradigm according to which the various categories of finite theology,

Luther clearly accepted paradox as a logical anomaly that must be accepted by faith. He is commonly known as the theologian of paradox and substantiates the moniker in his discussion of the Trinity.

> I hear that Christ is of one essence with the Father and that there is, nevertheless, not more than one God. . . . When I hear the word sounding from above, then I believe it although I cannot grasp it nor understand it nor let it enter my head, as I can grasp with my reason that two and five are seven and let me tell no one otherwise. But if He should say from above, no, two and five are eight, then I should believe it against my reason and feeling. If I am resolved to judge then I cannot believe, but I am resolved to believe him who judges and decides. To this I cling in life and death, for I trust in him whom I consider wiser and who can count better than I; although I also know it I am going to believe him; what he says I will consider as truth even if the whole world should say otherwise. Thus you must do here: although reason cannot conceive that two persons are one God—it is as if I would say: two are not two, but two are one—word and reason are here in conflict, nevertheless reason should not play the master nor be the judge and doctor, you rather take off your hat and say: two are one although I cannot see nor understand it, but I believe it. Why? For his sake who said so from above.[43]

One of the most well-known instances of Luther's view on paradox is his understanding of the Eucharist based on Christ's incarnational omnipresence. Luther openly concedes that it is unreasonable for two substances to become one. "All this every rational being in creation must acknowledge; nothing else makes sense." In the case of the Lord's Supper, "reason takes offense". But based on verses such as 2 Corinthians 10:5, human reason must be captive to the authority of Scripture. Even if we cannot comprehend the meaningful content of a theological truth, we should accept it and "simply repeat his words after him as he pronounces them for us".[44] Luther goes on to argue that the Trinity and the Incarnation are examples in which the logically contradictory actually does happen—two distinct substances become one. Therefore, believers should accept the impossible and logically inexplicable reality that occurs in the Lord's Supper—the elements of the sacrament can also be Christ's body and blood.[45] Luther's view on paradox, therefore, places total confidence in the biblical text as it stands and shows very little concern for the logical disjunctions that might arise as a result.

---

classified according to their mode of communication, could be grouped together under the divine archetype, while on the other hand, epistemological concerns somewhat different from those of Scotus brought about modification of the terms and their use."

[43] Quoted in M. Reu, *Luther and the Scriptures* (Columbus, Ohio: Wartburg, 1944), 151.

[44] LW 37:295-96.

[45] Luther also argues from Psalm 104:4, which refers to angels as winds and flames of fire. This he claims is an example of two substances paradoxically functioning as one entity. Ibid., 37:298. On the other hand, Luther does go on to speak of these examples as synecdoche and compares them to several linguistic examples. Ibid., 37:294-303.

Calvin was also unafraid of paradox and the limitations of human knowledge, but he was generally more responsible than Luther. Regarding the Trinity, Calvin cautions,

> On this, indeed, if on any of the secret mysteries of the Scripture, we ought to philosophize with great sobriety and moderation; and also with extreme caution, lest either our ideas or our language should proceed beyond the limits of the Divine word. For how can the infinite essence of God be defined by the narrow capacity of the human mind, which could never yet certainly determine the nature of the body of the sun, though the object of our daily contemplation? How can the human mind, by its own efforts, penetrate into an examination of the essence of God, when it is totally ignorant of its own? Wherefore let us freely leave to God the knowledge of himself. . . . But if the distinction of Father, Son and Spirit, in the one Deity, as it is not easy to be comprehended, occasions some understandings more labour and trouble than is desirable, let them remember that the mind of man, when it indulges its curiosity, enters into a labyrinth; and let them submit to be guided by the heavenly oracles, however they may not comprehend the height of this mystery.[46]

Calvin also discusses the objection that "if nothing happens but by the will of God, he has in him two contrary wills, because he decrees in his secret counsel what he has publicly prohibited in his law".[47] For Calvin, the problem is simply that

> The weakness of our understanding comprehends not how the same thing may be in different respects both agreeable to his will, and contrary to it. . . . Rather, while we comprehend not how God intends that to be done, the doing of which he forbids, let us remember our imbecility, and at the same time consider, that the light which he inhabits, is justly called inaccessible, because it is overspread with impenetrable darkness.[48]

Like Luther, Calvin defended the weaknesses in his view of the Eucharist by appealing to mystery. Calvin's presentation of the Eucharist as mystery is more devotional than Luther's, focusing on how mystery limits what anyone can say about the Eucharist. Still, the theology of the Eucharist in both reformers illustrates the danger inherent to paradox—all too easily it substitutes as a defense for theologically weak positions.

Calvin also speaks of a "beautiful coherence" even in such "great mysteries" as the Incarnation, and he confidently emphasizes the logical sufficiency of the orthodox formulations.[49] Two observations can be made about his theology: (1)

---

[46] John Calvin, *Institutes of the Christian Religion*, trans. John Allen, Vol. 1, 2 vols. (Philadelphia: Presbyterian Board, 1921), 137-38. Book 1, chapter 13, section 21.

[47] Calvin, *Institutes*, 215.

[48] Ibid., 216. Elsewhere Calvin also refers to the mysteries of the Trinity (133, 136, 138), the Incarnation (435-436), divine sovereignty with human responsibility (231, 424), and specific questions about the angelic hosts (158).

[49] Ibid., 439. Also, 196-97. Calvin also uses "mystery" for the truths of Scripture that mature believers receive through illumination, in keeping with the Pauline musth/rion

Calvin labels certain theological concepts as "mysteries"—usually distinguished because they contain an inscrutable element or a problem that is particularly challenging to explain. (2) He emphasizes the attitude that mystery requires. Theologians must exercise extraordinary care and sobriety, studiously avoiding vain speculation.[50]

Following but codifying Calvin, the post-reformation scholastics largely reproduced Calvin's content and at times clarified it with helpful distinctions. At a few points their clarification also removed Calvin's intentional ambiguities, but the existence and relevance of theological paradox remained. The scholastics did add one critical distinction. Archetypal theology is infinite, and only God can know it absolutely because it represents the truth as it is in reality. Ectypal theology is the limited, relative knowledge of human minds, received by revelation.[51] This is the knowledge of all rational creatures and includes Christ's human knowledge in the Incarnation, the knowledge of angels, the understanding of humans before the fall, knowledge after the fall that is informed by revelation, and the heavenly knowledge of the blessed.[52] Ectypal theology relates to the archetypal by analogy—human knowledge parallels what God knows of the reality, but only incompletely and partially.[53] In essence this results in a broad dualism between God's understanding and every other instance of knowledge.

In summary, the reformation contains examples of the three orthodox views of paradox—the *sui generis* view, complementarity, and the paradox-minimizing view. Luther seems the closest to the *sui generis* view, but his position also allowed him to accept and defend problematic conclusions. In the case of consubstantiation, it let his prior assumptions overwhelm plausibility problems in a rather dubious interpretation. Calvin's view was closest to complementarity, but Calvin successfully rooted his theological decisions in exegesis. For him logic played an important role in the theological process, but where exegesis makes logical correlation impossible, he suggests that theologians should accept problematic constructions as they stand.

(1:253, 531). However, he also uses the word more specifically for truths that no one can rightly understand in the present life (1:158).

[50] Ibid., 1:133, 136-37, 439, c.f. 1:561. Michael S. Horton, *Covenant and Eschatology: The Divine Drama* (Louisville: Westminster John Knox, 2002), 184-85.

[51] Muller, *Post-Reformation Reformed Dogmatics*, 1:128.

[52] Ibid., 1:133.

[53] Michael Horton, "Hellenistic or Hebrew? Open Theism and Reformed Theological Method," *JETS* (June 2002): 317-42, revitalizes the archetypal versus ectypal distinction, restating it as univocal versus analogical language. Using this distinction, he goes on to criticize open theism for denying paradox because it "makes ectypal knowledge archetypal and analogical language univocal" (337). Horton also helpfully points out that analogical knowledge is only possible because of the *imago Dei*. "When God accommodates us by speaking 'baby talk,' he is presupposing imaginative powers in the creature that he himself gave in the first place. Just as he has the archetypal ability to create imaginative analogies, human beings have the ectypal ability to understand and interpret them" (244).

Two observations from the reformation era are particularly salient. (1) Paradox may sometimes provide an opportunity for logical inconsistency that allows problematic formulations to stand. By implication any view that grants a meaningful role for paradox should also propose a method for distinguishing it from bad theology or blatant absurdity. (2) When God's knowledge is materially distinguished from all other knowledge (as opposed to distinguishing it purely by the amount of information known), it will result in a kind of universal, epistemological dualism.

Modern Theology

Following the Reformation, a large group of liberal theologians emphasized mystery to the point of devaluing propositional theology. Beginning with the influence of Immanuel Kant, continuing in Søren Kierkegaard, and most recently with Karl Barth, a whole segment of theology regarded contradiction as the ultimate demonstration of true faith. In the process, of course, they also made significant adjustments to the foundational faith commitments of orthodox Christianity.[54]

Conservative theologians, however, generally acknowledged the existence of paradox but tended to emphasize logical consistency and sought for resolutions wherever possible. When Charles Hodge speaks of God's timelessness, he acknowledges the conundrums the doctrine involves and concludes that "we should not pretend to be able to comprehend God".[55] Likewise, he speaks of the "incomprehensible nature of the Godhead, the mysterious character of the doctrine of the Trinity, [and] the exceeding complexity and difficulty of the problem which the church had to solve". At the same time he is confident that the orthodox formulation of the Trinity is free from contradiction and that intractable logical problems exist only in the evaluations of unbelieving philosophy.[56]

Shedd also avers that "the great mystery of the Trinity is, that one and the very same substance, can subsist as an undivided whole in three persons *simultaneously*".[57] Speaking of divine sovereignty and human responsibility, he comments that "the certainty of sin by a permissive decree is an insoluble mystery for the finite mind".[58] At the same time Shedd carefully qualifies that none of these

---

[54] The simplest critical evaluation of this theological trend is that it failed to grapple adequately with the propositional nature of biblical revelation and the paradigm of logical reasoning that is everywhere evident in biblical revelation. If Scripture itself reasons using logical derivations, or uses one set of propositions to eliminate others, it must be warranted for theologians to do so in at least some situations. Ultimately this theological program makes it impossible for any propositions to be true in a way that eliminates heresy.

[55] Charles Hodge, *Systematic Theology* (Grand Rapids: Eerdmans, 1973), 1:388-389.

[56] Ibid., 1:445, 478.

[57] William G.T. Shedd, *Dogmatic Theology* (Nashville: Thomas Nelson, 1980), 1:248, original emphasis.

[58] Ibid., 327.

questions are genuine contradictions.⁵⁹ Though he never discusses it clearly, Shedd most likely understood mystery as quantitative gaps in theological knowledge but not genuine logical conflicts.

Benjamin B. Warfield also tended to emphasize logical coherence. Discussing the popular concept of "spiritual leading," Warfield recognizes that one of the common defenses is actually an abuse of mystery. "The sober-minded seem often to look upon it as a mystery into which it would be well not to inquire too closely."⁶⁰ Similarly, Warfield criticizes Ritschl's distinction between religion and historical fact, saying that it "passes beyond the apparent absurdity of paradox into the actually absurd".⁶¹

Cornelius Van Til and Gordon Clark

Naturally the debate that shares the most in common with contemporary concerns is also the most recent. Two reformed apologists, Cornelius Van Til and Gordon Clark, clashed over the nature of knowledge and the existence of paradox, a debate that continues between their followers in the present.⁶²

Both thinkers tended to state their positions abstrusely, and at times the conflict involved confusion of terms. As John Frame comments, "neither man was at his best".⁶³ But it is possible to state the foundational elements in several points. First, Clark believed in the necessity of innate ideas as the *a priori* foundation of human knowledge, including logical principles such as non-contradiction and identity.⁶⁴ These ideas were foundational for the possibility of a natural theology—the basis of

---

[59] Ibid., 1:268 for the Trinity, 1:401-402 for divine sovereignty and human responsibility, and 1:193, 298 for the infinity of God; 1:51-52 for Shedd's view of contradiction.

[60] Benjamin B. Warfield, *The Power of God Unto Salvation* (Philadelphia: Presbyterian Board, 1903), 152.

[61] Benjamin B. Warfield, *The Right of Systematic Theology* (Edinburgh: T. & T. Clark, 1897), 58.

[62] D.G. Hart and John Muether discuss the historical background of the conflict from the Van Tilian perspective in *Fighting the Good Fight* (Philadelphia: Orthodox Presbyterian Church, 1995), 106-15, or in John R. Muether, *Cornelius Van Til: Reformed Apologist and Churchman* (Phillipsburg, N.J.: P&R, 2008), 100-113. A perspective sympathetic to Clark is available in Herman Hoeksema, *The Clark-Van Til Controversy* (Unicoi, Tenn.: The Trinity Foundation, 1995).

[63] John M. Frame, *Cornelius Van Til: An Analysis of His Thought* (Phillipsburg, N.J.: P&R, 1995), 112. Frame regards the entire debate as a matter of confusing terms and personal vendettas. Frame is accurate that the particular interchange regarding Clark's ordination involved more confusion than clarity and may have been primarily a matter of misunderstanding. But there were fundamental epistemological differences between the two thinkers that were evident far beyond this specific debate. If nothing else, Van Til willingly acknowledges the existence of unresolved paradoxical tensions, while Clark ridicules this idea. Frame himself discusses this very issue as a major difference between the two men (155-59).

[64] Gordon H. Clark, *Language and Theology* (Phillipsburg, N.J.: P&R, 1980), 139.

Clark's apologetics.[65] Van Til also spoke of innate ideas, but he used the term in an unusual way, describing the principle of general revelation in everyone bearing the image of God.[66] For him all human knowledge comes through divine revelation, whether general or special. For Van Til, the critical issue to reject was the existence of logic as a self-existent reality or a "non-revelational *a priori*."[67] While Clark anticipates that the natural person might be forced to recognize the implications of their innate knowledge in spite of themselves, as it were, Van Til believes that the natural person resists and suppresses the divine knowledge they possess. Therefore an apologist must confront people with their self-deceit, and only divine illumination will bring about repentant faith.

This leads to the second point of conflict: the relationship between God and ordering concepts such as the laws of logic. Clark and Van Til agree that logic rests on the foundation of God's own nature, rather than having an independent, external existence antecedent to God himself. For both thinkers logic defines the relationship between distinct propositions only because this is how they are ordered in the mind of God. Clark, however regards logic as unchangeable. To put it differently, fundamental logical principles are eternal and uncreated because they represent God's own unchanging, uncreated nature.[68] Van Til, however, emphasizes that all that exists is either God himself or that which he has created. "The whole of the created universe should always be kept distinct from and subordinate to its Creator. The laws of human thought and the laws of ethics are not eternal or unchangeable in the sense that God is unchangeable."[69] To put it differently, Van Til regards laws of logic as resting on God's creative act and working as a function of the created universe. This allowed him to go so far as suggesting that God's knowledge might not be propositional—transcending human logic in some way.[70]

The third point of conflict regarded the relationship between human and divine knowledge. Clark suggested that humans know a proposition in the same way that God does, while Van Til insisted on the qualification that all human knowledge is only analogical to the divine. Clark insisted that knowledge is meaningless unless

---

[65] Gordon H. Clark, *The Trinity* (Jefferson, Mass.: The Trinity Foundation, 1985), 64-65.

[66] Cornelius Van Til, *Junior Systematics* (Philadelphia: Theological Seminary of the Reformed Episcopal Church, 1940), 144-45.

[67] Cornelius Van Til, *In Defense of the Faith*, Vol. 5 (Philadelphia: P&R, 1978), 171.

[68] Gordon H. Clark, *Logic* (Unicoi, Tenn.: The Trinity Foundation, 1998), 112-17.

[69] Van Til, *Junior Systematics*, 10. Van Til does not mean by this that these laws are less epistemically certain, for on the same page he goes on to say that "once God has created the universe in accordance with certain laws, it is in accordance with these laws that we must learn to know the universe if we wish to know it at all. Then, if we do know the facts of the universe in accordance with those laws, our knowledge is just as certain with respect to them as our knowledge with respect to God is."

[70] Page 5, col. 2 of the unpublished "complaint," representing Van Til's position; quoted in Clark, *Trinity*, 85. Clark, by contrast, utterly repudiated the concept of "non-propositional truth." See Gordon H. Clark, "Reply to Ronald H. Nash," in *The Philosophy of Gordon H. Clark: A Festschrift*, ed. Ronald H. Nash (Philadelphia: P&R, 1968), 413.

its truth content is universal and unchanging. We cannot speak of "merely human logic" because true and logical thinking corresponds with God's.[71] Van Til argued that God's knowledge is qualitatively distinct from humanity's because he also knows every truth in relationship to every other truth. This is the sense of his statement that God's knowledge does not coincide with that of human beings at any single point and the reason that human knowledge can be analogical at best. Clark responded that to speak even of "analogy" required at least some point of coincidence between the two.[72] Entities that share nothing in common are not analogical.[73]

In this point of the debate, both thinkers overstated their positions, and neither made effort to understand the other. It seems that Van Til spoke of propositions taken in their entirety, while Clark analyzed distinct components of propositions. For Van Til no proposition could completely correspond between God and our knowledge in every way, since one of the meaningful components is certainly its relationship to every other proposition. God is all-knowing and humans are not; so at a minimum the context for every proposition is always different. But if a single component of a proposition could be isolated from its context, Clark was right in saying that analogy must require at least some points at which individual components are the same. In this part of the conflict, the debate echoed medieval debates, though neither thinker would have been happy with the parallel.[74] This was the least helpful part of the disagreement and has unfortunately received the most emphasis in subsequent discussion. Recently R. Scott Clark (unrelated to Gordon Clark) has argued that the roots of Van Til's distinction can be traced to the distinction in Reformed scholasticism between archetypal and ectypal knowledge.[75] Van Til himself did rely on this distinction at least once, but these terms were never introduced into the debate in any significant way.[76]

---

[71] Clark, *Logic*, 123-24.

[72] Gordon H. Clark, "The Bible As Truth," *Bib Sac*, April 1957, 163-67.

[73] Fred Klooster, *The Incomprehensibility of God in the Orthodox Presbyterian Conflict* (Franeker, Netherlands: T. Wever, 1951), 42-59, suggests that a number of passages support Van Til's understanding of the incomprehensibility of God, as opposed to the view of Gordon Clark (Job 5:9; 9:10; 11:7; Ps. 139:6; 145:3; Isa. 40:28; 55:8-9; Matt. 11:25-27; Rom. 11:33-34; 1 Cor. 2:6-16; 13:8-13). While the conclusion seems warranted, in several places Kooster's argument is weak, and it is not always possible to demonstrate from the passages he cites that Van Til's understanding is exegetically necessary.

[74] Clark's arguments against Van Til are fascinatingly similar to Ockam's: (1) Every analogy must contain at least one point of univocity. (2) Were there no points of univocal correspondence between God and man, knowledge of God would be impossible. See "Duns Scotus and William Ockam," 255-56.

[75] R. Scott Clark, "Janus, the Well-Meant Offer of the Gospel, and Westminster Theology," in *The Pattern of Sound Doctrine: Systematic Theology at the Westminster Seminaries*, ed. David Van Drunen (Phillipsburg, N.J.: P&R, 2004), 157-160.

[76] Clark, *Junior Systematics*, 203.

The final point of conflict regards the related issue of how human knowledge is limited. For Clark, the limitation on human knowledge was quantitative rather than qualitative. Quoting Bavinck, he writes,

> No doubt it is true that 'that which God reveals of himself . . . is so rich and deep [presumably Bavinck means extensive and complicated] that it can never be fully known by any human individual.' But this is not because the knowledge of God is a peculiar and different type of knowledge: It is because life is too short to gain an understanding of the Bible. The defect lies in the shortness of human life, and often in the mediocrity of the man, not in the understandability of the revelation, for all Scripture is profitable for doctrine.[77]

Van Til, on the other hand, maintained that the doctrine of incomprehensibility "is not the doctrine that God can be known only if he makes himself known. . . . It is rather that God because of his very nature must remain incomprehensible to man."[78] Later he writes that "the knowledge possible to man may never be conceived of merely in quantitative terms, as a difference of degree rather than a difference in kind."[79] To oversimplify, Clark believed that human knowledge is limited in information and that gaps in our understanding are matters of ignorance; we struggle to answer certain questions because we do not know enough information. For Van Til knowledge is also limited by comprehension, and gaps in our understanding might be paradoxical; we struggle to answer certain questions because our ability to understand and process information is limited.

The result from all of this is that Van Til accepted the idea of logical paradox, while Gordon Clark largely repudiated it. Clark commented that "he who says a given paradox cannot be solved, logically implies that he has examined every verse in Scripture, that he has exhausted every implication of every verse, and that there is in all this no hint of a solution".[80] Clark also "wrote that there was nothing objectionable in the human pursuit of comprehensive knowledge of God".[81] Van Til and Murray, on the other hand, believed that biblical theology contains propositions that are beyond our ability to reconcile.[82] Van Til saw apparent contradictions in the Trinity, the problem of God's freedom or necessary actions, the problem of evil, God's secret and revealed wills, prayer and God's sovereignty, the image of God in human beings, people's federal representation in Adam, sin's destructive power over God's creation, knowledge in unregenerate people, the humanity and deity of

---

[77] Clark, *Trinity*, 80-81. Brackets included in Clark's quotation.

[78] Quoted ibid., 84, taken from the complaint against Mr. Clark—an unpublished document that was central to the political conflict. Van Til did not write the complaint, but he did sign it, and it certainly represents his thought. John Muether, *Cornelius Van Til*, 104-105.

[79] Klooster, *The Incomprehensibility of God*, 16.

[80] "The Answer," 36 (unpublished).

[81] Muether, *Reformed Apologist*, 101.

[82] Hart, *Fighting the Good Fight*, 114.

Christ, and the free offer of the gospel.[83] This is probably the core of the conflict between Clark and Van Til, and it is unfortunate that the emphasis has been placed instead on whether divine and human thinking relate "analogically" or "univocally".[84]

It is not hard to see that this difference in starting points works out in a number of specific issues. Discussing the Trinity, Van Til comments that

> As Christians, we say that this is a mystery that is beyond our comprehension. . . . [The natural man will say] that such a notion claims to say something while it says nothing. To say that God is one person and at the same time to say that he exists as three persons he will say, is not merely to contradict yourself verbally, but is to say that all predication is analytic. . . . There is no possible way of softening this dilemma. Nor should we wish to tone it down. If we say that we can explain the doctrine of the Trinity to the satisfaction of the natural man by reducing the objectionable irrational element to his own non-objectionable irrational, we are in fact setting up an irrational that is objectionable from the Christian point of view.[85]

On the other hand, Clark attacks Van Til, confidently proposing that the Trinity contains no contradiction. Rather, if we clearly distinguish the three persons and one essence, the points of confusion involved with the Trinity will disappear. Clark quotes one of Van Til's students, who commented that "it would solve the apparent contradiction if we knew clearly what a substance (*ousia*) was, what person (*hypostasis*) was, and precisely how the two are related. But we don't." Clark comments that "there is not even an apparent contradiction if we say that God is one in one sense and three in a different sense. . . . Who can be so obtuse as to deny that *Substance* and *Person* are intended [in the Athanasian Creed] to have different meanings?"[86]

Clark was similarly confident with the problem of evil. He argued against free will as a theodicy, since the concept is unnecessary for both human responsibility and divine holiness. Instead, he argued that God can decree evil without being the efficient cause. As a result the theologian is no longer "compelled to disguise the obvious contradictions by the false piety of calling them mysteries".[87] Clark also criticized his denomination for maintaining "that the reconciliation of man's free agency and God's sovereignty is an inscrutable mystery. Rather the mystery is—

---

[83] *Analysis*, 155-156. It is worth noting that many of these points of conflict correspond to the five areas of mystery discussed in chapter 4.

[84] One of the most fascinating primary sources on this question is a letter from Van Til with critiques of one of Clark's journal articles. Clark highlighted the points of greatest contention by writing rebuttals of Van Til's thoughts in the margins. The primary point of conflict in the letter regards the status of human logic in relationship to the divine and to ultimate reality. Cornelius Van Til, *Letter of Dr. Cornelius Van Til to Dr. Gordon H. Clark*, December 5, 1938, http://www.pcahistory.org/findingaids/ clark/ cvtletter.html (accessed April 15, 2015).

[85] Van Til, *Defense*, 230-231.

[86] Clark, *Trinity*, 95-96.

[87] Gordon H. Clark, *Religion, Reason and Revelation* (Philadelphia: P&R, 1961), 220.

recognizing that God is the ultimate cause of the man's nature—how the Calvinistic solution could have been so long overlooked."[88]

What makes this example particularly poignant is the fact that Clark and Van Til shared so much in common across their other theological commitments.[89] Both were conservative Presbyterians; both regarded their view as faithful to Calvin's theology; both men even referred to their apologetic method as presuppositionalism; but their views on paradox were still at odds. This difference was great enough to extend to multiple theological questions.

On these bases it is legitimate to suggest several observations. (1) One's view on paradox is not inextricably based on a given theological system. In certain cases it might be entirely possible to hold to the same theological system in broad outlines while holding any one of the three major views on paradox. (2) When it comes to more complex, detailed issues, however, one's conclusions about paradox will certainly have a real influence on the answers we might be willing to make on a number of theological questions.

Observations from Church History

The common viewpoints on mystery in church history are far from simple or monolithic, but there are discernable trends as well. First, the historical pattern verifies the basic positions on mystery articulated in chapter 2.[90] In particular, the paradox-minimizing view and complementarity have had a constant presence throughout church history.[91] Though there are certainly variations in the specific details of these views, the various forms are strikingly similar—in some cases stretching across centuries. This suggests that fundamental philosophical or theological pre-commitments underlie each position—pre-commitments that every Christian philosopher must make.

Second, while historical precedents cannot certify a position independently, they eliminate the common charge that either complementarity or the paradox-minimizing view are recent innovations.[92] Both positions have existed throughout

---

[88] Gordon H. Clark, "Determinism and Responsibility," *EQ* (Jan 1932): 16. Clark argues that as the lawgiver, God has the right to define responsibility however he chooses, and he can condemn those who are not elect without bringing his justice into question.

[89] Clark, "Determinism and Responsibility," 22-23, and *Junior Systematics*, 1.

[90] The two positions that fall outside of orthodoxy have not been mentioned here because they are not a major concern of this study. However, examples of each do appear throughout church history. Arius, Peter Abelard, Michael Cervitus, Hartshorne, and others allowed over-emphasis on logic to lead them into heterodoxy. On the opposite extreme, Origen, Gilbert de la Porrée, Ian Ramsey, and others have made the same errors by an overemphasis on mystery.

[91] The *sui generis* view has been rarer in the history of the church. This is itself a significant consideration against the view, implying that it is further afield and carries more inherent problems than the other conservative views.

[92] Contra Norman Geisler, "The Incarnation and Logic: Their Compatibility Defended," *TJ* 6.2 (Fall 1985): 191.

the life of the church, and both have representatives within orthodoxy. Unfortunately, both positions have also functioned as the starting point out of which innovative and sometimes heterodox views have been born. In fact, most new theological challenges, debates on specific topics, or major doctrinal transitions in the history of the church have been accompanied by an underlying conflict that concerns the nature of theological paradox. At times, the church has assessed these underlying issues self-consciously; generally it has not.

Third, there is a specific issue at the core of many of the historical debates. All of the theologians surveyed here acknowledged the rather obvious insight that human knowledge about God is limited, but their viewpoints diverged in the response to that reality. For some thinkers we have an ethical responsibility to leave the unknown as it is. If God has not revealed a truth, people pursue further knowledge only at their own peril. For others it is completely acceptable to press on, seeking to understand as much as possible. This attitudinal difference toward unknown theological truths is one of the differences between the complementarian and paradox-minimizing views: if further reasoning or clarifying distinctions can be made, should theologians press on, and can they regard their suggestions with confidence? Or on the other hand, are there built-in limitations on what human thinkers can legitimately ask or seek to answer?

Fourth, the historical theology of paradox also exposes chronological development in the church's thinking on the question. Without a doubt contemporary discussions contain a level of sophistication surpassing the analyses of ancient thinkers. As the church's thought progressed and theology came under an increasingly consistent, systematic method, the problem of paradox also became clearer. The Church Fathers assumed that some theological truths were beyond human logic without exploring the implications of this assertion on faith and reason. The Middle Ages offered numerous variations on all of the views on paradox, but the church was largely complementarian, and doctrinal aberrations largely depended on extreme rationalism or mysticism. Most of the Reformers were complementarians but misused mystery in a few cases. In general, the Catholic Church's position was slightly more rationalistic than that of the Reformers, and most doctrinal aberrations during this era rested on extreme rationalism. Modern epistemology forced theologians to think more self-consciously about paradox, and theology has tended towards rationalism as a result. During this period the *sui generis* view diminished, and the conflict has been between complementarity and the paradox-minimizing view. Quite recently, open theism has brought the underlying questions to the fore again, and this specific debate will be one of the applications of this study later.

Fifth, the history of discussion on this question exposes an overemphasis on the preeminence of logic in contemporary discussion. This is not to say that logical gaffes should be acceptable or that theology is reduced to fideism. Still, it seems that theologians of the past were more willing to tolerate unresolved tensions or logical disparities without the *a priori* insistence that human knowers must know the relationship between theological propositions and have access to that knowledge in the present. Regarding the Incarnation, for instance, Geisler comments that "if the Incarnation as traditionally understood is indeed logically incoherent and therefore meaningless . . . , no other arguments need be offered against the Chalcedonian view, nor could there be any arguments mustered in favor of it. . . . The question of logical coherence is the most fundamental question in the whole debate."[93] It is hard not to contrast this framing of the question with Augustine's question—"who will explain in consistent words this single statement, that 'the Word was made flesh and dwelt among us?'"[94] Likewise, Charles Simeon's perspective is nearly a total contrast to Geisler's:

> It may be asked perhaps, How do you reconcile these doctrines, which you believe to be of equal authority and equal importance? But what right has any man to impose this task on the preachers of God's word? God has not required it of them; nor is the truth or falsehood of any doctrine to be determined absolutely by this criterion.[95]

Geisler's overemphasis may have arisen from the focus on logical consistency in the post-enlightenment era. Whatever the reason, historical comparison exposes it as a stronger contemporary concern. Modern theologians should note that theologians in the past assumed that some propositions would be logically irresolvable and did not regard that fact as a significant problem. Greater attention to the problem in contemporary thought is certainly positive, but theologians can also benefit from acknowledging the perspective of thinkers in the past and avoid epistemic hubris.[96]

Conclusion

Collecting these insights in Table 4.1, historical survey helps to evaluate theological paradox. More extended analysis of specific periods or specific issues would be helpful, but the broad themes lay a useful foundation.

Table 4.1. Summary of Historical Observations Concerning Paradox

---

[93] Geisler, "The Incarnation and Logic," 186.

[94] *Enchiridion,* Chapter 34. *A Select Library,* 3:249.

[95] Charles Simeon, *Horae homileticae,* vol. 15 (London: Holdsworth and Ball, 1833), xv.

[96] Historical theology has competing implications for the ongoing theological process. On the one hand, progressive illumination and the advancing clarity of theological debate mean that later formulations are often superior and it is legitimate to place greater confidence in the later conclusions of the church. On the other hand, it is far too easy to be historically myopic and parochial, prematurely dismissing ideas that enjoyed a high level of confidence in previous eras, or acquiescing to arguments that previous thinkers found insubstantial. At times, more recent emphases or concerns stand almost alone in theological history, calling their legitimacy or relevance into doubt. In the case of paradox, it is possible to articulate a model that is consistent and academically respectable in contemporary terms, but it is also helpful to acknowledge that theologians throughout church history have more readily accepted informational or even logical gaps. The understanding of paradox proposed here seeks as much as possible to take both observations into account.

Even from early times, the church has maintained that there are some theological issues and problems that cannot be completely resolved.
For many theologians paradox is connected to God's intellectual transcendence.
Paradox is inseparably connected to the problem of faith and reason.
A thinker's view on paradox is often dictated by his broader philosophical and epistemological pre-commitments.
A central point of debate is whether questions should be explored as much as possible or whether logical solutions should be proposed whenever possible.
Paradox may sometimes provide a window for logical inconsistency that inadvertently allows problematic formulations to stand.
When God's knowledge is materially distinguished from all other knowledge, it will result in a universal epistemological dualism.
It is often possible to hold to any one of several views on paradox while being committed to the same basic theological system.
On specific theological questions, one's conclusions about paradox will have a real influence on the answers he might give.
The basic positions on mystery have had a constant presence throughout church history. Thus none of these positions are novel.
While discussion of paradox has progressed in church history, contemporary discussion probably overemphasizes the preeminence of logical consistency.

This survey demonstrates that for all of the allusions to paradox throughout church history, very few theologians have analyzed the problem in depth. Theologians continue to discuss specific issues touching on paradox, but the problem itself has simply been set aside. Recent developments (particularly that of open theism) have forced theologians to reevaluate their positions and discuss paradox more self-consciously. The present theological milieu is ideal for a more extended analysis of paradox, which probably explains the burgeoning discussion of the topic. These recent developments are also the reason for a more extended application to open theism in this study. But it is necessary first to assess the orthodox views and establish a particular view of how to handle paradox properly.

CHAPTER 4

Understanding and Accounting for Paradox: Theological Examples

At some point in the debate over virtually every major Bible doctrine two roads diverge in the theological wood. It is vital to learn to detect where reason veers off from the road of explicit biblical statement. Once you step off the edge of the cliff of clear revelation, trusting in the power of logic to levitate your position, the fact is you are still standing out in thin air with nothing under you.[1]

Models for analyzing paradox are completely unnecessary unless paradox exists as part of theological discourse. Are there actually theological propositions that are true and must be accepted even though they seem to contradict one another? What of the far-reaching epistemological implications of this situation? There are no simple answers to these questions. But one way forward is to examine specific examples: problems that have driven at least some theologians to appeal to paradox. The method will be a combination of biblical theology and simple logic. If it is possible to support clear propositions with biblical theology, and then using simple logic demonstrate that they have contradictory content, then a method for paradox is imperative. Though other minor examples may also exist, there are five major areas for antinomy: the Trinity, the Incarnation, the problem of evil, sovereignty and free will, and the infinity of God.

Several introductory observations are in order. First, some interpreters question whether each of these examples contains an actual paradox. That is to say, they disagree with either the biblical propositions or the logical analysis suggested here. Naturally, most of these interpreters belong to the paradox-minimizing view, since neither of the non-orthodox views are bound by biblical data and both of the other conservative views are willing to tolerate paradox. Part of the purpose of this chapter, therefore, is to demonstrate that Scripture faces us with logical conflicts that it does not explicitly resolve.

Second, the idea that some theological propositions may conflict is highly controversial, and theologians rarely state the genuine issues clearly. A number of qualifications and clarifications appear in the next chapter. For the present, this study does not suggest that paradoxical truths are ultimately contradictory. On the contrary, paradoxical truths completely cohere in God's understanding. Perhaps

---

[1] Layton Talbert, *Not by Chance* (Greenville, S.C.: BJU, 2001), 252-53.

given further revelation, human minds will understand these truths as well. This study simply argues that some theological propositions do have apparently contradictory content as they presently stand in the biblical text.

Finally, the most natural way to resolve biblical paradoxes is to introduce a distinction. A contradiction both denies and affirms the same truth at the same time and in the same way. Thus theologians can relieve the tension if they suggest a plausible distinction between the two terms of the conflict—precisely what they have done in all five of the antinomies discussed here. But even where theologians proffer distinctions from outside the text, they cannot solve the problems completely. In fact, generally these distinctions simply relegate the problem to a deeper logical level. Retreat into the unknown can generate only more unknowns. In other cases the distinctions distort one or more strands of biblical data. Ironically, the biblical data stubbornly resists simple solutions, very often crossing over clear distinctions and combining incommensurable ideas in shocking ways.

The Trinity

One of the most intractable problems of systematic theology is the doctrine of three persons in one essence.[2] This conflict is inescapable if Scripture indicates that (1) the Father, Son, and Holy Spirit are God, (2) the Father, Son, and Holy Spirit are distinct from one another, and (3) God is one.[3]

Biblical Support

Scripture clearly supports proposition (1): all three persons are God. The deity of the Father is essentially undisputed (Matt. 6:26-32; John 6:27; 1 Cor. 8:6; 1 Pet. 1:1-2). Of course, some theologians dispute the Son's deity, but Scripture also clearly supports it (Isa. 9:6; John 1:1-4; 20:28; Rom. 9:5; Col. 2:9; Titus 2:13; Heb. 1:3, 8). The deity of the Spirit is well accepted, and passages that teach his deity are not difficult to find (Acts 5:3-4; Ps. 139:7-8; 1 Cor. 2:10-11). It is more common for theologians to question whether the Spirit is a person, suggesting instead that the Spirit metaphorically describes God's power. But Scripture records that he performs personal actions (John 14:2; Rom. 8:26-27; Acts 8:29; Eph. 4:30) and also distinguishes him from his own power (Luke 4:14; Acts 10:38).[4]

Scripture also states proposition (2): the three persons are distinct. Several passages list the three persons in parallel (Matt. 28:19; 1 Cor. 12:4-6; 2 Cor. 13:14;

---

[2] James Anderson, *Paradox in Christian Theology* (Eugene: Wipf and Stock, 2007), 11-59, works at length to demonstrate that the traditional, orthodox understanding of the Trinity is necessarily paradoxical.

[3] Throughout this study, propositions are numbered for the sake of clarity. Propositions that are not true but are included for the sake of argument (*reductio ad absurdum*) are listed with negative numbers. Each subsection is numbered separately.

[4] Wayne Grudem, *Systematic Theology* (Grand Rapids: Zondervan, 1994), 232-33, points out that if the Spirit refers only to the power of God, a number of these statements are redundant and nonsensical. In Luke 4:14, "Jesus returned to Galilee in the power of *God's power?*"—original emphasis.

Eph. 4:4-6; 1 Pet. 1:2). Another group of passages distinguishes them from the others by referring to inter-Trinitarian actions as interpersonal and relational (Matt. 3:16-17; John 14:26). A number of passages distinguish two of the persons, such as the Son from the Father (John 1:1-2; 17:24; 1 John 2:1; Heb. 7:25), the Spirit from the Father (Rom. 8:27), and the Spirit from the Son (John 16:7). Once again, many of these statements involve relational interactions between the persons.

Finally, Scripture states proposition (3): God is one (Deut. 6:4-5; Isa. 45:5-6; Rom. 3:30; 1 Cor. 8:6; 1 Tim. 2:5; Jas. 2:19). These passages do not emphasize the unity or simplicity of God so much as they eliminate polytheism as a possible understanding of the Trinity.

To summarize, Scripture indicates that (1a) the Father, (1b) Son, and (1c) Holy Spirit are God. (2) The Father, Son, and Holy Spirit are distinct from one another, as well as the fact that (3) God is one.[5] But this leads to proposition (-3): God is three, because of a simple logical syllogism:

(4) MP: By identity (counting), the Father, Son, and Holy Spirit are three.
(1) mp: The Father, Son, and Holy Spirit are God.
(-3) Conclusion: God is three.

But, of course, if there is any meaning to proposition (3) that God is one, proposition (-3) contradicts it. Polytheism is unbiblical because of proposition 3, but can it really fulfill that role if it is also possible for one to be three? For (3) to have any heresy-eliminating power, it must also eliminate (-3). Of course, there is a basic explanation for this problem, but at the outset, one should acknowledge that this is the beginning of a serious conflict.[6]

Another way to clarify the problem is in connection to the biblical statements about the economic Trinity. For instance, Scripture repeatedly states that (5) the Father sent the Son into the world (John 5:23; 10:36; 1 John 4:14):

(5) MP: The Father sent the Son into the world.
(1a) mp: The Father is God.
(-5) Conclusion: God sent the Son.

Of course, one could follow a similar process using proposition (1b) (the Son is God) to reach the conclusion that God sent God. Though Scripture never makes both substitutions in the same place, it does refer to both the Son and the Father as

---

[5] The Trinitarian and Christological heresies negated almost every combination of these propositions: Arianism or Macedonianism/Pneumatomachianism deny #1, Modalism/Sabellianism or Nocticism deny #2, and polytheism denies #3.

[6] Theologians may become inured to such jarring conflicts. Philosophers have long recognized that repetition and familiarity can sometimes substitute for comprehension. In other words, people can look past a genuine problem if they are very familiar with the concept. This is a common phenomenon with all of the theological paradoxes, and one of the reasons that this study returns to the basic starting propositions.

"God" without any additional qualification.[7] Furthermore, equally logical substitutions in statement (-5) yield the conclusions that the Father sent the Father, the Son sent the Son, or the Son sent the Father. All of this results from syllogisms in the following form:

(-5) MP: God sent the Son.
(1b) mp: The Son is God.
(-6) Conclusion: The Son sent the Son (substitution).[8]

Besides the obvious practical issue of how someone sends himself, the proposition that the Son sent the Son disagrees with biblical data, and the corresponding derivation that the Son sent the Father is only worse. Of course, the logical problem here rests on the meaning of the predicate relationship—in what sense should we understand our starting propositions, and what substitutions do these statements permit? Yet this only highlights the problem. Each predicate is capable of substitution in some cases but not in others, and consistent patterns are all but impossible to find.

Scripture also contains a few passages that cross over the paradox by recombining propositions in complex ways. Several texts seem to imply that the Son is separate from God, without explicitly identifying "God" as the Father (John 1:1-2; 1 Cor. 8:6; 1 Tim. 2:5). 1 Corinthians 8:6 indicates that the Father is the "one God" and distinguishes him from the "one Lord, Jesus Christ." More clearly, Peter equivocates between God (qeo/j) and the Spirit of the Lord in a way that attributes the same action to each (Acts 5:4, 9). A number of NT passages demonstrate that in the Old Testament *Yahweh* ambiguously referred to various persons of the Trinity.[9] Finally, John 17 juxtaposes the distinction (John 17:3, 8, 11, 24) and unity (John 17:11, 21-23) of the Father and the Son.

---

[7] Matthew 1:23 and John 1:18 both speak of the "Son of God" in this way. Scripture speaks of the Father as God in Acts 13:23; Romans 5:1; 15:6; Galatians 4:4; Hebrews 13:20 or in any occurrence of "Son of God" (Matt. 16:16). The best examples of reverse substitutions are from OT Yahweh to the Son (Isa. 40:3 with Heb. 1:6) or the Father (Lev. 11:44 with 1 Pet. 1:16-17).

[8] This is similar to a syllogism that John Frame suggests as logical but impossible in *The Doctrine of God* (Phillipsburg, N.J.: P&R, 2002), 732.
MP: Whatever the Father does, the Son also does (John 5:19).
mp: The Father begets the Son.
Conclusion: The Son begets the Son.

[9] A large group of passages equate OT Yahweh with Jesus of Nazareth: Matthew 3:3 with Isaiah 40:3; John 12:41 with Isaiah 6:1-3; Ephesians 4:7-8 with Psalm 68:18; Hebrews 1:6 with Psalm 97:7; Hebrews 1:10-12 with Psalm 102:25-27; 1 Peter 3:14-15 with Isaiah 8:12-13. But another group identify OT Yahweh with the Father: Matthew 22:32 with Exodus 3:6; Acts 4:24-25 with Exodus 20:11 and Psalm 2:2; Acts 13:33 with 2 Samuel 7:14; 1 Peter 1:16-17 with Leviticus 11:44. Recently an increasing number of interpreters have argued that 2 Corinthians 3:17 equates OT Yahweh with the Spirit. See Murray J. Harris, *The Second Epistle to the Corinthians* (Grand Rapids: Eerdmans, 2005), 311-312.

Theological Analysis

It is standard and orthodox to recognize a distinction between personhood (by which the three are distinct) and essence (by which the three are one). It is also common to say that this distinction relieves the Trinity of the charge of contradiction.[10] But in an otherwise unhelpful article, John Dahms points out that this distinction only pushes the problem to another level. Do the three persons each partake of a portion of the essence, or is there a division between each of the persons and the essence by which they exist?[11] Either understanding leads to further theological problems. Or should theologians really say that every passage that speaks of God as a unity and incorporating all three persons, refers to his essence but not his person? Should they really draw the natural conclusion that the one God (without distinction between Father, Son, and Holy Spirit) has no unified personal component—God's personality exists only in the individuated three?[12]

Turning again to the economic Trinity, the difficulties only become greater with the Incarnation. Orthodox theologians cannot maintain that the Father and the Spirit also came to earth, suffered and died. But it is equally untenable to say that when the Son took on a human nature, died, and rose again, it only involved his Trinitarian person and nothing of the undivided essence of the Trinity.[13]

The reason for this barrage of questions is to expose the logical conflicts that still exist beyond the distinction of person and essence. One could answer that these questions carry us beyond the revelation God has given, but this essentially

---

[10] Norman Geisler, "'Avoid . . . Contradictions' (1 Timothy 6:20): A Reply to John Dahms," *JETS* 22.1 (March 1979): 62. Also, William G.T. Shedd, *Dogmatic Theology* (Nashville: Thomas Nelson, 1980), 1:268-69 and R.C. Sproul, *The Mystery of the Holy Spirit* (Wheaton: Tyndale, 1994), 46-52. More philosophically and using formal logic, A.P. Martinich, "Identity and Trinity," *JR* 58.2 (April 1978): 169-81.

[11] John V. Dahms, "How Reliable is Logic?," *JETS* 21.4 (December 1978): 373-74.

[12] Gerald O'Collins, *The Tripersonal God* (New York: Paulist, 1999), 174. This is the sense in which to understand Cornelius Van Til's comments about the one, unified personality in the Trinity. See his *In Defense of the Faith*, Vol. 5 (Philadelphia: P&R, 1978), 229-30.

[13] Given the simplicity of God, we should not fully divide between his essence and person. In fact, if essence is understood as an ontic category, it is meaningless and impossible to divide the two—and yet this is exactly what the Incarnation should logically force us to do. In fact, the same problem could be applied to every distinction between the three persons, but the case of the Incarnation is the clearest example of one person's actions in which the other two must be excluded. Indeed, while otherwise attempting to show that the Trinity is not logically contradictory, John Feinberg, *No One Like Him* (Wheaton: Crossway, 2001), 495-96, recognizes this specific point as "the mystery that we can't understand." Feinberg goes on to say that references such as Matthew 3:16 force us to "grant that somehow each divine person can act distinctly from the other two, even though all three in some sense do every deed of each member of the Godhead." If Feinberg's goal is to demonstrate that the Trinity does not contain logical contradictions (493), this is a clear example that he never explains. Indeed, words such as "somehow" and "in some sense" imply a distinction that he never makes. This serves to illustrate the reality behind attempts to solve paradox by introducing distinctions—the problems are only pushed to a deeper level.

concedes the point—as the biblical data stands there are significant, unresolved, logical conflicts. The distinction between person and essence does not relieve the tension.

These difficulties only expose a deeper problem in the distinction: what exactly do person and essence mean? Though the distinction has theological utility, it never appears in Scripture, and theologians have always struggled to define it with meaningful content.[14] One wonders if the terms refer to little more than the logical necessities they represent. Several things are certain. (1) God is one in some sense and three in some sense. (2) Humans cannot fully account for how these propositions relate, but (3) God knows the resolution perfectly. Clearly, there is some way that these conflicting propositions cohere that we do not know. Based on the principle that a proposition and its opposite cannot both be true in the same way and the same time, we can assume that there must be some type of distinction between the senses of the propositions. Perhaps person and essence serve as a way of stating that fact. In other words, "essence" represents the sense (unknown to humans) in which one can accurately say that God is one, while "person" represents the sense (also unknown to humans) in which one can say that God is three.[15] If this is so, "person" and "essence" are primarily analytic rather than synthetic.[16] In other

---

[14] Millard Erickson, *Christian Theology* (Grand Rapids: Baker, 1998), 363, comments that the Trinity is not a contradiction because God is one and three in different respects—one *ousia* and three *hypostases*. "The problem is determining what these two terms mean, or more broadly, what the difference is between the nature of locus of God's oneness and that of his threeness." The major difficulty is with the meaning of *essence*. What can we really claim to know about the ontology of a self-caused being and how it works? Humans are incapable of defining or describing their own personality and ontology; what of God's? Gordon Clark, *The Incarnation* (Jefferson, Md.: The Trinity Foundation, 1988), 55, is something of an iconoclast on this point, dismissing substance and subsistence as meaningless terminology. He presses for a rigorous standard of meaning, demanding that we either "discard or define!" Even the easier concept—personhood—has its own challenges. Clark goes on to suggest an unusual definition of personhood as a composite of truths—i.e., a person possesses consciousness of facts that are true about them self (51-55). Stretching the idea of personhood even further, Gerald O'Collins, *Tripersonal God*, 178-79, distinguishes the divine persons almost exclusively by their relationships with one another. Some of the confusion also certainly stems from a fundamental difference between the way the church fathers understood personhood and the more modern, psychological understanding. See John Murray, *The Collected Writings of John Murray* (Carlisle, Pa.: Banner of Truth, 1982), 4:277-81. M. John Farrelly, *The Trinity: Rediscovering the Central Christian Mystery* (New York: Sheed & Ward, 2005), 17-18. See, also, Feinberg, *No One Like Him*, 225-31, for a helpful theological discussion of personhood.

[15] We can gather some information about the meaning of these terms (particularly "person") by observing the context in which statements about the Trinity appear. This is why it seems acceptable to give provisional definitions of personhood, such as self-consciousness, social interaction, and self-determination. Essence, on the other hand, is almost entirely elusive.

[16] Analytic notions are propositions that unassailably arise from deductive logic but state no new or external information. An example would be "all bachelors are unmarried men."

words, they stand by definition as the senses in which one or the other proposition is true of God, but the meaningful content one can assign to them is quite limited.[17] John Frame explains this concept clearly:

> What the Bible reveals is that there is one God in three persons, persons related to one another as Father, Son and Spirit. Much of the rest of Trinitarian theology, one suspects, is an attempt to get beyond this fundamental truth by multiplying forms of *Father, Son*, and S*pirit*. . . . Much of the reflection, it seems to me, really amounts to putting the names of the three persons into different forms, without any increase in knowledge or edification. . . . I cannot escape the notion that at least some of this discussion amounts to playing with words.[18]

Synthetic notions give new information by predicating something external about their subject. An example would be "John is a bachelor." D.W. Hamlyn discusses the complexities behind how "analytic notions" have been variously understood in "Analytic and Synthetic Statements," in *The Encyclopedia of Philosophy*, ed. Paul Edwards (New York: Macmillan, 1967), 1.105-109. It is actually quite hard to escape the assertion that the Trinitarian distinction between persons and essence is analytic. To the extent that "person" and "essence" arise exclusively from the biblical data (i.e., the propositions about the Trinity stated above) without going beyond it, they can bear only an analytic relationship to that data. The only other way for information to enter the question synthetically would be from philosophical notions of what is possible for God's personality and being. Regarding this, it seems safe to assume that we are not qualified to delimit what is possible or impossible for God's ontology. Therefore, unless a solution to the paradox of the Trinity arises from the biblical text or out of logical inferences built on it, these terms can only solve the problem analytically.

[17] In fact, it may be that the ontological distinctions (procession and spiration) arose from the need to differentiate the three persons in light of the radical unity of the essence. Gerald O'Collins, "The Holy Trinity: The State of the Question," in *The Trinity*, ed. Stephen T. Davis, Daniel Kendall and Gerald O'Collins (Oxford: Oxford University Press, 1999), 9. Exegetical support for this metaphysical impartation of essence is quite lacking.

[18] Frame, 7 *Cornelius Van Til: An Analysis of His Thought* (Phillipsburg, N.J.: P&R, 1995), 13-714. Stephen T. Davis, *Logic and the Nature of God* (Grand Rapids: Eerdmans, 1983), 137-138, interacts with Martinich and several other proposed solutions, finally concluding with the understanding of analytic terms presented here. Even in the context of denying that the Trinity is a contradiction, Shedd inconsistently gestures in the same direction when he writes, "To assert that there is but one divine *nature* or *essence*; that this undivided essence is common to three *persons*; that by *person* when applied to God, we do not mean the same as when applied to man, but only somewhat analogous to it; that we have no adequate idea of what is meant by the word person when applied to God, and use it only because distinct personal attributes and actions are ascribed to the Father, Son and Holy Ghost in Scripture, is no contradiction" (1:268). Wayne Grudem, *Systematic Theology*, 255, also supports this notion when he comments that "Christian theology has come to use the word *person* to speak of these differences in relationship, not because we fully understand what is meant by the word *person* when referring to the Trinity, but rather so that we might say something instead of saying nothing at all.". Also, Calvin, *Institutes*, I.xiii.5.

This is not in any way to mitigate either the doctrine of God's personhood or the clear biblical indication that each of the three members of the Trinity is fully personal. Both propositions enjoy definite biblical support. Only one aspect of the distinction is analytic—to the extent that theologians use it to resolve the logical conflict of the Trinity. Said differently, there is biblical data supporting the reality that three divine persons exist; there is also biblical data supporting the reality that God is one being. But in the absence of data explaining how these realities relate to one another, analytic expressions are the only solutions warranting complete confidence.[19]

Nor does this idea lead in any way to the unacceptable conclusion that theologians ought to abandon the person-essence distinction. On the contrary, the distinction elucidates heretical aberrations that deny either the personal distinctions among the three members or the essential unity of the one God. The mistake is to think that this distinction also fully resolves the logical tension in the biblical data concerning the Trinity.[20]

How should this logical problem be regarded? In order to avoid the conflict between these propositions, one must set aside either the exegetical support for the propositions or the logical analysis that leads to the conflict. Theologians simply do not know how these propositions harmonize, and the legitimate distinction between God's person and essence cannot solve the problem completely. Were these propositions not posited in Scripture, good theologians would dismiss them as nonsensical. One could propose an endless array of other arbitrary distinctions, but they either push the problem to another step or obfuscate it in unexplained terms.

The Person of Christ

Another long-enduring problem of theology involves the two natures in the one person of Christ.[21] The conflict is inescapable if two basic propositions are true: (1)

---

[19] Speaking for Van Til, Frame, *Cornelius Van Til*, 158-159, points out that the church has traditionally "made the claim that God is one and three in different senses, and . . . Van Til does not dispute this claim. But he does claim that we do not know precisely how God is one and precisely how he is three; so we cannot *demonstrate* the logical consistency of the doctrine. For that reason, some appearance of contradiction remains"—original emphasis.

[20] Grudem, *Systematic Theology*, 255-56. Berkhof, *Systematic Theology* (Edinburgh: Banner of Truth, 2000), 88-89, comments that "the Trinity is a mystery . . . in the sense that man cannot comprehend it and make it intelligible. . . . The real difficulty lies in the relation in which the persons in the Godhead stand to the divine essence and to one another; and this is a difficulty which the Church cannot remove, but only try to reduce to its proper proportion by a proper definition of terms. It has never tried to explain the mystery of the Trinity, but only sought to formulate the doctrine of the Trinity in such a manner that the errors which endangered it were warded off."

[21] As with the Trinity, James Anderson, *Paradox in Christian Theology*, 61-106, also demonstrates that the traditional, orthodox understanding of the Incarnation is paradoxical. The history of Christological heresies reveals repeated attempts to deny either Jesus' full deity (Arianism and Ebionism) or his humanity (Docetism,

Jesus possessed both full deity and full humanity in one person, and (2) deity and humanity involve incommensurable attributes.

Biblical Support

The fact that Jesus possessed both full deity and humanity is solidly established in orthodox Christology. Scripture clearly teaches that Jesus was fully God with all of the attributes of deity, including omniscience (Mark 2:8; John 1:48; 2:24; 6:64; 16:30; 21:17), omnipresence (Matt. 8:8-13; 18:20; 28:20), omnipotence (Matt. 8:26-27; John 2:1-12), and eternal preexistence (John 8:58; 17:5, 24; Rev. 22:13).[22] Scripture is just as clear that Jesus was fully man, including characteristics such as limited knowledge (Matt. 24:36; Mark 13:32; Heb. 5:8), limitations of space (John 11:15-17), limitations of strength (John 4:6; Luke 23:26), and limitations of time (Matt. 1:18; Luke 3:23).

It is also simple to demonstrate that the characteristics of humanity and deity are incompatible. Because of the *imago Dei*, humanity possesses many of the same capacities as deity, with one crucial difference—God is infinite while human nature is limited. This is why theologians have traditionally spoken of God's incommunicable attributes and also why many of the attributes are described apophatically.[23]

Given the fact that Christ possessed both divine and human traits and that the two are mutually exclusive, it is a simple matter to demonstrate the conflict. It would be impossible for Jesus to be fully deity without being infinite and also impossible to be fully human without being limited. Each of the attributes has the strong biblical support listed above, and all can be placed in a simple opposition leading to a logical contradiction:

(subset of 1)   MP: Jesus possessed limitless power.
(subset of 1)   mp: Jesus did not possess limitless power.

Eutychianism, and Apollinarianism). Speaking of the Incarnation in particular, Stephen T. Davis, "John Hick on Incarnation and Trinity," in *The Trinity*, ed. Stephen T. Davis, Daniel Kendall and Gerald O'Collins (Oxford: Oxford University Press, 1999), 258, comments that "virtually every theologian who has ever defended the classic doctrine has emphasized that there is an element of mystery or paradox about it".

[22] It is not common to speak of Christ's omnipresence during the Incarnation. Certainly it would be wrong to speak of the omnipresence of his human nature. But there is also significance in the perfect periphrastic followed by the present tense in Matthew 18:20: "where two or three *have gathered* in my name, there I *am* in their midst". There is no exegetical indication that the promise should be restricted to gatherings of believers after Christ's resurrection and ascension. The grammar seems to indicate that in some sense, Christ was present with such believers *during* his Incarnation.

[23] Apophatic language describes God's attributes negatively. The simplest way to describe omnipotence, omniscience, and infinity is by negating the limitations of humanity or the created world. Thus, omniscience means that God knows without any limitations. By definition, this demonstrates that these attributes are fundamentally incompatible with human characteristics on some level.

(subset of 2)   Conclusion: Jesus did and did not possess limitless power.[24]

Just as with the Trinity, Scripture includes a number of cross-over passages that combine both sides of this tension. Even before Christ's coming, Isaiah 9:6 prophesied that he would be "the mighty God" and yet he would be "a son" and "born to us"—a biological descendant of Abraham and David. John 17 repeatedly juxtaposes Jesus' limitations (John 17:4, 8, 12, 24) and infinity (John 17:5, 22, 24).[25] Hebrews 1 teaches that Christ is the perfect messenger from God because he is God, while chapter 2 emphasizes that he is the perfect high priest because he is a man. In Matthew 8:24 Jesus is weary enough to sleep (also implying a cessation of human consciousness), but as soon as he awakens, he exercises power over the forces of nature (Matt. 8:26-27). All three of the major passages on Jesus' limited knowledge specifically emphasize his deity by calling him the Son, rather than expressions that more naturally relate to his humanity (Matt. 24:36; Mark 13:32; Heb. 5:8).[26] In John 11 Christ learns of Lazarus's sickness from messengers (vv. 3, 6), has to ask where they laid him (v. 34), and grieves Lazarus's death (v. 35). But Jesus knew from the beginning that Lazarus would be raised (v. 11) and knew without being told that he had died (vv. 11-14).[27] In these instances the conflict is not merely theoretical, as though only systematic theologians would notice it. Any attentive reader of these texts is confronted with jarring inconsistencies and wonders how both kinds of statements could apply to the same individual.[28] A related form of the problem explores how Christ's natures integrated with each other.[29] The Chalcedonian model proposes two complete natures united in one

---

[24] Out of all of these attributes, the one with the most explicit exegetical backing is Jesus' simultaneous omniscience and limited knowledge, since Scripture clearly states at least one thing he did not know (Matt. 24:36; Mark 13:32).

[25] Most shocking is Jesus' reference to being one with the Father (v. 21-22), while also speaking of coming to him (v. 13).

[26] These passages could have used a title with less emphasis on his deity, such as "Jesus Christ" (c. f. 1 John 4:2). Hebrews is especially clear by using a concessive conjunction—"although he was Son, he learned obedience" (kai/per).

[27] One could assume that Jesus only asked these questions for the sake of his hearers. But (1) there is no exegetical data to imply this. (2) The sheer number of questions that Jesus asked and the nature of the questions seem to imply otherwise. Nothing about Jesus' responses indicates any pretense (c. f. 11:35). (3) There is clear biblical indication of things Jesus did not know (Matt. 24:36; Mark 13:32; Heb. 5:8). Therefore, it seems best to accept these as genuine questions.

[28] This relates to an observation that will be significant later: Scripture is not preoccupied with such conflicts as though their very presence lends a mystical authenticity, nor does Scripture avoid these types of logical conflicts as though their presence brings its authenticity into question. All in all, Scripture is remarkably indifferent to the presence of apparent contradictions and sometimes places conflicting propositions in close proximity.

[29] As A.A. Hodge, *A Commentary on the Confession of Faith* (Philadelphia: Presbyterian Board, 1869), 195, puts it, "It is impossible to explain philosophically how *two* self-conscious intelligences, how *two* self-determined free agents, can constitute *one* person. Yet this is the precise character of the phenomenon revealed in the history of Jesus." This

person "without confusion, without change, without division, without separation, the distinction of natures being in no way annulled by the union, but rather the characteristics of each nature being preserved and coming together to form one person and subsistence, not as parted or separated into two persons".[30] This leads to more complex questions such as how Christ's mind and will could exist in two natures but interface in one person. Since Scripture never explores these questions in depth, this tension is harder to state in propositional form with biblical supports.[31] Instead, the conflict rests on the foundation of the Chalcedonian formula— (3) one person with two natures. We could state the problem as follows:

---

conflict is because "the essential properties of divinity cannot be communicated to humanity; that is, humanity cannot be made to be infinite, self-existent, eternal and absolutely perfect" (196).

[30] Even the apophatic (negative) language of the formula implies that this doctrine is an unsettled tension between several biblical truths and that the framers were more comfortable with limiting the statements that could be made than giving more details about the Incarnation or satisfying the tension.

[31] One possible way to state it would be simply in the same form as above:

MP: Christ possessed all knowledge.
mp: Christ was ignorant of some things/Christ did not possess all knowledge.
Conclusion: Christ did and did not possess all knowledge.

(1) MP: Human nature includes human consciousness.
(subset of 3) mp: Jesus possessed a human nature.
(2) Conclusion: Jesus possessed human consciousness.

Of course, the same reasoning applies to the divine nature for proposition (6): "Jesus possessed divine consciousness." Joining these by identity, we can say that (7) "Jesus possessed two consciousnesses (human and divine).[32] In fact, this conclusion has enjoyed the support of the majority of the church.[33]

However, consciousness is a significant defining component of personhood. In fact, (8) there is hardly a component more central to personhood than consciousness.[34] Thus, we could reason that:

(7) MP: Jesus possessed two consciousnesses.
(8) mp: Consciousness defines personhood.
(-1) Conclusion: The incarnation involved two persons.

Of course, this conclusion contradicts the Chalcedonian formula. The response should be that Christ was one person with two consciousnesses. But this also produces a crisis of definition as a result, for there is no longer a way to define personhood distinctly, and the terms of the Chalcedonian model lack meaningful content that is sufficient to resolve the tension.

All of this is a complex way of saying that no one can explain how two complete and personal natures could coexist in one person.[35] Once again, the problem is not

---

[32] Donald Macleod, *The Person of Christ* (Downers Grove: InterVarsity, 1998), 193, is careful to say that Jesus did not possess two self-consciousnesses, but that "there are two levels of consciousness of the one self. These two forms of consciousness remain distinct, united in the one person, communicating through the Holy Spirit." Some type of distinction like this is probably necessary. The important point is that this distinction still does not solve the problem—it only pushes it to another level. What can it mean to have two levels of consciousness united in one person? It is simple enough to respond that Christ's mental states are completely different from ours, but one begins to wonder how meaningful the distinction is or how helpful terms like "level" really are if we cannot propositionally state their truth value. As with the Trinity, the problem is not with the distinction itself but with the idea that such a distinction can completely satisfy the logical conflict.

[33] Charles Hodge, *Systematic Theology* (Grand Rapids: Eerdmans, 1973), 2:405.

[34] John Feinberg, *No One Like Him,* 228, defines personality with self-consciousness and self-determination, i.e. the will. The issue of Christ's will could proceed along the same analysis as the reasoning here. It is fascinating that these two issues have been the very points where Chalcedonian Christology has most struggled to integrate the two natures. In fact, Monothelitism was condemned as a heresy. This is confirmation that the Chalcedonian problem is the struggle to unite two natures into one person, even though both of the natures contain respective personal components. Gordon Clark, *The Incarnation,* 68, uses this very problem to attack the more traditional understanding of the Incarnation, when he asks, "How can a human consciousness, mind, heart and will not be a human person?" Wayne Grudem, *Systematic Theology,* 558-61, offers an honest and direct discussion of this problem.

with Chalcedon, but with the idea—unsupported by historical theology—that Chalcedon can explain the problem of the Incarnation. What gives this problem special status is the fact that *as they stand* the biblical propositions are more than unexplained; they are an unresolved logical conflict.

Theological Analysis

The most helpful model is that Christ possessed the capacity for all power or knowledge while voluntarily limiting the free exercise of these abilities. Still, this cannot solve the problem completely.[36] First, this is only workable if the divine nature makes all concessions to the limits of humanity, since it is only possible for the greater to condescend to the lesser. There could hardly be a contrast as far-reaching as that between the nature of God and humanity. The result is that the divine nature must adjust in every attribute, leaving a very impoverished shadow of the second person of the Trinity during his Incarnation. This leads to a second and more intractable problem—the biblical data is not so simple. In fact, Scripture records that Christ simultaneously displayed *both* super-human knowledge *and* human limitations of knowledge; *both* super-human power *and* human limitations of strength. The reason for these tensions is also clear—Jesus exhibited both human and divine attributes because he was both a man and God (John 2:11; 3:2; 4:25-29; 10:20; Acts 2:22). Finally, this resolution is overly simplistic because the meaning of full deity and humanity require more. God's omnipotence includes the constant maintenance of all things (Heb. 1:3), meaning that Christ continued to exercise his full omnipotence even while he experienced human weakness. Likewise, full

---

[35] The idea of the *anhypostasia* or better, the *enhypostasia*, is not an answer to the problem, since the idea of the *enhypostasia* is that Christ's human nature never existed independent of the hypostatic union. See Macleod, *The Person of Christ*, 199-203. If Christ's divine nature has a special status as the foundation of his personhood in some sense, the implications only become even more problematic. As Gordon Clark *The Incarnation*, 69, points out, this results in the divine nature having a more ultimate role in the personhood and leads to the uncomfortable situation of the divine person suffering the weaknesses of the human nature.

[36] Kenoticism appears in various forms, but the essential concept is that Christ temporarily set aside the exercise of certain attributes so that he could possess both natures in one unified person. On this understanding, the attributes that he set aside are contingent rather than necessary. In other words, neither divine nor human nature requires these attributes in order to maintain their identity. This construction also requires that there are no necessary divine attributes that it is impossible for a human to exhibit, and the converse. "John Hick on Incarnation and Trinity," 262-63. Given these requirements, it is possible to understand the doctrine of the Incarnation in a way that is logically defensible. Nevertheless, using the very same type of analysis, Thomas Morris, *The Logic of God Incarnate* (Ithaca: Cornell University Press, 1986), 93-102, rejects kenoticism because of two problems: (1) It requires that so many divine attributes are contingent, there is very little left to distinctively define a divine nature. (This results when kenoticists require the divine nature to make all concessions to the limitations of the human nature.) (2) This impoverished view of the divine nature in Christ causes significant problems to the doctrine of immutability.

humanity implies a beginning, but preexistence is a fact of deity quite independent of voluntary limitation.

The standard answer for a conflict such as the proposition that "Jesus possessed all power and Jesus did not possess all power" is to distinguish between his person and natures. Norman Geisler is confident that Chalcedon relieves any charges of logical contradiction using this distinction.[37] But while Chalcedon is a necessary understanding of the theanthropic person, it cannot fully solve the problem, but only introduces another string of questions. As Wayne Grudem points out, biblical statements attach characteristics of either nature to the one person of Christ.[38] Each nature is so united with the person that what can be said of one of Christ's natures can also be said of his person. As in Figure 3.1, predicates of either nature can also be predicated to the theanthropic person. But there is also a divide between the natures—some predicates of the divine nature cannot be predicated to the human nature and the converse.

Figure 3.1. Predicate Relationships in Chalcedonian Christology

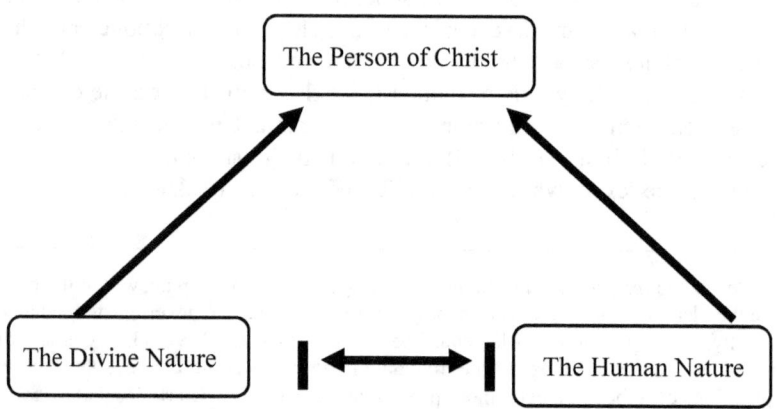

If the human nature is finite, the person can also be called finite. But of course, it follows that if the divine nature is infinite the person of Christ is also infinite. This leads to the impossible conclusion that the *person* of Christ was both infinite and not infinite—the exact form of an explicit contradiction. For example, one ought to affirm that Jesus Christ was omnipresent and that he was not in Galilee at the time of Matthew 19:1. Or one might say that Jesus Christ was dead for several days in the first century, while also affirming that Jesus Christ has been alive eternally—he never has and never will cease in his living existence.

As with the Trinity, this is not to say that the distinction between Christ's person and his natures is wrong or valueless. The distinction is still helpful because Scripture never mixes the characteristic of one nature with the other. There is no

---

[37] Norman Geisler, "The Incarnation and Logic: Their Compatibility Defended," *TJ* 6.2 (Fall 1985): 185-97.

[38] Grudem, *Systematic Theology*, 562.

biblical data, for instance, suggesting that Christ's physical body was omnipresent. But Chalcedon limits the distinction from being useful to the extent that would solve the problem. If every set of conflicting predicates is relegated to the separate natures, there is simply nothing left for the unity of the person.[39]

Just as with the Trinity, it is more helpful to recognize from the outset that the distinction is analytic rather than synthetic. In other words, *nature* refers to any predicates of Christ that cannot be predicated to him unreservedly—those human characteristics of the human that do not apply to the divine or the converse. *Person*, on the other hand, describes predicates that apply to Christ without distinction. Beyond this, it is very difficult to assign meaningful content to the terms of the distinction.[40] Essentially, they represent some necessary but unknown distinction that allows both sets of propositions to be true: one side of that distinction is called the person (unity), and the other is called the natures (differentiation). This is the reason that certain predicates and their opposite may both be true: the one person of Christ was omniscient and also ignorant of some things; omnipresent and locationally limited; omnipotent and limited in power. Perhaps theologians will come to a full knowledge of what the distinction means in eternity, but for the present no one can say.

As with the Trinity, any distinction that purports to resolve the paradox of the Incarnation introduces new problems on a deeper level. For instance, what about the problem of uniting two personal natures or explaining how they interface? The idea that Christ had two levels of consciousness nicely maintains both humanity and divinity, but it immediately begins to separate the natures and weaken the unity of Christ's person.[41] To explain how they integrate, one has to give a special level

---

[39] Conflicting predicates would include omnipresence/physical body, omniscience/ignorance, omnipotence/weakness, preexistence/birth and possibly impeccability/peccability. This last pair is the most controversial, but whatever one's position on Christ's impeccability, it should be necessary to agree that the Incarnation was unique in this respect. In other words, it is hard to imagine Scripture speaking of an analogous temptation for the Father or the Spirit. To whatever extent peccability might be true, Christ was uniquely temptable and therefore, theology must explain how this coheres with his essential equality with the Father and Holy Spirit. To this extent, there is a conflict between his unique peccability and the impeccability he shared with the Father and Spirit.

[40] Gordon Clark points out the challenge of defining *nature* in his final and uncompleted work, *The Incarnation*. After defining personhood in a rather eccentric way (54-55), he ridicules the ambiguity with which theologians use *nature* (74), and demonstrates the logical problems that arise when they fail to articulate the relationship between *person* and *nature* (64-74). Clark never completed his explanation of how the propositions do relate. Based on his positions in other areas, it seems probable that he would have proposed a model that he regarded as a coherent, rational solution to the problem. As it is, his editor (John Robbins) goes on to suggest that "Jesus Christ was and is both God and man, a divine person and a human person" (78)—a step well beyond Chalcedon with deeply alarming implications.

[41] Robert Reymond, *A New Systematic Theology of the Christian Faith* (Nashville: Thomas Nelson, 1998), 618-19, gives two versions of a double-consciousness hypothesis. Thomas

of ultimacy to one or the other level of consciousness.⁴² Since there is hardly a component more central to personhood than self-consciousness, it is even more difficult to explain how Christ could still be a united person with two levels of consciousness.

Perhaps other solutions are possible, but it is quite clear that the biblical text presents data that no one can explain, and that it never proposes a solution. If any escape from this problem is to be had, it will come from outside of the biblical text—not from within.

The Problem of Evil

The problem of evil is one of the most common and longest discussed theological problems.[43] The most common presentation involves three propositions, all of which can be clearly supported biblically: (1) God is good, (2) God is all-powerful, and (3) evil exists.[44]

Biblical Support

If goodness is defined as the desire to act in the best interest of all independent agents, omnipotence as the capacity to effect this, and evil as the reality that this has not taken place, these propositions do not cohere.[45] Substituting these definitions into the above propositions, we could syllogistically argue:

V. Morris, *Logic*, 102-107, 154-62, places the two-mind hypothesis at the core of his defense for the Incarnation, but he also runs dangerously close to Nestorianism and produces other logical problems, such as how a person with multiple minds can remain a single person who is also distinct from other persons.

[42] Human ultimacy would suggest that Christ was ignorant of all things except when the Spirit granted him additional information. Divine ultimacy would suggest that "the human (limited) mind of Christ did not have access to the content of the divine (unlimited) mind unless the latter permitted the former such access"—Reymond, *A New Systematic Theology*, 619, in his summary of Thomas Morris' position.

[43] C. Stephen Evans, *Faith Beyond Reason* (Grand Rapids: Eerdmans, 1998), 126-36, gives a good but concise discussion of the problem of evil and some of the major defenses that have been offered. He concludes with the need for faith that is satisfied not to have all the answers. Unfortunately, Evans' "fideism" is defective, sharing too much with Kierkegaard.

[44] Of course, the problem of evil involves two different forms of evil—moral evil (sin) and existential evil (suffering). Correspondingly, the first form challenges God's righteousness, while the second challenges his benevolence to creatures. Given that the first is causally ultimate to the second, the problem of moral evil is generally more difficult to answer than the issue of suffering.

[45] Alva McClain, *Doctrine of God* (Theology Notes, Grace Theological Seminary, Winona Lake, Ind.), defines the goodness or love of God as "that in God which moves Him to give Himself and His gifts spontaneously, voluntarily, righteously, and eternally, for the good of personal beings, regardless of their merit or response." Gordon R. Lewis, "God, Attributes of," in *Evangelical Dictionary of Theology*, ed. Walter A. Elwell (Grand Rapids: Baker, 1984), 456, defines it as "a settled purpose of the will involving the whole person in seeking the well-being of others". The same definition also appears in Gordon

(1,2)   MP: Since God has the capacity to effect anything, if he has not effected the best interests of all independent agents, he is not good.
(3)   mp: God has not effected the best interests of all independent agents.
(-1)   Conclusion: God is not good.

Together with the second starting proposition, this leaves us with the conclusion that (1) God is good and (-1) God is not good. A similar analysis can be used for each of the other propositions.[46]

A closely related question is the origin of evil. For the most part it involves the same propositions.[47] The difference is that this question adds the additional complication of causality and rests on two basic propositions: (4) God is the Creator and source of everything that exists (1 Chr. 29:14; John 1:3; Acts 17:28), and (5) God is not the source of evil (2 Chr. 19:7; Job 34:10; Ps. 5:4; 92:16; 1 Tim. 4:4; Jas. 1:13). The resulting syllogism could be stated as follows:

(4)   MP: God is the Creator and source of everything that exists.
(5)   mp: God is not the source of evil.
(-2)   Conclusion: Evil does not exist (evil is not part of all things).

Of course, this clashes with one of the starting propositions (3), leaving the proposition that evil simultaneously does and does not exist. Once again, Scripture never specifies how the propositions relate.

Theological Analysis

There have been myriad attempts to resolve the problem of evil.[48] Most open theists and some Arminians answer the problem by positing that the source of evil is a

---

R. Lewis and Bruce A. Demarest, *Integrative Theology* (Grand Rapids: Zondervan, 1996), 235. Erickson, *Christian Theology*, 318, defines it as "God's concern for the welfare of those whom he loves". Alternatively, God's goodness can be defined as the fact that he accomplishes his own eternal purposes, which are good by definition. But the biblical texts go beyond this to say that God provides for the good of his creatures out of his kindness (Matt. 5:45; Acts 14:17), and that in some way he desires their well-being for their own sake (1 Cor. 13:5; 1 Tim. 2:4). As Millard Erickson points out, God's love is not entirely for humanity's sake (which would jeopardize his glory) nor exclusively for his sake (which would compromise the intrinsic quality of love [i.e., its outgoing, giving nature]) (320). Clearly, God is intent on his own glory and purposes, but the biblical meaning of his infinite love is that his concerns are larger than that alone.

[46] An argument proving the opposite of (2) would begin, "Since God desires the best interest of all independent agents, he is not all-powerful if he has not done so." A syllogism designed to prove the opposite of (3) would begin, "If God desires, he is able to effect the best interests of all independent agents."

[47] Since this is more naturally a moral question, evil should be understood as moral (the origin of sin), and God's goodness should be understood as his righteousness—his total hatred of sin and separation from it (Hab. 1:13; Jas. 1:13).

[48] Some of the proposed solutions include divine weakness, John Hick's soul-making theodicy, and denying the reality of evil. John S. Feinberg, *The Many Faces of Evil: Theological Systems and the Problems of Evil* (Wheaton: Crossway, 2004), 33-203, lists

causal agency outside of God.[49] On this view, by choosing to create free moral agents with libertarian free will, God voluntarily limited his power. Subsequent to the fall, he uses his power to limit evil and even to redeem creation back to himself, but God still allows free moral agents to act out their own decisions.[50]

There are some logical problems with this explanation, but it struggles most to integrate the biblical data.[51] Scripture records numerous instances in which God has intervened in human decisions (Exod. 7:3-4; Acts 4:27-28) or declared the outcome of events that were contingent upon human choices, long before they occurred (Isa. 41:25-26; Matt. 26:34, 56).[52] But if God is able to determine human choices even once, why is it definitively impossible for him to do so at other times? At best, open theism can only partially ameliorate the problem of evil; at worst, it only pushes it to another level. In either case it cannot solve the problem.[53]

---

seven major theodicies in addition to his own view. John Frame, "The Problem of Evil," in *Suffering and the Goodness of God*, ed. Christopher W. Morgan and Robert A. Peterson (Wheaton: Crossway, 2008), 141-64, also discusses and dismisses evil as privation of good, greater good, and the free will defense. In addition, Alvin C. Plantinga, *God, Freedom, and Evil* (Grand Rapids: Eerdmans, 1974), has demonstrated that this problem need not destroy the apologetic credibility of the Christian faith, through his free-will defense.

[49] Describing libertarian free will, Stephen Wellum comments that "the most basic sense of this view is that a person's act is free if it is not causally determined. For incompatibilists this does not mean that our actions are random or arbitrary. Reasons and causes play upon the will as one chooses, but none of them is *sufficient* to incline the will decisively in one direction or another. Thus, a person could always have chosen otherwise than he did. David Basinger, "The Importance of the Nature of Divine Sovereignty for Our View of Scripture," *SBJT* (Summer 2000): 77, states it this way: for a person to be free with respect to performing an action, he must have it within his power to choose to perform action A or choose not to perform action A. Both A and not A could actually occur; which will actually occur has not yet been determined.'"

[50] John Sanders, *The God Who Risks: A Theology of Providence* (Downers Grove: InterVarsity, 1998), 289-91.

[51] The logical problem is that even after huge emendations to the traditional understanding of omnipotence and omniscience, the libertarian model still does not solve the problem of evil. In light of God's perfect wisdom, can anyone really say that he was completely unaware of the potentially disastrous results that could stem from creating free moral agents? And if he understood even the possibility of the pain, suffering and horror that could unfold, why did he choose to create a world that contained that possibility? Anyone who knowingly risked causing one of the world's great disasters deserves harsh censure. But if the meaning of free moral agency is the ability to do either right or wrong, would it not be obvious to God that such horrors could occur? To completely avoid truncating the goodness of God, open theism would have to limit God's wisdom to a level hardly above our own.

[52] Daniel Elmer, "Critique of John Sanders and Clark Pinnock on the Prophetic Necessity and Certainty of the Crucifixion" (Th.M. thesis, Capital Bible Seminary, 2007), 39-55.

[53] John Frame, "The Problem of Evil," 148-49, criticizes libertarian free will on five bases: (1) It violates biblical data on God's sovereignty. (2) Scripture never explicitly teaches it. (3) Scripture never bases human responsibility on the foundation of free will. (4) Glorified believers cannot sin, meaning that the highest human state will have no

Another common solution is to adjust the definition of good so that in spite of the evil in the universe, it is still the best of all possible worlds. This model is used by strong Calvinists and Arminians alike, though in different senses. For the Calvinist, good should be understood as that which glorifies God, rather than good in human terms. Since God works all things to his utmost glory, everything in the universe serves this final end and is therefore the best of all possible worlds. For the Arminian, there are certain givens that must function consistently for the universe to be good, such as libertarian free will and consistent physical laws. Unfortunately, these givens may also have negative results in human suffering or moral evil. Still, the present universe is the best that could be had, given these rigid requirements.

The Arminian view seems to place certain metaphysical realities as *a priori* before God himself. If God could not craft a universe that contained these givens without also including evil, is he not limited by structures of being that are even greater than he?[54] Even granting this, the model is still vulnerable to the question of why God had to create in the first place. One also has to question whether the evil in human history is truly an unavoidable consequence of a consistent world that also contains free will. When biblical data confirms that God can intervene and has intervened by redirecting in human decisions, why would he not do so with some or all human tragedies?

Regarding the Calvinistic view, there is real value in understanding good and evil from God's perspective rather than in human terms. But Scripture itself complicates this analysis when it speaks of God's goodness, his concern for the welfare of even those that rebel against him, and his desire that all people would live (Ezek. 18:23; 33:11; 1 Tim. 2:4; 2 Pet. 3:9). Furthermore, this distinction does not relieve the moral problem of evil, since God is not the cause of sin under any definition of terms.[55] Though eternity will resolve many injustices and mitigate the problem of evil, it is interesting that it also represents the greatest depth of the problem in both existential and moral respects. Existential suffering could not be greater than eternal, conscious torment in hell for those that refuse salvation, and the eternal state of separation from God is the ultimate moral nadir for unregenerate humanity. The fact that an omniscient, moral God allowed certain human beings to

---

libertarian free will. (5) God holds people responsible for actions that were not within libertarian free will (Pharaoh, Judas, and Jesus' crucifiers).

[54] J.L. Mackie, "Evil and Omnipotence," in *The Philosophy of Religion*, ed. Basil Mitchell (New York: Oxford University Press, 1971), 93-97, highlights this recurrning problem in traditional theodicies.

[55] Mackie, "Evil and Omnipotence," presents this problem effectively by distinguishing between lower order and higher order good (109). Though theists can legitimately defend God's goodness by arguing that lower order evil ultimately contributes to a higher order good (God's glory), the intractable problem is with higher order evil (the fact that sin detracts from his glory). Said differently, if an individual's believing obedience contributes to God's glory, how can the damnation of a different individual contribute to the same end? And would it not also be reasonable to say, therefore, that this person's eternal damnation is a higher order good, and that God's own response to it is mixed? The problems with this understanding quickly multiply and overwhelm it.

enter the world with the knowledge that they would spend eternity in hell is beyond any simple explanation, but all of these facts are biblically demonstrable.[56]

Another point that adds to the challenge of the problem is the doctrine of foreknowledge. If God knew that creating the universe as he did would result in so much suffering, why did he actualize anything at all? By the same token, if he knew that certain human actors would act diabolically, could he not have avoided their creation and actualized only individuals who would freely choose the good? Not surprisingly, some theodicies have made significant adjustments to the doctrine of foreknowledge.[57]

When it comes to the moral problem of evil (how God is not the cause of sin), reformed theology is particularly vulnerable.[58] Reformed theologians typically introduce a distinction at this point, placing an additional causal step between God and evil: God acts for good and for the creation of the world, but passively allows evil to happen. Therefore, sin arises from the choices of fallen creatures.[59] While this distinction is warranted, it hardly eliminates the problem. Secondary causation still rests on the final cause to some degree, and God knew that catastrophic sin would ultimately appear in the creation.[60] Scripture never explains how these

---

[56] This problem has been one of the major motivations behind why some writers minimize the horror of the doctrine of hell.

[57] In spite of confidently maintaining that the free will defense solves the philosophical problem of evil, Stephen T. Davis, *Logic,* 116, nevertheless concedes that this question is one of several that cannot be answered. Instead he confesses to the fact that Christians must accept questions they cannot answer, and trust leads us not to question God inordinately.

[58] This is one of several points where the problem of evil intersects with the problem of God's sovereignty and human being's free will. A number of theologians, starting with Augustine, have defined evil as the absence of good so that it has no independent metaphysical reality. But Scripture never suggests this distinction, and worse, Scripture seems to describe evil with as much independent reality as good (Gen. 3:22; Job 2:10; Rom. 5:12; 7:21). In addition, it is still unclear how this distinction resolves the problem. In whatever sense Scripture speaks of evil when it says that God hates it and qualifies that he did not create it, it is also necessary to answer how evil exists. JoAnn Ford Watson, "Contemporary Views on the Problem of Evil," *Ashland Theological Journal* (1992): 27-28.

[59] Hodge, *Systematic Theology,* 1:547-48; Reymond, *A New Systematic Theology,* 372-76; Berkhof, *Systematic Theology,* 174-75.

[60] The origin of evil may be another form of this same antinomy. Karl Heim, *Jesus the World's Perfecter* (Philadelphia: Muhlenberg, 1961), 71, articulates the problem well. "That in a world in which God works all things there should be a will that wants to destroy God, is, as we saw, to our minds a Gordian knot which we cannot undo. We are restlessly thrown to and fro between the two statements which our reflexion can never unite. One is: God is the sole agent, even in the devil. For without this certitude we cannot pray and trust in God. For without it God's power would be limited by an opposing power whose victims we might become at any moment. But the other is: God must have no part in the diabolical rebellion. For if God Himself receives diabolical characteristics, then He can no longer call us to account when we have taken part in the demoniacal rebellion."

biblical facts cohere with the truth that God is not the cause of sin. In the words of Berkhof, "the problem of God's relation to sin remains a mystery".[61]

In short, some of the standard theodicies have real value by qualifying how to understand the problem of evil and by mitigating its argumentative force. But none of them can resolve the problem entirely without raising just as many questions at a deeper level. As it stands, the biblical data presents a logical problem that cannot presently be resolved.[62]

Divine Sovereignty and Human Responsibility

Another recurring theological problem involves divine sovereignty and human responsibility. Some statements of the problem essentially reduce to the problem of evil, but the tension between sovereignty and free will is still an independent logical problem.[63] Specifically, the problem arises from how God's sovereignty over all things accords with human responsibility. The propositions could be stated as follows: (1) God determines every event including human salvation, and (2) man is responsible for his choices.

---

[61] Berkhof, *Systematic Theology*, 175. Frame, "The Problem of Evil," 149, also comments that "I do not see any real difference between effectual permission and efficient causation, and I do not know why God should be responsible for what he causes efficiently, but not for what he permits effectually." Frame also helpfully points out that this is a form of the privation of good defense.

[62] Carson writes, "In a strict sense, there is no ultimate theodicy in the Scriptures: there is no attempt to vindicate God by beginning with human observations, perspectives, and reasonings. Theodicy makes God's power and goodness a deduction of human reason; this the biblical writers will not allow. Their closest approach to theodicy comes in the recognition of their inability to comprehend many aspects of God; and even this divine 'unknownness' is known to be such only because it has been revealed. Thus it attacks man's arrogance, defines the limits of his knowledge, and makes the only 'solution' one of faith"—*Divine Sovereignty and Human Responsibility* (Eugene, Oreg.: Wipf and Stock, 1994), 217-18. John Frame, "The Problem of Evil," 149, 157, also commends compatibilism and the greater good defense but adds that it cannot fully explain the mystery involved. For him some of the theodicies help to demarcate the limitations of our knowledge and rebuke the critic for demanding an explanation when the burden of proof is really on him. Still, Frame maintains that major aspects of the problem of evil must remain a mystery that believers accept in trust. See, also, John Frame, *No Other God: A Response to Open Theism* (Phillipsburg, N.J.: P&R, 2001), 137. Frame's position is significant because he never purports to resolve the problem but also outlines biblical limits on what can be said. This supports the important concept of "epistemic space" articulated in chapter 5.

[63] Statements that are closer to the problem of evil often move to the negative side of election—if God elects some individuals to certain salvation, it is only a short logical move away to say that individuals that are not elect will certainly be damned. From there, many advocates of libertarian free will polemically ask how this is in keeping with the goodness of God. Stated differently, if God's effectual grace is necessary for any individual to respond, why does He allow anyone to go without it and ultimately perish?

Biblical Support

Scripture offers multiple pairs of conflicting propositions in this subject. The gospel should be freely offered, and all unbelievers are invited to salvation (Isa. 55:1; Acts 2:21; Rev. 22:17), but only those whom God enables can or will come (John 6:44, 65; Rom. 3:11; 8:7). Likewise, salvation can be accessed only by a human choice (Deut. 30:19; Josh. 24:15; Isa. 55:1-3; Rom. 10:13; Rev. 22:17), but only those whom God has chosen will be saved (Acts 13:48; 2 Thess. 2:13). Believers must continually choose to live obediently (Rom. 6:11-13; 13:14; Gal. 5:16; Eph. 5:18; Col. 2:6), but they will certainly endure to the end (John 8:31-32; Col. 1:23; Heb. 3:14; 1 John 2:19), and their lifestyle will be characterized by good works (Rom. 8:12-14; Heb. 6:7-9).[64] On the other hand, unbelievers are responsible for choosing to reject God's free offer (Ezek. 18:30-32), even though it is certain that they will not and cannot respond positively apart from his work in their hearts (John 10:26; Rom. 9:16). In every moral scenario, right choices are commended and wrong choices are condemned, but given God's sovereignty, every choice is predetermined. In each instance it is hard to explain why there is every appearance of genuine choice—even in Scripture's own description of events—while the outcome is actually predetermined.

Scripture also includes a number of passages that juxtapose God's sovereignty and our responsibility within a few sentences or even in the same sentence (Matt. 11:20-28; 23:37; Luke 22:22; John 6:37, 44-45, 64-65; Acts 2:23; 4:27-28; 13:48; 16:14; 1 Cor. 3:6; Phil. 2:12-13; 1 Thess. 1:3-4; 2 Thess. 2:13-14; 1 Pet. 1:2,5).[65] Scripture seems to indicate that human beings are especially responsible *because* they have the power of choice, linking the two poles logically (Ezek. 18:27-28, 30-32; Rev. 3:19-20).

In his extended discussion of the problem, D.A. Carson recognizes several problematic areas involving free will. The first is the definition of "free will" for which neither compatibilism nor libertarian free will offer a complete solution. Another area is time and eternity—the issue of how God's foreordination and predestination can be genuinely precedent to the actions of independent agents. A third challenge is the nature of divine "ultimacy," since God cannot be the cause of sin. Fourth, Carson points to the "will(s)" of God. God does not desire sin or the destruction of the wicked, but at the same time, he is completely in control while he allows it to happen. Later, Carson adds an additional challenge, involving anthropomorphism, anthropopathism, and personality. God interacts with his creation personally, and this is often difficult to square with divine transcendence. Carson also points to experience and theory—the fact that these questions come

---

[64] In fact, Scripture sometimes directly juxtaposes commands that believers choose to live righteously with the fact that they will certainly be characterized by righteousness as the regenerated children of God (2 Cor. 6:14-18; Eph. 5:3-5).

[65] This list is taken from *Not by Chance*, 257-259, where Layton Talbert helpfully displays the specific words that indicate each emphasis.

into focus for each individual as they face their own crisis of faith before God's transcendence (with the problem of evil in particular).[66]

Carson's discussion is very helpful even though it combines sovereignty and free will with the problem of evil—two problems discussed separately here. Using his analysis, the tension might be grouped in several ways.

At the foundation, the conflict is essentially a contrast between biblical ontology (God is sovereign over all) and phenomenology (humanity's responsibility to make right choices). In other words, while the biblical description of the universe is that there is no pure contingency, there is every appearance that human beings make significant choices with real consequences. This is especially evident in Scripture's appeals to the human will—whether direct ethical commands or invitations for people to repent (Acts 17:30). Since God, in fact, controls the factor that permits a positive response (irresistible grace or effectual calling), these appeals seem disingenuous, as though the offer of the gospel is a play act, or as though some of the most pertinent information is hidden.

Another class of references involves God's will.[67] A group of passages clearly teach that God desires the salvation of the wicked (Ezek. 18:23; 33:11; 1 Tim. 2:4; 2 Pet. 3:9), and others seem to say that God's intentions might be frustrated in some way by the human will (Deut. 5:29; Matt. 23:37). But how do these cohere with the clear teaching that God can affect his will without any limitations (Dan. 4:35; Rom. 9:19)?

What's more, Scripture connects the fact that men and women sinfully resist God's will with another locus of tension: sovereignty and free will involve a conflict of responsibility. Scripture clearly places the responsibility for sin on individual sinners (Isa. 66:3-4; Eccl. 7:29; Rom. 9:19-20; Luke 22:22) while also affirming that God is in control of every event (Ps. 33:14-15; 75:6-7; 139: 16; Phil. 2:13). In the biblical presentation God is responsible for any positive response, while human beings are fully responsible for any rejection. If God's causal relationship to these choices is such that he is responsible for positive responses, how can he be absolved when it comes to the negative? As in Table 3.1, there is incongruity in how Scripture assigns responsibility for moral actions.

---

[66] Carson, *Divine Sovereignty*, 205-19.

[67] D.A. Carson, *How Long, O Lord?* (Grand Rapids: Baker, 1990), 202-12, 221-22, offers impressive biblical support for this problem. One group of passages speak of God "repenting" of something (Gen. 6:6; Exod. 32:7-14; 2 Kgs. 20:1-6; 1 Sam. 15:11; 2 Sam. 24:16; Jonah 3:10). Yet another group says that he does not repent (Num. 23:19ff; 1 Sam. 15:29; Jer. 4:28; Ps. 89:34). In Genesis 22 God directs Abraham to do something he apparently never intended to allow. Scripture also teaches that God longs for the repentance of the wicked (Isa. 30:18ff; 65:2; Hos. 11:7-9; Ezek. 33:11; Lam. 3:33-36), though it is also clear that he is in control of these things. God also sends a messenger with a message of doom, along with the assurance that it will be rejected (2 Chr. 18).

Understanding and Accounting for Paradox: Theological Examples

Table 3.1 Incongruity in Divine Sovereignty and Human Responsibility

	Good	Evil
God is sovereign over everything.	"Every good gift is from above" (Jas. 1:17).	"God is not the author of evil" (Ps. 5:4).
Humanity is responsible for their actions.	"It is not of [man], but God who shows mercy" (Rom. 9:16).	Human beings are fully responsible for their own sin (Jas. 1:13-14).

The negative side of election illustrates this principle. Scripture teaches that the elect will certainly be saved, and this fact explains their believing response. The converse truth is that those who are not elect will certainly be damned and this fact explains their rejecting response. But Scripture is unwilling to make this link. In fact, the condemnation of the damned is always connected to their own chosen response. Scripture stops short of affirming the logical implications of its own teaching. To be sure, this involves emphases in biblical data and not direct, exclusive statements. It is a definite distortion of biblical emphases for someone to credit his receipt of eternal life to his own choice, or conversely to say that someone was damned because God chose not to elect him.[68] Yet how are these statements distortions when they represent the converse propositions to major biblical emphases? As Wayne Grudem concludes, we must "come to the point where we confess that we do not understand how it is that God can ordain that we carry out evil deeds and yet hold us accountable for them and not be blamed Himself." Still, "we can affirm that all of these things are true, because Scripture teaches them".[69]

Even though it is helpful to discuss this problem separately from the problem of evil, additional complexity arises from integrating the two tensions. Evil is only more difficult to explain if God is in control of every detail of every event.[70] As

---

[68] The closest example of the former statement is Ezekiel 18:27-28, where a person's believing actions are the reason that he lives. Here and elsewhere, Scripture does speak of the human response as an intermediate cause in a causal chain, just as one might speak of hearing the gospel as a step in the causal chain of conversion. Still, Scripture firmly attributes the final responsibility for obedient human responses to God (Phil. 2:13; Rom. 9:16). The closest example of the latter statement is Romans 9:10-22, where God "hardens whom he desires" and "endures the vessels of wrath prepared for destruction". Still, Scripture always speaks passively and with the sinner's own choice in view.

[69] Grudem, *Systematic Theology*, 330. The statement that "God can ordain that we carry out evil deeds" seems to press troublingly towards the implication that God is responsible for sin, but in general, seems to represent the biblical data accurately.

[70] In fact, to some extent these problems also have a relationship to the infinity of God when it comes to his relationship with time. Since God has complete foreknowledge of future events, an entire series of questions arise about his determination of his events. Likewise, it is more difficult to defend the presence of evil given that he knew before creation it

John Frame points out, the only biblical passage that directly answers the problem of evil (Rom. 9:19-21) includes a strong emphasis on God's sovereignty.[71] Just as with the divine response to Job's suffering, Scripture answers the problem by silencing the accuser.

Both the problem of evil and divine sovereignty and human free will also reach their nadir in eternity. How can a good and omniscient God create humans who will, within his sovereignty over every detail of their lives, ultimately be damned? There are no simple answers to these questions. This is why most attempts to solve either problem make adjustments in the propositions for the other. Open theism answers the conflict by making adjustments in the problem of sovereignty and free will. A few Reformed theologians solve the problem by making adjustments in the problem of evil, implying that God's relationship to evil is mixed.[72] Neither type of explanation is acceptable.

Theological Analysis

One of the classic solutions to this problem is compatibilism—the idea that individuals will always act in keeping with their own motivations and nature. In this model, events are determined while individuals still freely act according to their will. When it comes to salvation, fallen individuals left to themselves will always reject God's gracious offer. Scripture clearly affirms that God governs his creation concurrently with the decisions of his creatures (Prov. 16:1, 9). Furthermore, the NT directly traces our predicament back to the content of our sinful heart (Rom. 3:10-18). Compatibilism is probably the clearest statement of the biblical data.

Still, compatibilism cannot solve the problem entirely. To take the problem areas identified by Carson, compatibilism does not answer the issues of ontology vs. phenomenology. Carson comments that such perspectives "may provide helpful working models of the problem, but no solutions, for they are less than precise on the question of the boundaries of this 'free agency', and are equally unclear on how this special control of God operates. . . . At times they are in danger of losing the tang of the Scriptures they purport to explain."[73]

---

would certainly arise. Thus the problem of evil, sovereignty and free will, and the infinity of God all share at least one theological connection.

[71] Frame, "The Problem of Evil," 164.

[72] R.C. Sproul Jr. illustrates this with his comments in *Almighty Over All* (Grand Rapids: Baker, 1999). Regarding sin's cause, "the trail ultimately leads back to God" (57). Since Adam, Eve, nature, and Satan were created good, only God could have "introduced evil into his world" (51) in keeping with what he most wished to come to pass (54). "It was [God's] desire to make his wrath known. He needed, then, something on which to be wrathful. He needed to have sinful creatures" (57). Sproul even suggests that God desired humanity's fall into sin (53). He qualifies that "I am not accusing God of sinning; I am suggesting that he created sin" (54). 1 Timothy 4:4, on the other hand, teaches that "every created thing from God is good."

[73] Carson, *Divine Sovereignty,* 207.

When it comes to the negative side of election, compatibilism argues that God's sovereignty and people's choices are companion, interchangeable ways of describing the same realities. The problem is that Scripture disallows believers from interchanging these two in certain combinations. A similar analysis applies when it comes to God's will. If God's will and human being's are fully compatible descriptions of the same realities, how can our choices work against the genuine desires of God? Likewise, compatibilism proposes a fusion of God's and humanity's agency in human choices, but Scripture explicitly divides these, placing responsibility for some events on God's agency, and others on ours.

Another proposal for this paradox is the Arminian solution, or to a greater degree, open theism. Essentially these models work by minimizing the first proposition, resulting in the conclusion that God's control of all things is limited to some extent. It is important to note that the problem of sovereignty and responsibility is a significant polemical keystone of the argument in these positions. The problem with these views is simply in the statements of the biblical text. Scripture describes God's ultimate control over human decisions so clearly that this approach cannot reasonably escape it.

The Infinity of God

As a class of mysteries, the infinity of God is more challenging to define, support with clear biblical data, and state in propositional logic. Still, this is probably an example of antinomy because in a number of respects it is impossible to explain how God's infinity relates to the limitations of time and space. In both cases the problem arises from how God can be infinite but still exist in a finite universe. With both space and time, God is antecedent to everything, including the metaphysical givens of existence. In other words, God not only fills all space; he transcends the category entirely. Likewise, he has existed throughout all time, but he also transcends time itself and exists beyond it.[74]

God's Relationship to Time

God's relationship to time is a matter of significant debate, and the principal question has been whether God exists within or outside of time.[75] Scripture is clear that God interacts with creation within the framework of time, and it is hard to reduce this to mere anthropomorphism (Jer. 50:31; Acts 17:30-31; Gal. 4:4; Titus 1:2-3). A number of passages even represent God experiencing time as a succession

---

[74] It may be that these mysteries are more difficult to state propositionally simply because we have no way to clearly define time and space. As Augustine said, "What then is time? If no one ask of me, I know; if I wish to explain to him who asks, I know not"—*The Confessions of St. Augustine*, trans. J.G. Pilkington (Edinburgh: T & T Clark, 1876), 301.

[75] John Feinberg offers an extended discussion of the views on this question in *No One Like Him*, 375-427. Richard Swinburne argues against the timelessness view in *The Coherence of Theism* (Oxford: Clarendon, 1977), 215-22. According to Carl Henry, *God, Revelation and Authority* (Waco: Word, 1982), 5:239, divine timelessness has been the historic position of Christian orthodoxy.

of moments (Ps. 90:4; Jer. 31:1; Rom. 3:25-26). At the same time, Scripture indicates that God exists beyond time (Job 36:26; Ps. 90:2; John 1:1; 8:58; Jude 25; Rev. 1:8; 4:8). Scripture is less clear about what this means or how it works. Nevertheless the concept of time assumes limitations. As Wayne Grudem points out, if God has eternally existed in time, how could we have ever reached the present point?[76] What can it mean that God has existed eternally, unpreceded and uncaused? Or what can it mean that God experiences all chronological moments *simultaneously* when time itself refers to an ongoing progression of events?[77]

Here also, Scripture uses language that crosses over this conflict and makes it even more challenging. For instance, while Psalm 90:4 (c. f. 2 Pet. 3:8) supports the assertion that God experiences time as a succession of moments, it also indicates that his experience of time is completely different from ours. The expression seems to be a phenomenological way of expressing timelessness. More clearly, Psalm 90:2 describes God as stretching beyond time itself. All of this points to the conflict within human conceptual frameworks. The psalmist has to use chronological language to express God's transcendence over time. The same is true of every other biblical passage that supports timelessness (Ps. 90:2; John 1:1; Jude 25). What can it mean that God existed "before" time itself? But on the other hand, how else could the concept possibly be communicated?

God's Relationship to Space

Scripture is clear that God is present everywhere and interacts with the material universe in ways that appear to be authentic dimensionality (Ps. 139:7-10; Jer. 23:24; Acts 17:28). God can act in one place in ways that he does not act in others. But Scripture is also clear that God is by no means constrained by dimensional limitations (1 Kgs. 8:27). In terms of systematic theology, God is present everywhere in the *totality* of his being. How then, is it possible for God to relate to the world dimensionally, without being limited by it? Another way to state the problem is as a conflict of definitions: dimensionality involves limitations by definition, because something is either present at a given point or it is not. In other words, if an entity or part of an entity is present at one place, it cannot be present in the same way at any other. On the other hand, God is also infinite by definition, and the meaning of omnipresence is that God is not limited by location in any way. Thus the statement that God is locationally infinite is something of a contradiction in terms.

Biblical Integration

We might place both of these problems in a provisional framework. The starting point is a philosophical notion. The entire conceptual fabric of time collapses unless

---

[76] Grudem, op cit, 172.

[77] Wayne Grudem op cit, represents this conflict when he defines God's eternity as the truth that he "has no beginning, end, or succession of moments in his own being, and he sees all time equally vividly, yet God sees events in time and acts in time" (168).

we maintain that the same event cannot occur at two different times. Likewise, the meaning of spatial dimensionality is dependent on the concept that the same matter cannot be present in two different places at the same time and in the same way. Thus we could form proposition (1): if something dwells in time and space, it is limited by them.

If this proposition is taken as it stands, the conflict becomes quite clear. The biblical evidence supports the fact that (2) God dwells in time and space (as well as outside of it), but the evidence also indicates that (3) he is not limited by time and space (or any created limitation for that matter). These propositions take the following form:

(1)   MP: If something dwells in time and space, it is limited by them.
(2)   mp: God dwells in time and space.
(-3) Conclusion: God is limited by time and space.

Of course, this conclusion violates the biblical reality of proposition (3): God is not limited by time and space, and is clearly traceable to a flaw in the starting proposition—proposition (1). The point is that God's relationship to these fundamental principles forms an impossible conflict. From a human vantage point, time and space do not permit anything external to them. This is why it is impossible even to articulate the concept without using dimensional terms—"God exists *outside* of dimensional space; God existed *before* time began." Since God exists beyond these principles, either the meaning of time and space collapses, or theologians must hold the ideas in a standing tension.

Another way to state this conflict (perhaps more clearly) is with the principle that infinity cannot exist in a limited universe. If it did, a number of irresolvable paradoxes would emerge, and consistency within the dimensional world would be impossible.[78] But, of course, God does exist within the universe, and he is an infinite being.[79]

Theological Analysis

The simplest solution to the conflict proposed above is to deny the philosophical link stated in proposition (1): if something dwells in space and time, it is limited by

---

[78] William Lane Craig, *The Existence of God and the Beginning of the Universe* (San Bernardino: Here's Life, 1979), 35-53, artfully demonstrates this with the example of an infinite library in which the number of books is represented by A. If someone removed 100,000 volumes from the shelf, the number of books on the shelf would still be the same: A, which is infinite. At that time, the total holdings of the library would also be the same: 100,000 + A, which would also be equal to A alone. A more philosophical treatment is available in J.P. Moreland, *Scaling the Secular City: A Defense of Christianity* (Grand Rapids: Baker, 1987), 15-34.

[79] Gordon Clark, *The Incarnation*, 55-64, denies that God is truly infinite for precisely this reason. It is true that God is not infinite in the truly unlimited sense that he possesses every attribute and on to infinity. But he does exhibit infinity as an accurate description of the various attributes he does possess. See John Feinberg, *No One Like Him*, 243-49, for an extended discussion of this problem.

them. This is a simple solution for two reasons. First, as a philosophical assertion, it necessarily enjoys a lower epistemic status than propositions stated in Scripture. But even more simply, one can suggest that the proposition is not universal. In other words, though time and space imply limitations in the way that we experience them, this simply is not true of God. As acknowledged earlier, the biblical data teaches that God relates to time in a completely different way from humans. Thus proposition (1) could simply be restated: any finite beings that dwell in space and time are limited by them.[80]

Though this qualification is correct, the conflict is more fundamental and still arises at various theological points. For instance, it is meaningless to speak of God's existence before the beginning of time, since there can be no chronological precedent to time itself. On this basis some have argued that to avoid the conceptual muddle, God must exist within time, which must itself exist eternally and without differentiation. A similar point could be made about God's dwelling beyond or outside of dimensionality—the statement is inherently meaningless, and therefore we should speak of God as existing within both dimensionality and time.[81]

But there are two problems with this conclusion. The first was already mentioned—infinity itself is philosophically impossible and meaningless within the dimensional world. But the second is even more crucial—God's ultimacy. God is the only cause of anything that exists, and there cannot be anything that is metaphysically prior to him. Were there to be a metaphysical framework in which he necessarily exists, it would limit him in some way, for by definition it would require that he exist within it. Furthermore, there is a serious problem of causation, for what can be the causal basis for something more ultimate than God?

Ultimately, this question is a crisis of meaning more than a direct propositional conflict. Humans are incapable of saying that God transcends the metaphysical and dimensional givens of their existence without using those very metaphysical and dimensional givens to describe it, so by default they use dimensional categories to describe realities beyond those categories. Simply put, human language and mental categories cannot describe these concepts without self-stultification, and yet they are theologically necessary. The result is that theologically necessary propositions are also internally contradictory or at least incoherent.

---

[80] Of course, the resurrected Christ would also fall under this proposition, though he possesses omnipresence and transcends time in the same way that the Father does. However, this particular form of the problem properly belongs under the antinomy of the Incarnation.

[81] Hugh Ross, *Beyond the Cosmos* (Colorado Springs: NavPress, 1996), offers a rather novel approach to this question. String theory proposes at least ten dimensions, and Ross suggests that God transcends the four dimensions humans experience by existing in all ten dimensions. Ross' proposal rests almost entirely on a scientific theory that has not been confirmed, and Ross' conclusions inadvertently cause other theological problems. See William Lane Craig, "Hugh Ross's Extra-Dimensional Deity: A Review Article," *JETS* (June 1999): 293-304.

Evaluation

This discussion has examined five examples of paradox with biblical support and logical correlation for each.[82] Not every example of paradox is equivalent. The Trinity and the Incarnation are probably the clearest and are also the only paradoxes in which a particular distinction is part of orthodoxy. Like these, the problem of evil can also be stated in a clear propositional form. The problems of divine sovereignty and free will or the infinity of God cannot be stated as clearly with biblical propositions and logical oppositions. The basis of these tensions is probably phenomenological and definitional.

But though it is true to varying degrees, the conclusion is the same in every example—Scripture confronts readers with conflicting propositions that cannot be resolved. Thus, theologians have made distinctions and articulated models to ameliorate these tensions, and those distinctions fall into three basic categories. First, some represent biblical emphasis and may not violate biblical revelation in any way. This would include compatibilism and the legitimate qualification that evil should not be defined in strictly human terms. These insights are helpful as far as they go and may even ease tensions somewhat, but they do not solve the problems entirely.

A second category also avoids violating any biblical propositions. These distinctions represent the problem in analytical terms that communicate no new information. In general, they only push the problems backwards to another level. Hypothetically, one could simply continue to suggest successive distinctions, but it would only produce successive logical problems. The result is to solve the problem largely by obfuscating it or hiding it in the indescribable. In some cases these distinctions do provide a helpful framework or model for representing biblical propositions. The distinctions are legitimate; the idea that they can fully resolve their logical problems is not. The distinction between the three persons and the essence of the Trinity fits this category, as well as the distinction between Christ's dual natures and his person.

A third category includes concepts that violate one or the other pole of the biblical data and must be rejected. Distorting biblical evidence in order to forcibly make ideas cohere is hardly a solution. Examples include open theism or some aspects of the free will defense, though myriad others have been proposed.

Regardless of the distinctions or qualifications proposed, these five examples of paradox defy simple resolution. There are many points of theology where theologians could ask questions that Scripture does not answer or where they might want more details. But the group of problems discussed here is unique because the

---

[82] There are other ways of categorizing these mysteries, and there may be other theological antinomies in addition to these. Vernon Grounds, "The Postulate of Paradox," *BETS* 7 (1964): 3-21. lists seven, including the ontological (divine unity and plurality), cosmological (God and the universe), epistemological (Scripture as exclusive theological truth), anthropological (original sin and human responsibility), Christological, soteriological, and eschatological (damnation). See, also, Kenneth Boa, *God, I Don't Understand* (Colorado Springs: Victor, 2007).

information believers possess seems to be at odds with other revealed information. Drawing certain deductions from this type of biblical data (as here), one quickly ends up contradicting other biblical data. In some cases key terms have so eluded clear definition that one wonders if some of the power of the distinction lies in obfuscating the problem. If one cannot define what we mean by "person," "nature," and "essence," or clearly state the difference between them, how well can they claim to have resolved the logical tension in the biblical data?

Is there any value, then, to making these distinctions? There probably is, because they can still usefully mitigate the force of the tension. In several cases they function as a model for how to bracket further reasoning based on the biblical data. For instance, the distinction between Christ's person and his natures keeps better track of which predicates correspond with which subjects and makes Christological language more precise. The Trinitarian distinction between persons and essence codifies biblical data in a way that makes heretical aberrations more obvious. The problem of sovereignty and free will and the problem of evil are certainly mitigated to some extent by theological distinctions and definitions. Defining good and evil primarily in terms of God's prerogative purposes helps restore a more biblical perspective—that God, not human beings, is at the center of the universe. Compatibilism restores a biblical emphasis: our decisions grow out of our character, and the problem with unbelievers is deeper than their choices; it extends to their character. With the infinity of God, it is true and necessary to recognize that God does not have to be limited by time and space, because he relates to them in a completely different way than humans experience either. But as much as these distinctions can mitigate the tension, they can do only that. They cannot set aside the tension altogether.

Conclusion

Does all of this mean that Scripture is in fact contradictory? What of the broad implications that this assertion would have on theology and the theological method? It is inescapable that these doctrines contain conflicting propositions *as they stand,* but this is short of proving that the doctrines are inherently and irresolvably contradictory. Is the proper response to seek for a solution or to demarcate barriers against further inquiry? What is needed is a systematic analysis of contradictory relationships and the possibilities that exist for that epistemic category.

CHAPTER 5

Understanding and Accounting for Paradox: Systematic Analysis

The discussions and definitions of the more formal and scholastic theologians, concerning the personal distinctions in the Godhead, have always seemed to me to present a striking instance of the reluctance of the human mind to confess its own weakness. For, let any read them with the closest attention, and he will perceive that he has acquired little more than a set of terms, whose abstruseness serves to conceal from him their practical lack of meaning.[1]

The discussion so far has been restricted to exegetical data and the struggle to harmonize it, but that argument has led to a difficult sticking point. It seems that as it stands, the biblical data leads to unavoidable contradictions. Philosophically, any proposition can be derived from a contradictory proposition—clearly an intolerable situation for theology.[2] How should theologians regard these contradictions, and more importantly, how are they to proceed in the theological endeavor?

Understanding Theological Antinomy

To evaluate the five theological paradoxes that chapter 4 explored, one must begin with a better understanding of contradictions and a clear definition of apparent contradictions. The challenge is how to understand this epistemic category and how to distinguish it from other kinds of propositions.

---

[1] Robert Dabney, *Systematic Theology* (Edinburgh: Banner of Truth Trust, 1985), 202.

[2] The principle of explosion is an established philosophical dictate, stating that "anything follows from a contradiction". Given that two contradictory statements are both true— (1) the moon is round, and (2) the moon is not round—one can prove that (3) Martians must exist. Based on statement (1) we can prove the disjunctive statement that (4) either the moon is round or Martians exist, since we know that one of the two statements (here, statement 1) is true. Connecting this with statement (2) allows us to negate the first part of statement (4) with the result that (3) Martians must exist. That being said, recent developments in philosophy have explored paradox and the possibility of dialetheism. R.M. Sainsbury *Paradoxes* (New York: Cambridge University Press, 2009), 150-59, discusses the logical implications of contradiction at some length, along with the more contemporary reevaluations of paradox. Still, philosophical dialetheism is closer to the *sui generis* view than to theological complementarity, and dialetheism also violates the fundamental logicality of God's nature. James Anderson, interview by Camden Bucey, *Paradox in Christian Theology*, www.reformedforum.org /ctc132/, July 23, 2010.

The Meaning of Contradictions

While discussing the problem of evil, Alvin Plantinga distinguishes three types of contradictions.[3] Explicit contradictions simultaneously affirm a proposition and its negative, such as

(1) Socrates is immortal.
(-1) Socrates is not immortal.

A formal contradiction, on the other hand, includes several propositions that are contradictory in their implications. As a result, the propositions in a formal contradiction can be deductively linked together to form an explicit contradiction. For example, in the following set, propositions (2) and (3) form a categorical syllogism that implies proposition (-1)—the explicit contradictor of (1).

(1) Socrates is immortal.
(2) All men are mortal.
(3) Socrates is a man.

The third type, an implicit contradiction, increases the distance between the two propositional sets by leading to conclusions that contradict another unstated but generally accepted proposition. These propositions can take multiple forms, but they will contradict only after another reasonably apparent truth is added. For instance, an implicit contradiction could share something in common with explicit contradictions if someone starts with (1) and adds the well-known historical reality that Socrates died, to reach (-1). It could also share something in common with a formal contradiction if someone started with (1) and (2). Because proposition (3) is a rather obvious and well-known truth, one could quickly derive (-1), and the starting propositions would be implicit contradictions. Said another way, implicit contradictions are contradictions stated as enthymemes.

Based on this distinction, are the antinomies of Scripture explicit, formal, or implicit contradictions? The *sui generis* view has no problem with identifying them as full and explicit contradictions. Of course, this requires broad epistemological adjustments to make logical consistency possible. Typically this view has criteria for the propositions that are not subject to the laws of logic, allowing the problematic data to stand as true in spite of being contradictory. The problem is that since logic is so central to all human discourse, these criteria must be objective and recognizable in order to have any real practical worth. Most theologians and philosophers have found it a daunting task to articulate universal criteria guiding reasoning for all of human knowledge. Even more daunting is the task of substantiating these criteria. The challenges are simply too great for this approach to be workable and defensible.

After surveying the three types of contradictions, James Anderson concludes,

> The type of contradiction, apparent or otherwise, involved in paradoxical Christian doctrines is best characterized as *implicit* contradiction. The problem is that certain

---

[3] Alvin C. Plantinga, *God, Freedom, and Evil* (Grand Rapids: Eerdmans, 1974), 13-17.

statements of Christian doctrine seem to imply further claims that in turn explicitly contradict *other* statements of Christian doctrine (or certain natural implications of those statements). For example: while the Definition of Chalcedon may not explicitly state that Jesus *was* aware of everything (including the date of the Parousia) and also that Jesus *was not* aware of everything, it nonetheless appears to *imply* those very claims by virtue of the balanced Christology its authors sought to articulate.[4]

Still, the fact that biblical antinomies are only implicit contradictions does not mitigate the problem. The three types of contradictions differ in the degree to which their conflict is stated clearly and therefore in the epistemological space between the two sides of the conflict. A formal contradiction becomes explicit to the extent that the logical process is valid; an implicit contradiction becomes explicit to the extent that the supplied premise is true and that any logical processes it might use are also valid. Stated conversely, formal or implicit contradictions are less problematic than explicit contradictions only to the extent that the logical links (formal) or added premises (implicit) are epistemologically weak. All of this means that an implicit contradiction is only a few logical steps away from an explicit one, and both confront us with serious logical problems. In the case of some biblical antinomies, the added propositions and logical links are remarkably strong, meaning that the epistemological space between these implicit contradictions and their explicit form is actually rather narrow.

It is notable that Scripture never states biblical doctrines in explicitly contradictory ways. There are no propositional statements, for instance, that the Holy Spirit is one with God and that he is also distinct, or that Jesus knew all things and that he also did not.[5] In contrast to other religious traditions (not to mention trends in modern theology), Scripture does not highlight apparent contradictions by juxtaposing them in an explicit form.[6] On the other hand, Scripture does not seem embarrassed of these conflicts either, as if they are logical gaps that might cut against its credibility as a source of truth. In fact, the attitude of Scripture towards potential logical conflicts seems to be indifference: there is no particular reason to pursue logical conflicts nor to avoid them. As Carson writes, "[The texts of Scripture] juxtapose divine sovereignty and human responsibility at every turn, manifesting little if any awareness of the theoretical difficulties that

---

[4] James Anderson, *Paradox in Christian Theology* (Eugene: Wipf and Stock, 2007), 109.

[5] The latter antinomy comes the closest, since Scripture teaches that there are things Jesus did not know (Matt. 24:36) as well as the fact that he knew all things (John 16:30). Still, all of the biblical antinomies require a logical process and additional presuppositions to transform them into explicit contradictions.

[6] William H. Austin, "Complementarity and Theological Paradox," *Zygon*, (December 1967): 365-81, lists several examples from the Upanishads: "'That [Brahman] art thou' (Chandogya, CI.8.7). 'That One, the Self, though never stirring, is swifter than Thought . . . though standing still, it overtakes those who are running. . . . It stirs and it stirs not' (Isa 4-5). '[Brahman] is both far and near; It is within all this and It is outside all this' (Isa 5)." Of course, within the Christian worldview, Søren Kierkegaard and Karl Barth exalted the role of logical conundrums as the ultimate tests of trusting faith.

later thinkers discover in such a juxtaposition."[7] Should this attitude in Scripture be one of the considerations that guides theologians' attitude towards antinomy? Is it a problem that contemporary theologians seem more concerned than Scripture itself is to deliver Christian theology from any appearance of contradiction, implicit or otherwise?[8]

Perhaps the fact that Scripture never states theological contradictions explicitly does point to something. The distinction between implicit and explicit contradictions cannot remove the problem, but it does open up the epistemological space in which an entire world of distinctions is possible. Later, this observation will be significant to understanding paradox.

The Meaning of Apparent Contradictions

Most theologians with a complementary view of paradox qualify that antinomies are apparent contradictions—logical conflicts that appear to be contradictory even though they are not genuine contradictions.[9] Can this distinction deliver theology from the disastrous implications of a contradiction?

Apparent contradiction assumes that there is a deeper epistemological reality in which these antinomies do actually harmonize. Said differently, for this distinction to work, it must assume a soft epistemological dualism—at least between human perceptions of reality and God's complete knowledge of that reality.[10] Taking all of this for granted, it would be entirely possible that propositions that are quite incommensurable for us are completely commensurable in the mind of God. For the time being they must remain unresolved, but there is no damage done to logical systems since there is no actual contradiction in the mind of God. Figure 5.1 represents the dualism between divine and human perspective, as well as the fact

---

[7] D.A. Carson, *Divine Sovereignty and Human Responsibility* (Eugene, Oreg.: Wipf and Stock, 1994), 206.

[8] Of course, this also applies in the opposite direction. The tendency in some modern theologies to emphasize perceived conflicts as the core of genuine faith is simply unsupported in the Bible's own emphases.

[9] Writers occasionally combine "paradox" with "apparent contradiction" to speak of an "apparent paradox." Since the meaning of a paradox is something that appears to be contradictory in spite of being true, this is a convoluted redundancy. Paul Henebury, "Robert Reymond's Systematic Theology: A Dispensational Appraisal," *Conservative Theological Journal*, August 2004: 254. For instance, Jim Halsey uses "apparent paradox" interchangeably with "apparent contradiction" while critically reviewing Frame. Frame's original work, "A Preliminary Critique of Van Til: The Theologian—A Review Article," *WTJ* (Fall 1976): 131-32, however, never speaks of "apparent paradox."

[10] The epistemological framework assumed in this discussion is the correspondence theory, with the final epistemological resting point in God's knowledge. In other words, something is true if it corresponds with God's knowledge that it is true. This also presses back further to the final metaphysical basis of reality—God's creative causation or his aseity.

that propositions cohere in God's understanding while they are incompatible in ours.

Figure 5.1. Soft Dualism in the Epistemology of Paradox

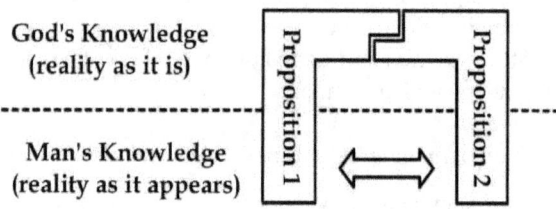

Several things can be said about this diagram. To begin, some degree of epistemological dualism does rest on solid biblical data. Chapter 2 demonstrated that there is a strong continuity between God's thoughts and that of human beings, but at times also a radical discontinuity. On this basis it is legitimate to represent a division between the two, with some propositional elements in common.[11] Of course, the challenge is to discern which elements of this analogical relationship are shared in common and which are distinct.

Second, this model easily comports with more fundamental philosophical givens. Our entire experience of the universe is limited to a lower level of understanding that cannot account for itself. Metaphysically, no cause can exist within the universe that is self-sufficient or great enough to cause the universe. Epistemologically, there can be no absolute starting point for any knowledge without comprehensive knowledge. Ethically, there can be no absolute moral law transcending human actors without an absolute lawgiver. In each case the universe requires realities that transcend it and that function as pointers to God. Human beings in the lower sphere of knowledge experience realities that cannot account for themselves and find their ultimate explanation only in the inscrutable realities of the divine. Theological paradox exemplifies this same principle using theological propositions.

Third, this model has several benefits. It clearly represents what it means for something to be apparently contradictory and how that differs from a genuine contradiction. Apparent contradictions conflict only on the lower level of knowledge; genuine contradictions would be at odds both in human understanding and in God's. The distinction between apparent and genuine contradictions is important because it points to the fact that antinomies do not force theologians to

---

[11] It should also go without saying that the dualism here involves only epistemology. Many other dualisms have been proposed in the history of theology, and some types of metaphysical dualism are warranted, but that is not the subject of the model proposed here.

abandon logic altogether. True propositions can appear to be logically contradictory to human minds as long as they can be harmonized in the mind of God. In other words, this epistemological dualism works by making the lower (human) level an incomplete version of the upper (divine) level. Logic and truth in the lower level is dependable only to the extent that it reflects the upper (divine) level. This model has the additional benefit of answering one of the primary charges against apparent contradictions: that they destroy the possibility of consistent meaning.[12] There is no crisis of meaning for apparent contradictions because they are fully known and certified in the mind of God—the most absolute possible foundation for truth.

Finally, this epistemological dualism is soft, because the lower level (human perception) is only a truncated form of the upper level (God's thinking). Aspects of the same propositions exist in both, and any truth that is available to human knowledge necessarily depends on the truth that only God knows. Revelation is God's act of moving information from the upper level into that which is available to humanity. In fact, all of our knowledge about God is dependent on revelation in the sense that even the capacity to know is a result of general revelation—the fact that God made human beings in his own image. In any case truth in the upper level is only the fuller, more detailed, and complete extension of the truths available in the lower level.

This raises the difficult question of how the same truths can be contradictory on one level and harmonized on another. The answer is that they are not. The problem arises from a misunderstanding of the lower level, which describes only the human perception of truth or what is presently available to human knowers. In other words, certain revealed truths (the propositional analysis in chapter 4, for instance) would be contradictory without further qualification. Since human knowers are restricted to a lower epistemological level, they only know these propositions as they stand in the biblical text. Through revelation they also know that God's knowledge extends beyond theirs and that in some way these propositions must cohere in his perfect knowledge of reality. But none of this changes the fact that human knowers can go no further than accepting these problems as apparently contradictory—contradictory as they presently stand without further qualification.

It becomes important, therefore, to distinguish the framework or vantage point from which theologians speak. By default they can speak only as human knowers in the lower level of knowledge. But based on Scripture's teaching about God's transcendent knowledge and his logicality (the biblical data from chapter 2), it is clear that his knowledge of paradoxical propositions extends beyond our own and that these propositions cohere in his mind in some way that they do not in human understanding.[13] Thus when speaking in absolute terms it is legitimate to say that

---

[12] This is the tenor of David Basinger's comments in "Biblical Paradox: Does Revelation Challenge Logic?," *JETS* 30.2 (June 1987): 205-13.

[13] Dualistic epistemological models face a chronic problem that emerges here. How can we speak of the upper level of knowledge if by definition it represents the things about which we cannot know anything? How can we say that there are truths about God we do

every paradox has a solution (our awareness of God's perspective), but the fact that a solution exists in God's mind cannot authorize anyone to act as though he presently knows it. The simple fact remains that as they stand apart from further revelation, the biblical paradoxes involve propositions in an implicitly contradictory relationship that no one can presently resolve.

James Anderson gives the hypothetical situation of a student listening to a lecture and hearing the statement, "the kingdom of God has arrived" before falling asleep. Several minutes later, the student awakens just long enough to hear "the kingdom of God has not arrived," and these two statements are all that he remembers from the lecture. Perhaps the lecturer genuinely contradicted himself; but more likely, the student missed the broader context that allowed both of these statements to be true.[14] The answer could be as simple as two different senses in which each statement can be understood. For instance, if the lecture is on progressive dispensationalism, the speaker might maintain that some of the kingdom promises are being fulfilled as Christ reigns in the hearts of his people. But discussing the promises of a physical home for the restored national Israel and the earthly reign of Jesus Christ over all nations, the lecturer might also maintain that the kingdom has not yet arrived completely.[15]

In the absence of any further qualification or explanation, it would be completely accurate to say that these two statements are contradictory. But perhaps the student knows externally that the teacher would not contradict himself—based on the word of a student who stayed awake, the academic credentials of the speaker, or the student's own previous experience with the professor. In such a case it would be quite reasonable to say that the statements contradict as they stand in the student's limited knowledge and also to be confident that a real solution does exist. The fact that the student does not know the solution in no way negates the existence of a solution; nor can the fact that a solution exists permit the student to proceed as though he already knows it. In the meantime the best way to describe the situation might be as a temporary or apparent contradiction.

---

not know, if these facts are themselves in the lower level of knowledge? The answer lies in a more precise understanding of what the two spheres represent. The lower level is defined as that which we know by revelation, and the upper level is that which is still unrevealed. On this basis there is nothing inconsistent about predicates in the lower level that apply to subjects in the upper level. Because we know that God's knowledge is higher than ours but that he also shares logicality with us, both of these facts are in the lower level of knowledge. Thus, we can know information (lower level) that applies in some way to information that is unknown (upper level). This should not be surprising. If every piece of information is related in some way to other pieces of information, these are just relationships that straddle the divide between revealed and unrevealed truth.

[14] Anderson, *Paradox in Christian Theology*, 223.

[15] Darrell L. Bock, "Covenants in Progressive Dispensationalism," in *Three Central Issues in Contemporary Dispensationalism*, ed. Herbert W. Bateman (Grand Rapids: Kregel, 1999), 202-203.

Understanding Resolution

If there really are propositions in the biblical text that contradict apart from any further qualifications, a second issue demands analysis: What is the nature of resolution? What does it mean to resolve the conflict between two propositions? More importantly, what logical solutions can theologians place their confidence in, how confident should they be in them, and what are the limits on the resolutions they should propose? These questions lead further into more fundamental questions about the nature of human and divine knowledge.

The Nature of Human Knowledge

If soft epistemological dualism is the way to regard paradox, what does it mean to be limited to a lower level of knowledge? Most importantly, how does human knowledge relate to divine knowledge?

The natural starting point for these questions is with human knowledge. An earlier chapter considered exegetical proof that our knowledge is fundamentally limited. Even the consistency of logic in human knowledge is derivative: realities in the universe relate to one another consistently because they are derived from the same preceding reality—the Creator. All human knowledge is likewise dependent on revelation in some way—whether general or special revelation.

But no single fact can be known veridically without knowledge of every other connected fact, spreading into a network that extends to the infinite realities of God's own being. This is the power of revelation—it can come only from someone who knows every fact and chooses to veridically reveal and confirm certain facts for human knowledge. Revealed truths are the only realities in the universe that can be known by humans absolutely and veridically, because God provides their epistemic warrant. Implications can be drawn that have real epistemic merit, but the further they move away from the propositions of Scripture, the greater their loss in epistemic certitude.[16]

Similar frameworks apply to every other part of reality. It is impossible for limited reality to contain genuine infinity, but conversely, limited reality cannot account for itself apart from infinity. In short, the created realm necessarily looks to something outside of itself for its fundamental bases. If all of reality is interconnected and if it also necessarily stretches beyond itself, one should expect to encounter truths whose epistemic contexts are entirely beyond human comprehension.[17] The universe is not a self-contained reality; revelation is not comprehensive. Since knowledge is an organic, inter-related whole with truths

---

[16] Of course, certain propositions have such a close relationship to biblical propositions, that for all *practical* purposes they hardly bear a diminished epistemic status. Kevin T. Bauder explains a helpful way to understand this truth category: "In the Nick of Time," *Central Seminary,* November 3, 2006, www.centralseminary.edu/publications/20061103.pdf (accessed March 19, 2010).

[17] Of course, this assumes that human knowledge is not infinite and that human comprehension has necessary limits.

resting on other truths, for human knowers the fabric of truth must eventually reach a point where it is beyond explanation.[18] As a result two truths may interrelate outside of the sphere of human knowledge. In other words, the specific way that two truths should be integrated may be unrevealed and beyond human capacity to discern.[19]

Several biblical passages seem to point to this final limitation in human understanding. Romans 9:19-21 carries the reader to an intolerable logical conclusion for which the simple answer is that God has the right to do what he wishes. Even more clearly, Job's struggle with the problem of evil ends without a theodicy or even an attempt to resolve his problems, but with the person of the incomprehensible God.[20] Postmodernism and presuppositional apologetics have exposed the fact that all knowledge must search for an independent foundation and cannot rest until it has been found. Revelation provides that foundation, but to the extent that it does not specify the logical relationships between many revealed truths, theologians should expect to encounter paradoxes they cannot explain. In fact, the marvel is not so much that problems like this arise but that that they do not arise more. It is miraculous that God provided a complete and sufficient revelation that is accurate as it stands, communicating clearly to limited creatures while still genuinely representing realities about him.[21]

The problem is that in the attempt to defend Christian doctrine from the charge of contradiction it is all too tempting to declare the specifics of how paradoxical propositions relate. This might be stated for the purpose of demonstrating that a resolution could potentially exist, or it might be stated as an analytic representation of the relationship. Either way, theologians profess to know more than they properly can. As a basic fact Scripture has not revealed this information, and any proposals are guesswork at best.

---

[18] As Stephen T. Davis, *Logic and the Nature of God* (Grand Rapids: Macmillan, 1983), 140-41, comments, "Perhaps it is not surprising that we find mysteries in the Christian doctrine of God. For this understanding is based on the premise that a transcendent being has revealed himself to us. . . . Not being ourselves transcendent or infinitely wise, it is obvious that we will not be able to comprehend God with the same skill or insight with which we comprehend rats or pencils or triangles. Perhaps all our thoughts about God are halting, inadequate and partial. Perhaps mysteries will inevitably appear if it is true that God who in his essence is unknowable to us reveals himself to us."

[19] Anderson, *Paradox in Christian Theology*, 237-43, for an excellent discussion of this concept.

[20] D.A. Carson, *How Long, O Lord?* (Grand Rapids: Baker, 1990), 171-78.

[21] Calvin describes this miracle well in a well-known quotation: "Who, even of the meanest capacity, understands not, that God lisps, as it were, with us, just as nurses are accustomed to speak to infants? Wherefore, such forms of expression do not clearly explain the nature of God, but accommodate the knowledge of him to our narrow capacity; to accomplish which, the Scripture must necessarily descend far below the height of his majesty"—John Calvin, *Institutes of the Christian Religion*, trans. John Allen (Philadelphia: Presbyterian Board, 1921), 1:116.

The Nature of Divine Knowledge

Since human knowledge is limited, it is only natural—even philosophically necessary—that some propositions would be beyond understanding. But what about divine knowledge? As mentioned earlier, there is definite evidence supporting continuity between God's knowledge and humanity's. Scripture reasons with humans and teaches that human reasoning is analogous to God's. But does this mean that God's reasoning processes must always mirror his creatures'? More specifically, is there any requirement that the fundamental laws of logic must hold for all of reality just as they hold in human experience? Is it absolutely certain that these requirements hold for God?

A number of philosophical theologians think it is crucial to answer affirmatively. For instance, David Basinger argues that suspending reasoning at any point compromises the possibility of meaning.[22] Norman Geisler also argues that a proposition must have logical coherence for it to carry any truth value, even with truths about God such as the Incarnation.[23]

But these arguments push toward an even more fundamental question: is God limited by a greater epistemic reality, as though some metaphysical framework preceded his existence and limits him? Furthermore, how can anyone know that axiomatic and philosophical realities that are basic to human existence are basic to all of reality? How would anyone know that all of reality must operate on causality, dimensionality and logicality? How could one ever confirm that existence as he knows it is the only mode of existence possible? By granting these assumptions an irrevocable status *even outside of the universe*, some theologians have elevated certain metaphysical phenomena above God himself, giving them an existence that logically antedates and controls even him.[24]

This points to a fundamental problem in the analyses claiming to resolve biblical antinomies—they each directly extrapolate from human experience of reality to God's. The assumption seems to be that because human beings have experienced reality only within certain givens, all of reality must be subject to those same givens.

---

[22] David Basinger, "Biblical Paradox: Does Revelation Challenge Logic?," *JETS* 30.2 (June 1987): 208.

[23] Norman Geisler, "The Incarnation and Logic: Their Compatibility Defended," *TJ* 6.2 (Fall 1985): 186.

[24] It is certainly valid to recognize that God cannot logically create a square circle *in this universe*, because in the matrix of reality that we inhabit he has created fundamental axioms such as identity, consistency and logicality. To then create a contradiction in terms would violate these fundamental axioms by producing something cross-current to the nature of the universe within the matrix of the universe. But there is no reason to presume that this must be the case outside of the sphere of reality we are accustomed to. Without a doubt the proposition of a square circle presumes a mental construct of both and makes sense only given those constructs. But it is philosophically presumptuous indeed to extend human experience in this universe outside of it and take as axiomatic that every reality must also include identity, dimensionality, causality and logicality, not to mention the mental constructs that men have built on these presumptions!

But if God transcends time and space, is there any *a priori* reason that he cannot also transcend the fabric of logic as we know it? Of course, there are important qualifications here. Even as he transcends time and space, God does not violate the way in which his creatures relate to these fundamental givens but goes beyond in a way that incorporates them. In a similar way God's relationship to logical laws such as non-contradiction or *modus ponens* would incorporate them without violating their true status. At the same time he could go beyond them in a way that exceeds our limited experience or categories for understanding.[25]

Regardless, the fact is that no one knows how God relates to logic.[26] This fact is a double-edged sword. On the one hand, it restricts anyone from affirmatively declaring that God relates to logic in a unique way. But it also corrects the *a priori* assumption that he must relate to logic in a way that is coextensive with our logical processes in order for meaning to be stable.

Concerning meaning, Richard Swinburne points out that "meaningless" is probably not the best description for such conflicts, for even if someone makes an impossible claim such as "1=3," readers do understand what he is communicating, even if it cannot possibly be true.[27] When applied to Scripture, there is no *a priori* reason that God could not reveal two propositions without also revealing how they relate. Wherever he did, the truth value of the propositions would simply rest on biblical authority.[28] The unrevealed aspects of truth would force believers to trust

---

[25] Even proponents of the paradox-minimizing view recognize that there must be some type of distinction between human understanding and God's, but they still require that logical laws must function as they do in the sphere of our present experience. Hugh Ross, *Beyond the Cosmos* (Colorado Springs: NavPress, 1996), 56, resolves theological paradoxes by toggling between multiple theoretical dimensions. Essentially his resolutions work by placing the two sides of paradox in separate dimensions. But without offering substantive proof he is quite confident that "the rules of logic do not change as one travels from one specific dimensional system to another." As with Immanuel Kant's noumenal realm, one wonders how someone can know so much about a realm which by definition cannot be directly known.

[26] John Frame, *Van Til, The Theologian*, 31, n.114, comments that "Van Til leaves open (as he must, to avoid speculation) the question of how God resolves these apparent contradictions, whether by a better-than-human logic, by fuller knowledge of the facts, or by somehow transcending the whole logic/fact problematic."

[27] Richard Swinburne, *The Coherence of Theism* (Oxford: Clarendon, 1977), 14.

[28] Michael S. Horton, *Covenant and Eschatology: The Divine Drama* (Louisville: Westminster John Knox, 2002), 186, points out that "God is the basis for existing and knowing. If God has spoken, then human speech has a foundation but not an *autonomous* foundation. Truth is established as both a goal and a possibility of communicative acts—it has its archetype in the communicative action of the creator of the human race. Although our knowledge doesn't penetrate the archetypal self-knowledge of the Trinity, it is ectypal of it. Our knowledge does have ultimate reality as its foundation, even if the former has an analogical relation to the latter. The old theologians spoke of God as the *principium essendi* (foundation for existing) and the *principium cognoscendi* (foundation for knowing), but this should be extended to include the claim that God is the *principium loquendi* (foundation of saying). Language is a divine construction, just as the reality that language both apprehends and is apprehended by."

Scripture as it stands, but it would not reduce the propositions to meaningless utterances.

Theological Distinctions

The standard way of handling apparent contradictions is to make a distinction. This has a legitimate epistemological basis, since two sides of a contradiction cannot both be true at the same time and in the same sense. Naturally enough, if theologians distinguish two different senses in which to understand conflicting propositions, the purported contradiction evaporates. Some theologians even maintain that in order to disprove the charge of contradiction, they need to propose only one plausible distinction, whether that particular distinction has any basis in fact or not. For them, if there is even a single workable distinction that can remove the conflict, the contradiction is no longer intractable and the charges of a logical problem dissolve.[29]

There are several additional requirements, however, before such a solution can genuinely solve the problem. To begin, it should be taken for granted that any proposed solution must also cohere with the rest of biblical revelation. Plantinga recognizes this requirement and seeks to proceed accordingly.[30] Still, a number of the proposed resolutions for biblical paradoxes rub against one or the other poles of the conflict.[31] Biblical data is the only kind of epistemic evidence of which anyone can be absolutely certain. Any attempted resolution that must adjust, distort, or set aside any biblical datum in order to resolve a paradox pays a premium that is far higher than the return.[32]

---

[29] An example of this type of argument appears in Plantinga, *God, Freedom, and Evil*, 24-29, where he argues that a defense against the charge of contradiction must only specify a state of affairs in which the contradiction does not stand.

[30] Alvin C. Plantinga, *Warranted Christian Belief* (New York: Oxford, 2000), 168-70. Depending on one's view of sovereignty and free will, however, it is questionable whether his free-will defense fulfills this requirement. See Alvin C. Plantinga, *God, Freedom, and Evil*, 29-34. As discussed later, one of the faults of the free-will defense is the assumption that God exists within a metaphysical framework that defines what is good, acceptable, or possible, and constrains his actions. Worse, the biblical evidence simply differs with Plantinga's understanding of libertarian free will.

[31] This is particularly the case with the problem of evil or the problem of sovereignty and free will. Open theism is a conspicuous example of an entire theological model built on the attempt to resolve such conflicts. As one might expect, the proponents of open theism universally subscribe to the paradox-minimizing view of antinomy. In this case, however, the attempt to resolve two paradoxes leads to a reinterpretation or even outright denial of significant biblical data. See Daniel Elmer, "Critique of John Sanders and Clark Pinnock on the Prophetic Necessity and Certainty of the Crucifixion" (Th.M. thesis, Capital Bible Seminary, 2007).

[32] To be sure, systematic consistency does play a role in interpretation. James 2:24 must be interpreted in a way that coheres with its own surrounding context as well as Romans 3:28, Galatians 2:16, Ephesians 2:8-9, and even Habakkuk 2:4. If the exegetical data is ambiguous enough to allow for more than one legitimate reading, systematic consistency is one of the various factors that can determine the best interpretation. The problem

This points to a further requirement. The fact that one can envision a distinction that solves one of the paradoxes does not mean that the distinction represents reality. Truth is only a function of the realities that underlie it, and in biblical terms something is true only if it represents God's knowledge of those realities. On this basis, how helpful is it really to propose distinctions that may have no basis in actual fact?[33] The student who wakes only to hear two contradicting propositions might be completely confident that his professor's position is cogent and self-consistent. He might even go so far as to be confident that some distinction must exist that makes both statements true. But it would be foolhardy for him to imagine an arbitrary possible distinction and then declare that he has vindicated his professor. In reality the student simply does not know how the propositions relate, because he was asleep when the professor explained them.[34]

Finally, a distinction or explanatory model must be meaningful. Terms such as *person*, *essence*, and *nature* have a measure of meaning that can be defined and biblically supported, but they fail at the very points where their meaning is most crucial. In many cases the distinctions reduce to little more than stating the problem using different terms. Returning to the comparison, without knowing the professor's distinction our hypothetical student might solve his dilemma by speaking of the "realized kingdom" and the "unrealized kingdom," but one wonders if this goes much beyond "sense A of the kingdom" for which it is true that the kingdom has arrived and "sense B of the kingdom" for which it is true that it has not. In either case these are only analytic notions and add no real information to our understanding of the concepts. Had he heard the lecture, he could give specific, meaningful content about how the professor actually distinguished the ideas, but as it is, the distinction only forces us to ask what these terms mean and hides the problem in terminological ambiguity.

On the other hand, it is fascinating that this result exactly fits the needs of the paradox-minimizing view. Though theologians who ascribe to this view recognize that there are genuine mysteries, they prefer to describe them as gaps in the information about theological realities and not any sort of genuine logical conflict.

---

comes when the drive for systematic consistency overwhelms or excessively controls the exegetical process. See Brian Collins, "Scripture, Hermeneutics, and Theology: Evaluating Theological Interpretation of Scripture" (Ph.D. diss., Bob Jones University, 2011).

[33] In fact, this very kind of argument is widely used in apologetic contexts to demonstrate that antinomies need not destroy the rationality of the Christian faith. The idea is that if even one reasonable solution can be proposed, it proves that the propositions are not inexorably contradictory. This may have a limited apologetic utility, but it does not solve the conflict between paradoxical propositions. Rather, this technique seems to take advantage of the vacuity of the unknown. The fact remains that no human being can know how the propositions actually relate.

[34] Hypothetically, a distinction could be proposed for any logical conflict. In order to distinguish forced resolutions from genuine answers, one must always apply the same controls that guide every other epistemic process. It is not enough that the distinction appears to resolve the basic conflict; it must also be warrantable on other, external bases.

Distinctions that mask logical tensions in analytic terms accomplish this very purpose—logical conflicts are replaced by an informational vacuum when the theologian is unable to define his own terms specifically and meaningfully.

Epistemic Space

Earlier, we discussed implicit and explicit contradictions, concluding that the only essential difference is the epistemic uncertainty of logical links in implicit contradictions. In other words, implied contradictions are less troublesome than explicit contradictions only to the degree that their linking inferences and supplied propositions are uncertain. It was also significant that Scripture never presents opposing truths in the form of an explicit contradiction. An explicit contradiction of the form "X is Y and X is not Y" implies that the two propositions are true in the same sense, at least by parallelism. Scripture leaves conflicts that it never explains by stating truths that *imply* that "X is Y" and other truths that imply that "X is not Y." But by stating these contradictions implicitly rather than explicitly, it leaves plenty of epistemological space in which distinctions could be made and resolutions could exist.[35] This epistemic space is crucial to understanding biblical paradox. D.A. Carson states this well in his discussion of sovereignty and responsibility:

> For us mortals there are no rational, logical *solutions* to the sovereignty-responsibility tension: it should be clear from the foregoing that neatly packaged harmonizations are impossible. But on the other hand, it is difficult to see why *logical* inconsistency is *necessitated*, especially in view of the many ambiguous parameters and numerous unknown quantities. The whole tension remains restless in our hands; but it is the restlessness of having a few randomly-selected pieces of a jigsaw puzzle when thousands more are needed to complete the design.[36]

It is also necessary that this epistemic space be of a certain kind. James Anderson bases his understanding of paradox on the incomprehensibility of God. As a result, "The relevant component claims of [a paradoxical doctrine] ought to involve metaphysical affirmations about *God*: his nature, his actions, his relationship to the creation, and suchlike."[37] Elsewhere, he speaks of the fact that antinomies involve significant metaphysical assumptions about what is possible, the connections between underlying realities, or what is involved in certain concepts.[38] Stephen

---

[35] Of course, it would be possible, at least hypothetically, that Scripture might explicitly (non-inferentially) state two apparently conflicting propositions in two different contexts. In this case, naturally, the epistemological space would exist in the context. The closest biblical example is probably Paul's statements about works in Romans 3:18 or Galatians 2:16 compared to James 2:17. However, this is probably an interpretational issue more than an antinomy, and none of the theological antinomies discussed here have this type of explicit statement.

[36] Carson, *Divine Sovereignty*, 206.

[37] Anderson, *Paradox in Christian Theology*, 266, original emphasis.

[38] Ibid., 225-226.

Davis points out that antinomies must involve subjects "we would expect to be puzzled about (not things like pins or pigeons but things like God)."[39]

Likewise, it seems completely reasonable that propositions straddling the divide between our knowledge and God's are particularly challenging, and it is hardly accidental that almost all of the problems discussed in this survey are exactly of that nature. God's infinity, the problem of evil, and the problem of sovereignty and free will all involve God's interaction in the physical world—something at the boundary of human understanding and that Scripture never explains. The Incarnation highlights this even more clearly with the consummate instance of mutual and unexplained interaction between the earthly and the divine. The Trinity stands out by not seeming to fit this analysis, isolated almost as an epistemological island. But even here the primary problem is understanding how ontology relates to personhood in the case of a being whose fundamental ontology theologians know almost nothing about. In that sense they struggle to describe or even imagine how the Trinity might exist, because there are no analogous models for such existence in human experience.[40] In each case the problem arises from the overlap and interaction of thought categories from limited human experience with realities that transcend them.

Resolution does exist for each problem, but it exists in God's knowledge. Those resolutions might be in keeping with the givens of reality as humans know them; they might not be. Perhaps God could reveal a simple distinction that would explain these antinomies within human thought structures. This would demonstrate that the problem was only informational—no one could understand because he lacked all of the data. But it could also be much more—traceable to something deeper in God's understanding of logic itself that in some way transcends human understanding. The simple fact is that no one knows, and it is never warranted to extend the givens of the known to the unknown with the assumption that they limit reality in the same ways in both places.

Apologetic Warrant

One final issue in the definition and analysis of antinomy is the apologetic problems they raise. How can anyone be warranted in believing two truths that contradict, or how can they establish these truths with any degree of epistemological warrant? Other works discuss this problem at greater length than is possible here, and the focus of the present study is the impact of paradox on prolegomena. Still, a few comments are in order.

---

[39] Davis, *Logic and the Nature of God*, 142-143.

[40] Granted, this entire argument somewhat conflates epistemology with metaphysics while the model of soft epistemic dualism mentioned earlier divides knowledge and not metaphysical realities. Still, the two are connected. The fundamental ontological divide between Creator and creature places each in separate ontic spheres that mirror the epistemological division suggested earlier.

In the last section of his work on logic and theology, Stephen Davis defines a mystery as "an apparent contradiction which there is good reason to believe".[41] Davis gives two criteria for rational belief in mysteries in order to distinguish them from nonsense or any arbitrary contradictory doctrine. First, something must suggest that the contradiction is only apparent. That is, there must be something that admits of further clarification or distinction (epistemological space), and the propositions must involve subjects that would naturally be puzzling.[42] Davis's second criterion is that it must have solid external support—specifically, there should be reason to believe that the apparently conflicting truths were both revealed by God.

These criteria are a helpful starting point, but James Anderson provides much fuller discussion in his extended work on paradox and apologetic warrant. Anderson proposes a model for the rational affirmation of paradoxical propositions. He begins with Aristotle's famous dictum that nothing can be both X and non-X at the same time and in the same sense and Aquinas's recommendation that when faced with a contradiction, one should make a distinction. Theologians may not be able to specify what the distinctions are, but if an apparent paradox allows for such a distinction in principle, it could be a MACRUE—a Merely Apparent Contradiction Resulting from Unarticulated Equivocation.[43] Anderson defines a mystery as "a metaphysical state of affairs the revelation of which appears implicitly contradictory to us on account of present limitations in our cognitive apparatus and thus resists systematic description in a perspicuously consistent manner".[44] He goes on to argue that his model for mystery can function as a defeater-defeater or a defeater-insulator: it refutes the charge that paradoxes destroy Christianity's apologetic credibility or inoculates believers to that charge.[45] As long as there is epistemic warrant to the biblical testimony, paradoxes contained in it can still have warrant as well.[46]

Both of these discussions reduce to the same two basic requirements that also comport with the preceding discussion of paradox. The first is "epistemic space"—an inferential relationship between the propositional poles that could permit distinctions. Because the biblical antinomies are implicit contradictions, all of them fit this requirement. The second basic requirement is for a surrounding epistemological field that supports the conflicting propositions. If a given worldview leads to certain truths that will be beyond full explanation, and the worldview is otherwise warranted, there is reason to accept some problems as they

---

[41] Davis, *Logic and the Nature of God*, 142.

[42] Ibid., 142-43. This accords with the previous suggestion that most paradoxes involve propositions that straddle the known and unknown.

[43] Anderson, *Paradox in Christian Theology*, 222.

[44] Ibid., 245.

[45] Ibid., 246-56.

[46] Ibid., 256-61.

stand.[47] Simply stated, if the propositions are clearly revealed in Scripture, apparently conflicting propositions have as much warrant as the Christian worldview in general.

This analysis is also the answer to a more general problem: if apparent contradictions appear to be contradictory from a human standpoint, how are they distinguished from genuine contradictions?[48] The same two criteria answer the problem: (1) Is the proposition an implicit contradiction with enough epistemic space to permit a distinction that could resolve it—at least hypothetically? (2) Is the proposition clearly taught in Scripture? More detailed discussion of this problem will appear in the following chapter.

Assessing the views of paradox

In light of these analyses, we are now in a position to return to the conservative strategies for paradox, evaluating how well each view comports with the biblical data and how helpfully it handles the theological challenges. Like any model, each of the three conservative strategies have both pros and cons.

The Sui Generis *View*

The advantage of the *sui generis* view is that the model is under no pressure to resolve the logical tensions in Scripture. The problem of integrating logic and paradox is settled by a matter of simple definition. However, since the *sui generis* view places a certain type of proposition beyond logic, there are two basic problems. First, the *sui generis* view must define what propositions qualify as exceptions to logical laws and specify criteria that limit deductions. Most attempts to do so prove to be abstract and ambiguous, ultimately failing to define any specific propositional set. But without such criteria the logical implications of this view threaten to destroy the entire theological program. Even if this problem could be overcome, the second issue is justifying the distinction. Why do some propositions have a special epistemic status? Why is it only those and not others? In application most presentations of the *sui generis* view fail in plausibility, workability, or both. In addition proponents of this view often fail to investigate theological tensions as much as they could or proffer helpful explanatory models—they simply do not regard these problems as requiring further analysis.

---

[47] Of course, this is hardly anything exceptional in models for explaining reality. Every worldview has problems or questions it does not explain, but it is still rational to accept them as they stand if they otherwise provide coherent explanations for reality. This returns to a fundamental concept mentioned earlier—limited reality is insufficient to explain or account for itself. At some point every worldview must seek out an external basis for itself. The cosmological argument argues for theism on this basis.

[48] When Norman Geisler (paradox-minimizing view) referred to John Dahm's (*sui generis* view) examples as "apparent contradictions," Dahms responded with this very problem—how can anyone profess to absolutely distinguish the two? See both, Geisler, "Reply," 62, and Dahms, "Rejoinder," 139.

One other consideration against the *sui generis* view is that apparently, very few thinkers in the history of the church have adopted it. In fact, it is quite difficult to identify even a moderate number of proponents. While this is hardly an absolute argument, it is an interesting and valid consideration.

The Paradox-Minimizing View

Most of the arguments for this view are essentially arguments against complementarity, since the paradox-minimizing view has primarily been articulated in the context of conflicts between the two views. Robert Reymond, for instance, gives four reasons for rejecting complementarity. The first is the problem of the universal negative—whether theologians can declare that a problem has not been resolved nor ever will be. Second, Reymond suggests that talk of "apparent contradiction" is unworkable, since there can be no way to distinguish apparent from genuine contradiction. Third, Reymond contends that paradox leaves theologians in a crisis of meaning. What, for instance, would a "four-cornered triangle" mean? Finally, Reymond opposes complementarity because it breaks the exclusionary power of theological propositions. In other words, the statement that "God is always good" should eliminate a set of contradictory propositions such as "God is evil" or "God is only good at certain times." Once propositions that are at odds are both allowed to stand, any theological proposition becomes possible. Its proponents need only to claim that it is part of an antinomy, and no logical considerations can be brought to bear against it. [49]

These are legitimate questions, and only a fully articulated model for paradox can answer them.[50] But it suffices to observe that one of the major advantages of the paradox-minimizing view is apologetic. In the attempt to reduce theological tensions as much as possible, this view also offers great explanatory power and logical coherence.[51] If the goal is to demonstrate that Christianity is the most cogent of the worldviews, it is immensely profitable to minimize logical conflicts. The weakness, however, is that the pressure to resolve tensions where possible can also skew the theological process and lead to illegitimate reevaluations of the biblical data. The text simply does not allow for complete solutions for every paradox, even though it is tempting to try to develop them anyway.

---

[49] Robert Reymond, *A New Systematic Theology of the Christian Faith* (Nashville: Thomas Nelson, 1998), 103-107.

[50] These questions are answered in depth elsewhere in the present study. Briefly, (1) Complementarians are not required to demonstrate a universal negative; if one can demonstrate that none of the current solutions are adequate, the problem of paradox stands. (2) Apparent contradictions are simply those that Scripture compels readers to accept; genuine contradictions are those without exegetical support. (3) Even a paradoxical formulation has meaning to the extent that readers understand what it says. (4) Paradoxical propositions can still eliminate heresy by designating inferences that should not be made.

[51] In fact, a good case can be made that one of the major motivations behind the paradox-minimizing view is apologetic defensibility.

The greatest weakness of the paradox-minimizing view is that it fails to achieve its goal plausibly. In their attacks on complementarity, these theologians place overwhelming epistemic importance on minimizing paradox and eliminating any logical tensions, but in practice their own view is no more capable of relieving these tensions completely.

In order to make its goal more attainable, the paradox-minimizing view must also define contradiction in a rather limited way. Discussing the problem of evil, Feinberg suggests that

> we must clarify what it means to say that a system or a set of propositions contains a contradiction. It doesn't mean that there may be a way to fit a theology's views together consistently but neither the critic nor the theist knows how. Nor does it mean that someday we shall understand, even though we don't now. It doesn't even mean that God knows how ideas fit together without contradiction, even though we don't. Instead, a charge of contradiction means that there is no possible way for *anyone ever* to harmonize these view, for they both affirm and deny the same thing at the same time and in the same way.[52]

On this definition it is a wonder that Feinberg can clearly designate anything as a contradiction.

Complementarity

The next chapter will present a full-fledged complementarian model, along with evaluation of its strengths and weaknesses. It is worth noting here that in many contexts the proponents of complementarity and the paradox-minimizing view have talked past one other. Complementarians define paradox as propositions that appear to be contradictory. Proponents of the paradox-minimizing view vigorously maintain that contradiction would cause the entire epistemological framework of theology to implode. Instead, they regard these tensions as informational gaps rather than logical conflicts.

The paradox-minimizing view ignores a critical distinction in complementarity—the difference between God's knowledge and limited human understanding. Complementarity maintains only that there is contradictory material *as our knowledge presently stands* but that the propositions themselves are completely coherent in the mind of God. For complementarity the fundamental issue is unclarified ambiguity—areas where two propositions appear to contradict and theologians lack enough information to know how they actually relate. Ironically, this is quite similar to the paradox-minimizing view, where advocates qualify that tensions cohere even if no one can explain *how* they relate.[53]

---

[52] John S. Feinberg, *The Many Faces of Evil: Theological Systems and the Problems of Evil* (Wheaton: Crossway, 2004), 28.

[53] R.C. Sproul, *The Mystery of the Holy Spirit* (Wheaton: Tyndale, 1994), 58, comments that "mystery is often confused with contradiction—for an obvious reason. Both are not presently understood. The difference is that a mystery may be understood with additional

Putting all of this together, it is natural enough to wonder whether the two perspectives are actually different, or whether there is merely a difference of terminology and emphasis. They are distinct for several reasons. (1) The two viewpoints differ in their attitude. The paradox-minimizing view values coherence and logical resolution highly, recommending that all reasonable attempts should be made to resolve logical tensions. Complementarians, on the other hand, place some type of limit on what attempts at resolution can and should be made. (2) The viewpoints lead to different theological conclusions. Complementarians are much more willing to leave questions unanswered and problems unsolved, while their counterparts generally find unanswered tensions unacceptable. Conversely, the paradox-minimizing view is willing to say that various solutions have resolved biblical tensions, while complementarity has no such confidence. (3) If nothing else, the views must be different because the proponents of each view clearly find the other perspective unacceptable. While it is hypothetically possible that each has so misunderstood the other that the difference is only terminological, the continued and unresolved nature of the conflict seems to indicate otherwise.

Conclusion

Partial knowledge is an inescapable function of finite minds trying to apprehend an infinite and interrelated truth. In fact, one should expect that paradox would occur, given several conditions: (1) an infinite reality (God), resulting in infinite truth. (2) Finite revelation to human minds. (3) Causal or logical relationships between propositions, forming an inferential network among all propositions that are true. Where revealed truth ends and unknown realities continue on, the process of integrating propositions with one another will be especially complex.

Still, the simple governing principle for all biblical paradoxes is that no one knows the resolutions, and theologians must be careful not to proceed rashly as though they do. This raises the difficult problem of how to proceed in the meantime. How can theologians carry out the task of deriving inferences from propositions that are implicitly contradictory? This is the subject of the next chapter.

---

information, but a bona fide contradiction can never be understood. We cannot understand contradictions because they are *intrinsically unintelligible*."

CHAPTER 6

Coexisting with Paradox: A Way Forward

Verbally speaking the enigmas of Jehovah seem darker and more desolate than the enigmas of Job; yet Job was comfortless before the speech of Jehovah and is comforted after it. He has been told nothing but he feels the terrible and tingling atmosphere of something which is too good to be told. The refusal of God to explain His design is itself a burning hint of His design. The riddles of God are more satisfying than the solutions of man.[1]

All of the previous considerations set a foundation for the crucial issue of this study—how is it possible to draw inferences and engage in theological reasoning if such reasoning might be invalid at any point? This problem is apparent in two ways. First, there is the problem of knowing the limits of logic. For example, in a perfect system a theologian could consistently rely on logic as an epistemological tool and always be confident that it will guide him to accurate conclusions as long as he uses it legitimately. But if there is even a single point at which logic should not be used, then the theologian needs a set of criteria for all of his reasoning. Now, every additional step into the unknown might turn out to be a misstep, and the entire process is hamstrung without some set of guidelines for identifying the limits of logic. The existence of a single paradox changes the entire process of theological reasoning and reflection.

A second issue is even more problematic. If two propositions can both be true and yet be apparently contradictory for human knowers, what of the whole field of implications drawn from them? A single pair of such propositions extends into an almost endless set of propositions at odds. The results are a widening cleavage in the fabric of systematic theology and an incoherent worldview. With multiple apparent paradoxes the problem is only multiplied further, and in several cases the logical problems they cause come together, producing even more challenging theological questions and anomalies.

With all of this complexity, it is not hard to see why some theologians try to avoid a complementarian view of paradox. Yet the chapter that examined the views on paradox demonstrated that theologians must accept paradox at some level in order to protect orthodoxy. This produces pressure away from the two extreme margins—rigorous logic on the one hand and the renunciation of logic on the other—and toward the middle with a modicum of both concerns. Without any

---

[1] G.K. Chesterton, *Introduction to the Book of Job* (London: Wellwood, 1907), xviii.

guidelines that allow logic and paradox to coexist, however, the theologian faces an additional pressure, away from the middle. As in Figure 6.1 (see the next page), this is why there is a natural appeal to the views at the equilibrium point between these pressures. The paradox-minimizing view limits paradox as much as possible (so that logic and paradox can coexist) while still granting that paradox does exist (in order to remain within orthodoxy). On the opposite extreme, variants of the *sui generis* view usually appear in a partial form—limiting logic enough that it can coexist with paradox but also sustaining a coherent meaning for the text in order to remain orthodox.

And yet, as previous chapters have demonstrated, there are challenges with the paradox minimizing and *sui generis* views as well. Since application requires logical processes, the *sui generis* view risks barring Scripture from any extra-textual application.[2] This model also handicaps the crucial interpretational role that passages should play for one another—guiding the readings that are legitimate through the analogy of faith.[3] On the opposite extreme, the paradox-minimizing view is unable to truly mitigate the force of the theological tensions. In short, the paradox-minimizing view pursues a worthy objective, but it is hard to say that the goal is realistic or achievable.

All of this leaves both the *sui generis* and paradox-minimizing views in an awkward position, attempting to avoid complementarity but arriving at a weaker position as a result. Because of the two problems mentioned above, complementarity may be the orthodox view with the most challenges, but not if it is possible to develop a workable model for identifying the limits of logic. If logic and paradox can coexist without causing prolegomena and theological systems to collapse, complementarity is the view with the greatest strength because it seems to represent the biblical evidence regarding both logic and paradox most accurately. The challenge is to articulate a self-consistent model for complementarity—the ambition of this chapter.

---

[2] John Frame, *The Doctrine of the Knowledge of God* (Phillipsburg, N.J.: P&R, 1987), 84.

[3] Brian Collins, "Scripture, Hermeneutics, and Theology: Evaluating Theological Interpretation of Scripture" (Ph.D. diss., Bob Jones University, 2011).

Figure 6.1. Competing Pressures in the Views of Paradox

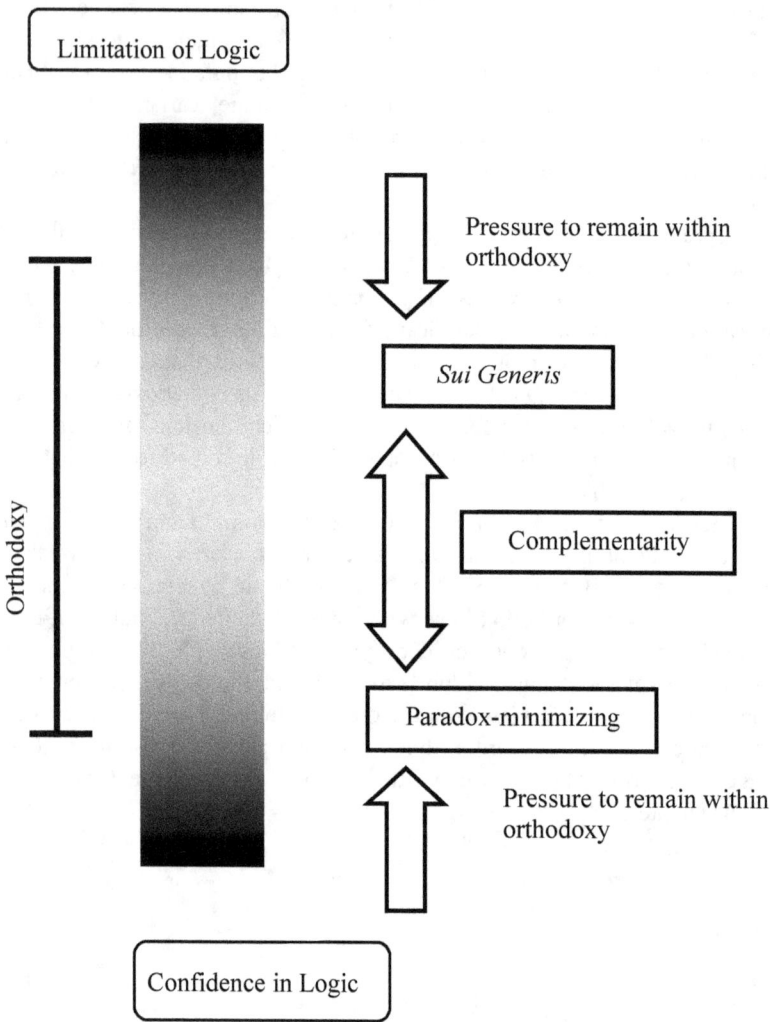

Components of a Complementarian Theological Method

Since a complementarian model exists to solve a problem of prolegomena, the clearest explanation is by comparison to the discipline of hermeneutics. Five foundational concepts can be gleaned from hermeneutics for analyzing paradox—inter-propositional ambiguity, the methodological spiral, epistemic warrant, diminishing epistemic certainty, and apophatic inference.

Inter-Propositional Ambiguity

Within biblical interpretation, if two or more texts seem to contradict, good interpreters adjust their understanding by reevaluating one or more elements in the interpretation. The lexical and semantic elements of a proposition involve enough ambiguity that some arrangement or combination of interpretational choices will yield a meaningful reading.

Likewise, for the theologian assessing paradox, the conflict follows after interpretation and involves logical consistency. Inter-propositional ambiguity describes the fact that two theological propositions might form a direct conflict because of an undescribed ambiguity in one of the terms. In the example of the Trinity, for instance, propositions state that God is both one and three, requiring that there be two different senses for understanding the statements. Considering that the biblical text never elucidates this distinction, it can be regarded as an unclarified ambiguity.

Where there is a conflict between logical coherence and the biblical data, the completed model must absorb that pressure somewhere. At its best, the paradox-minimizing view absorbs the pressure by drawing possible distinctions that are either non-explanatory or lack strong confirmation from the biblical data; at its worst, the view adjusts biblical data to make it cohere. The *sui generis* view, on the other hand, absorbs the pressure by adjusting the laws of logic in a way that is inconsistent with the rest of the theological method. But in the conflict between biblical data and consistent logical laws, is it not best that both epistemological principles stand, and the pressure is instead exhausted in the ambiguities that the biblical text itself suggests? Naturally, this means that some questions will go unanswered and some problems will be unexplored, but on the whole, ignorance or ambiguity is better than the logical problems of the *sui generis* view or the exegetical struggles of the paradox-minimizing method. This is not to say that there is no place for further theological clarification or specification. Complementarity does not limit theology to only the explicit affirmations of the biblical text. The principle of inter-propositional ambiguity simply suggests that it is sometimes better to let ambiguities stand than try to remove them.

The same is true when theologians propose a theoretical "bridge" between theological tensions—distinctions or models that purport to explain the conflict. If there is an unknown, the most sophisticated response is to recognize and acknowledge it as unknown. There is no epistemological advantage in proposing a possible solution if in reality it is an unknown variable. The important question is not whether a given model is possible or even represents a potential resolution of the problem. It does not in fact solve the problem unless there is reason to believe it is true.[4]

---

[4] Alvin Plantinga has argued that one must defend only a single plausible solution to theological antinomy to demonstrate that the problem of evil does not produce a *necessary* logical problem. Of course, Plantiga also acknowledges that the solution must comport with other propositions known to be true. But this still makes a solution relatively simple so long as the epistemological context for an antinomy is unknown—a

The Methodological Spiral

One tempting solution for the problem of paradox is to specify a rigid order for the theological disciplines. Some theologians have suggested that systematic theology must be separate from exegesis. In other words, theologians should work toward understanding texts apart from theological categories before moving on to develop an integrated theology. This results in a linear, sequential progression through the theological process and flattens the reciprocal, dynamic cross-interaction that ought to characterize it.[5] In this respect as well, theology in general and paradox in particular should recognize insights from hermeneutics.

In his influential work on hermeneutics, Grant Osborne models the interpretational process as a spiral. Interpreters move incrementally closer to the proper rendering of a text by reevaluating it and their own understanding as they proceed. In this analysis (Figure 6.2), the spiral represents the interpreter's understanding of the text at each stage of the process, and the center of the spiral is the divinely intended meaning.[6] The distance between the two represents hermeneutical noise—the extent to which the interpreter's understanding differs from an accurate understanding of the text.

There are two major benefits to analyzing paradox using the same framework. On the one hand, there is an inescapable circularity to the process that keeps interpretation constantly in development and never completely at rest. But the other

---

condition that is true for all of the antinomies discussed here. In other words, in the vacuum of specific knowledge about God's essential being (the Trinity), the union of Christ's nature (Incarnation) or the metaphysical nature of evil (problem of evil), it is all too easy to suggest arbitrary solutions that appear to bring the propositions together. Saying that such models relieve the tension lowers the epistemological bar in order to make it attainable. Kenneth Surin, "Evil, Problem of," in *The Blackwell Encyclopedia of Modern Christian Thought* (Oxford: Basil Blackwell, 1995), 193-194. Alvin Plantinga, *God and Other Minds* (Ithaca: Cornell University Press, 1967), 122-24. Also, Jay Wesley Richards, "Is the Doctrine of the Incarnation Coherent?" in *Unapologetic Apologetics*, ed. William A. Demski and Jay Wesley Richards (Downers Grove: InterVarsity, 2001), 138, 143.

[5] This is one of the issues in the correspondence between John Frame and Richard Muller, though to some extent they seem to be talking past one another. Richard Muller, *The Study of Theology* (Grand Rapids: Zondervan, 1991). See John Frame, "Muller on Theology," *WTJ* 56.1 (Spring 1994): 140-43; Richard A. Muller, "*The Study of Theology* Revisited: A Response to John Frame," *WTJ* 56.2 (Fall 1994): 409-17. A brief but helpful discussion of this problem appears in D.A. Carson, "Unity and Diversity in the New Testament: The Possibility of Systematic Theology," in *Scripture and Truth*, ed. D.A. Carson and John D. Woodbridge (Grand Rapids: Baker, 1992), 90-93.

[6] The concept of a divinely intended meaning is hardly taken for granted in many of the recent discussions of hermeneutics. See David K. Clark, "Narrative Theology and Apologetics," *JETS* 36.4 (December 1993): 511-13. The position assumed in this study is chastened foundationalism—the confidence that there is an objective truth, even though an individual knower or interpreter has no immediate or purely objective access to it. In biblical terms Scripture contains specific truths that God intends for readers to know. If the truths contained in Scripture do not eliminate some other propositions, a meaningful doctrine of revelation is impossible.

crucial component is the fact that legitimate progress is possible. As long as every stage eliminates at least some interpretational options, the spiral can continue inwards to greater clarity, and the interpreter can be increasingly confident of his conclusions.[7] The key to the process, therefore, is that at each given point, the method must eliminate some possibilities, steadily narrowing the field of available interpretational hypotheses.[8]

---

[7] As Grant Osborne describes this model, "The major premise of this book is that biblical interpretation entails a 'spiral' from text to context, from its original meaning to its contextualization or significance for the church today. . . . I am not going round and round a closed circle that can never detect the true meaning but am spiraling nearer and nearer to the text's intended meaning as I refine my hypotheses and allow the text to continue to challenge and correct those alternative interpretations, then to guide my delineation of its significance for my situation today"—*The Hermeneutical Spiral* (Downers Grove.: InterVarsity, 2006), 22. D.A. Carson, "A Sketch of the Factors Determining Current Hermeneutical Debate in Cross-Cultural Contexts," in *Biblical Interpretation and the Church: Text and Context*, ed. D.A. Carson (Grand Rapids: Baker, 1984), 12-13, points out that the interpreter's definition of "pre-understanding" makes all the difference in his hermeneutical approach. Those who recognize that they bring a pre-understanding to the process but are willing to let it be changed by the text can make steady, incremental progress towards accurate interpretation. But if pre-understanding is absolute, "it becomes *impossible* for the Scriptures to exercise corrective authority over our thoughts and lives in those matters where our 'pre-understanding' is immutably non-negotiable."

[8] D.A. Carson, "The Possibility of Systematic Theology," 90-93, develops this concept while discussing the relationship between exegesis and systematic theology. The relationship between the two is not strictly linear, as though theologians can carry out their exegesis prior to and separate from analysis; nor is it completely circular, as though systematic theology controls the outcome of exegesis. Rather it is a partial combination of both. Exegesis should come before systematic integration in both chronology and priority. But systematic theology does feed back into exegesis in an ongoing feedback loop. Of these, linear progression is the more ultimate, but the feedback loop is also a real part of the process.

Figure 6.2. The Hermeneutical Spiral

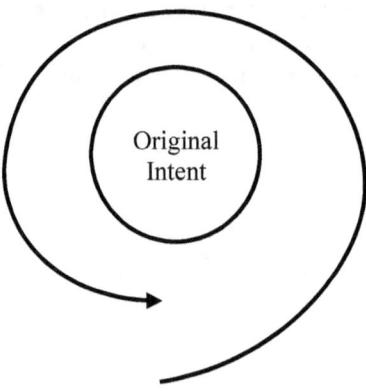

This analysis is relatively simple as long as interpretation pertains to only one text; it becomes more complicated when interpreting two closely-related texts together. For instance, the interpretation of Romans 3:21-24 is hardly complicated by the task of interpreting Galatians 2:16. This is the simple process represented in the first diagram of Figure 6.3—the hermeneutical spiral with multiple texts. Certainly each text contains content not found in the other, and both texts help to illumine the interpretation of the other. Still, the similarities are sufficient that an interpreter can work with both together and do so almost simultaneously. In such a scenario the texts nearly function as a propositional unity, with the interpretation spiraling around the ideas in both.

Theologians face greater complexity, however, when interpreting two texts together that initially appear to be at odds. Such an apparent conflict is illustrated in the case of Galatians 2:16 and James 2:14-17, because at first reading the two seem to be contradictory. Closer examination reveals interpretations for the texts that allow both to stand. If the interpreter failed to take James 2:14-17 into account in his analysis of Galatians 2:16, he might reach the invalid conclusion that good works are not a legitimate soteriological concern. Or conversely, interpreting James 2:14-17 without attention to Galatians 2:16 might lead to the conclusion that justification rests on the basis of works rather than faith. The most adequate interpretation emerges only when both texts stand together at the center of the hermeneutical spiral.[9]

---

[9] See Robert V. Rakestraw, "James 2:14-26: Does James Contradict the Pauline Soteriology?" *Criswell Theological Review* 1 (Fall 1986): 31-50, for a specific analysis of how the texts differ. Rakestraw argues that the meaning of "faith" differs between the two texts and that the works in view differ sequentially—Paul is concerned with works before justification and James speaks of the works that follow from believing justification. Rakestraw also uses these insights to exegete James 2, confirming that significant interpretational insights do emerge from cross-textual analysis and resolution.

More importantly, a result of bringing these texts together is additional information that is not obvious in either independently but emerges as a necessary inference. Specifically, Protestant interpreters clarify that God justifies sinners on the basis of their faith alone but that genuine justification will always result in good works. This intertextual resolution is hermeneutically necessary and guides the interpretation of both passages towards a more sophisticated and complete reading, but it also demonstrates that additional information emerges when interpreters legitimately integrate separate components of biblical revelation. The additional information is the bridge or interpretational resolution that brings the texts together and is represented in the shaded portion of the second diagram in Figure 6.3.

Figure 6.3. The Hermeneutical Spiral with Multiple Texts

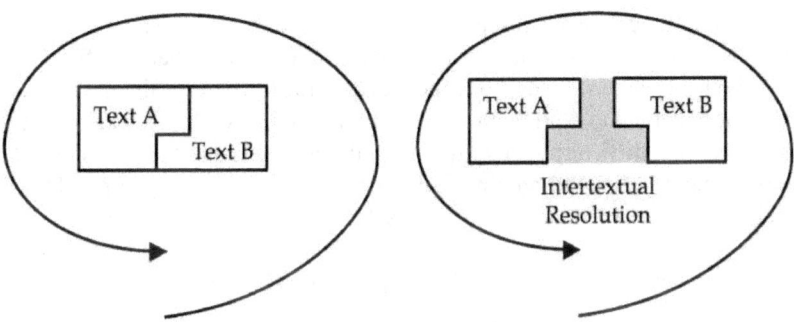

What makes paradox stand apart from such an analysis is the simple fact that no persuasive intertextual resolution exists to integrate paradoxical propositions. Instead, paradoxical propositions exclude resolution in some way, and any of the possible extrapolated inferences produce more logical problems than they solve. If an interpreter takes both sets of data and follows the hermeneutical spiral for both together, he finds himself in a middle ground that both texts exclude. With resolvable conflicts, such as Galatians 2:16 and James 2:14-17, the process is a matter of deciding between options for understanding each text and choosing two interpretations that are compatible. In the case of antinomy, however, there are no such options, and both data sets exclude one another absolutely, as in Figure 6.4. It is simply impossible, for instance, to harmonize the data suggesting Jesus' omniscience with his ignorance in a way analogous to the passages on justification and good works. Thus, insofar as one pursues logical correlations between two sets of paradoxical data, the interpretation of both will be skewed toward the middle, with impossibly contradictory formulations.

Figure 6.4. The Hermeneutical Spiral with Paradoxical Data Sets

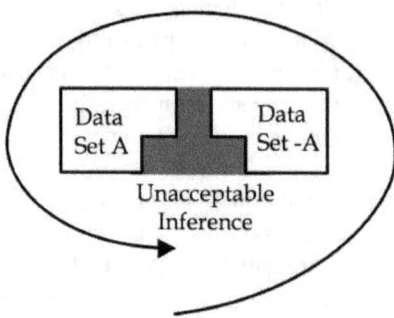

The hermeneutical spiral elucidates how paradox differs from resolvable conflicts such as the emphases in Romans and James. As a theologian spirals toward a better understanding of multiple theological propositions, he should pursue logical resolutions that allow both data sets to stand. By seeking logical coherence within the controls of the biblical data, he simultaneously pursues a clearer understanding of both data sets and their resolution. If he reaches a conclusion that satisfies the demands of both data sets, and the conceptual bridge between them is also theologically acceptable, the problem is merely a difficulty. In the case of a paradox, however, the difficulty will shift among the data sets and their resolution. A construction that satisfies the requirements of two elements will raise problems in the third, and no construction exists that can satisfactorily maintain all three.

Hermeneutical Support and Epistemic Warrant

An additional helpful comparison to hermeneutics is in the evaluation of evidence or legitimate support for a conclusion. Good hermeneutical decision-making bears in mind the weight of evidence behind the possible interpretations. All readers come to the text with an exegetical hypothesis or multiple hypotheses about how it should be rendered. Clearly, it is insufficient to settle on an explanation because it is a possibility. Skilled exegetes measure out the weight of each viable rendering and look for the option with the best support. If an exegete carries out the hermeneutical process correctly, it will lead him to the most probable hypothesis while eliminating the less likely options.

This type of analysis extends to the level of each exegetical decision. Polysemous words, for instance, might include more or less exotic meanings, but where the more basic and common meanings are workable, they should be preferred. As Moisés Silva explains, exegetes should select the meaning of a word that adds the least semantic information to the finished proposition or that causes the least disruption in the meaning.[10] In other words, unusual or forced lexical glosses decrease the relative plausibility of the total interpretation.

---

[10] Moisés Silva, *Biblical Words and Their Meaning* (Grand Rapids: Zondervan, 1994), 153-56.

To borrow an example, it is best to understand ο9 presbu/teroj in Luke 15:25 as "the elder one" rather than as the technical term for the office in the NT church.[11] As with most interpretations, this rendering is the best because it is the simplest and most natural and because it adds the least extraneous information—it has a minimum disruption to the total context. The same is true with complexity. Exegetes should move to readings that are more complex or not intuitively obvious only when it is necessary. The goal in every decision should be to maintain the highest level of hermeneutical support possible. The best hermeneutical choices are those that have the highest interpretational support while causing the least interpretational disruption or complexity.

To bring this analysis to paradox, it is never sufficient to settle for a model that resolves the problem; one must also ask how well that model comports with the biblical data. The basic goal is to provide a model that causes a minimum of "epistemological disruption"—logical inconsistencies or pressure against the biblical data. One conclusion from this is obvious—if the biblical text is the only element in the epistemological process that is absolutely certain, it only follows that violations of biblical data are always more problematic than violations of logical laws. Many of the proposed solutions for paradox apparently solve the problem, but at a high cost—neglecting rigorous attention to the biblical data or making significant and dubious adjustments to exegesis. In a few cases the desire for logical explanations leads to a direct denial of biblical evidence. This, for instance, is the problem with open theism's solution to the problem of evil.

The same dynamic is at work when it comes to evaluating the level of support a conclusion has. As theologians seek to integrate biblical data into a coherent whole, they must make decisions about which understanding of the evidence to use. It is insufficient to offer theological conclusions merely because they are possible, without also evaluating the relative merit of the supporting evidence. The goal of logical correlation is to maintain the highest possible level of epistemic warrant.[12]

To illustrate this analysis with a financial metaphor, each theological or inferential decision involves epistemic costs and benefits. Constructions or clarifications that helpfully alleviate theological problems add epistemic viability to the total system.[13] Other conceptual actions levy epistemic costs. These costs might be insignificantly small as in the case of deductive conclusions from unambiguous propositions, or they might be larger as in the case of introducing distinctions, offering new constructions, or building elongated chains of reasoning. A conclusion

---

[11] Ibid., 143.

[12] The context for the concept of "epistemic warrant" assumed here is from Alvin Plantinga's *Warranted Christian Belief* (New York: Oxford University Press, 2000). Also, James Anderson, *Paradox in Christian Theology* (Eugene: Wipf and Stock, 2007), 155-216 (largely based on Plantinga).

[13] Of course, there are many other forms of value in theological reflection. There is obvious value anytime that theological reflection can remove ambiguities, state theological truth in a clearer, more situationally relevant way, or answer questions the biblical text does not directly raise.

with small explanatory value and large epistemic costs has a total negative value for the viability of the system at large. If the goal of theological resolution is to maintain the highest epistemic warrant and create minimal epistemic disruption, conclusions that bring a negative total value should not be made.[14]

This becomes a powerful tool for evaluating some of the solutions proposed for theological antinomy as theologians develop ways to harmonize divergent sets of data. As much as possible, theologians seek to explain and resolve apparent discrepancies by proposing any number of distinctions or qualifiers, but an explanation is helpful only if it contributes positive explanatory value to the completed system. More specifically, the explanatory power of a resolution and the epistemic warrant it brings must be greater than the negative epistemic costs of its assumptions or its adjustments to the natural understanding of the data. A position that is long on epistemic costs and short on benefits is an unworkable model.

This explains why there is little value in deferring biblical antinomies to a deeper level of complexity by introducing external distinctions. Plantinga's free-will defense, for instance, only delays the problem, forcing the inquisitive thinker to ask how God could choose to create free actors or even create at all, knowing the catastrophe of eternal anguish that would result. In the final analysis there is little epistemic warrant gained by the explanation since the fundamental problem remains. At the same time, increasing the complexity of the model only introduces a number of new problems, leaving one asking whether the benefits can possibly be worth the cost. This also explains why there is little benefit in proposing possible distinctions without any grounds to think they have any basis in reality—the costs behind such a presumption are simply too great.[15]

---

[14] Vincent Brümmer, *The Model of Love* (Cambridge: Cambridge University Press, 1993), 25-26, discusses the requirement of comprehensive coherence in evaluating theological models. "There is a conceptual price-tag attached to each theological model, and to a large extent the task of systematic theology has to do with calculating the cost of our models in order to determine whether we are willing and able to pay the price." These considerations force "the choice between accepting the model at the calculated price, or deciding that the price is too high to pay and hence rejecting the model. The only possibility which [these concepts] exclude is that we should accept the model and refuse to pay the conceptual price." John Frame, *No Other God: A Response to Open Theism* (Phillipsburg, N.J.: P&R, 2001), 137, exemplifies this analysis well in the context of answering open theism: "Some theologians seem to be willing to pay any price for a solution to the problem of evil. So open theists insist on libertarianism, a doctrine that is both unscriptural and incoherent, and which actually destroys moral responsibility, as we have seen. And they are even willing to sacrifice God's exhaustive knowledge of the future, another doctrine that, as we shall see, is not biblically negotiable. Would it not be better to leave the problem unsolved than to resort to such drastic measures? Is there no point at which we should be silent and take God at his word? Open theists do not seem to have considered how large a price we should pay to solve this theological problem."

[15] Given the conflict between P^1: A is B and P^2 A is not B, some theologians simply distinguish them semantically with the form P^1:A is B and P^2: A is not B', or P^1:A is B and P^2: A' is not B. But in fact, this involves a critical logical flaw, since any contradiction could be "resolved" by similar means. For the resolution to have merit, the difference between the terms should be definable, explicable, and ideally supported by

On the other hand, it is easy to see on this analysis that an integrated understanding of Galatians 2:16 and James 2:14-17 adds real clarity to the final analysis of both passages and certainly to the relationship between the two. This is what makes such a correlation legitimate and warranted—it adds real epistemic value, and therefore the conclusion should be made. The critical difference, therefore, between resolvable conflicts and genuine antinomy is the workability of the suggested resolutions. In both cases there is a logical gap that must be filled (the logical space between conflicting data sets), but in one case that gap is filled plausibly, and in the other it is not.

There is also an attitudinal conclusion that arises from this comparison. Done properly, the goal of hermeneutics is not to draw as much meaning as possible out of the text—it is to draw as much *warranted* meaning out of the text as possible. Thus Vanhoozer speaks of the balance between humility and confidence—humility to recognize that not all truth can be known, and confidence to affirm that truth does exist that can be known and stated authoritatively.[16] Likewise, the goal of systematic theology should not be to derive as many conclusions as possible about God and reality. These conclusions are only as helpful as they are warranted. Theologians must have the honesty to stop short of conclusions that lack sufficient evidence, combined with the confidence to affirm what conclusions do have strong support. The ideal is to affirm everything that can be known and stop short of everything that cannot.

Diminishing Epistemic Certainty

Postmodernism has served to reveal the deep complexity of the interpretational process and the uncertainties that attend every interpretation. Within biblical hermeneutics this pressure has also made interpreters more cautious and aware of the assumptions they bring to the interpretive process. Each interpretive option is only as accurate as it represents the original text, and the more assumptions that are involved, the less certain an interpretation will be.

Turning to the theological process, the analogue to this concept is diminishing epistemic certainty. The foundation for this concept is a basic principle: the only meaningful propositions that can be trusted absolutely are those contained in divine revelation.[17] Of course, the challenge is in the process of interpreting and knowing

---

actual biblical data. Without any way to confirm that there is in fact a correspondence between the theological distinction and reality, such reasoning has an obviously negative epistemic net value. There is also, in fact, a formal problem with this reasoning. From the starting proposition that "a distinction does exist which *could* resolve the paradox," it does not follow that the paradox is demonstrably non-contradictory, but only that if the distinction could be demonstrated to be real and actual, then the paradox *would* be non-contradictory.

[16] Kevin J. Vanhoozer, *Is There a Meaning in This Text?* (Grand Rapids: Zondervan, 1998), 462-67.

[17] A legitimate case can be made that analytic propositions might be absolutely certain by definition. Statements such as "all bachelors are unmarried men" or "2+2=4" are true absolutely because speakers of English have agreed on the definition by convention or

these propositions.[18] Every step away from the uninterpreted text and toward understanding or analysis moves the proposition further from its original state of absolute epistemic certainty. This is natural enough, since every inferential move introduces additional possibilities for mistakes.[19] It simply is not the case that inferences drawn from Scripture are as absolute as the biblical data themselves.[20]

This is not to overstate the problem. Invoking the mathematical concept of limits, some interpretational and logical steps have such certainty that they are, for all practical purposes, almost as solidly grounded as the original statements of the text.[21] For instance, a move such as the following diminishes almost nothing from epistemic certainty:

---

because mathematicians have defined the system this way. On the other hand, this type of proposition is meaningless either because it fails to add any new information (Immanuel Kant's analytic-synthetic distinction) or at least because it adds only a negligible amount of information (as in W.V. Cline). Regardless, only Scripture conveys the meaningful, certain propositions necessary as a starting point for an adequate worldview.

[18] Kevin T. Bauder, "In the Nick of Time," *Central Seminary*, October 27, 2006, http://www.centralseminary.edu/publications/20061027.pdf (accessed July 29, 2010), comments that necessary inferences drawn from biblical premises are just as authoritative as the text of Scripture itself." Yet if this were true, it would mean that there is information extending beyond the biblical text that actually enjoys the exclusive authoritative status of Scripture. Furthermore, without a clear definition of what constitutes an unavoidable or necessary inference, this leaves open the window through which a whole variety of logical suppositions might be posited as bearing biblical authority. It is crucial to recognize that the biblical text is the only truth that can be known with absolute certainty. Taken in context, Bauder is attempting to answer anti-deductivists who may overstate diminishing epistemic certainty. As stated here and in Bauder's thought, there is a sense in which some inferences are almost as certain as the biblical data for all practical intents and purposes. In substance, this discussion of diminishing epistemic certainty rests on some of the same concepts Bauder articulates. Still, he is guilty either of overstating his own position or of stating it without sufficient clarity. Nor is it sufficient to distinguish, as Bauder does, that this kind of absolute certainty applies only in the case of deductive arguments. The challenge of reasoning from biblical propositions is never this simple, since there are always aspects of inductivism and areas of undistinguished propositional ambiguity in every part of the theological process.

[19] Exegetically, this principle is illustrated in Paul's repeated mh\ ge/noito response to unacceptable conclusions that might appear to be natural logical inferences. See Thomas R. Schreiner, *Romans* (Grand Rapids: Baker, 1998), 150. Obviously, Paul uses this expression rhetorically, without implying that the inferential conclusions have any real merit. Abraham J. Malherbe, "Mh Genoito in the Diatribe and Paul," *HTR* 73 (April 1980): 234-35. Still, there is an inferential connection in each case, demonstrating that legitimate-sounding inferences often lead in completely unacceptable directions.

[20] As John Frame, *Doctrine of the Knowledge of God*, 84, helpfully points out, the question of epistemic certainty is separate from authority. To the extent that they are true, inferential propositions have the same applicational force as statements of Scripture.

[21] If a curve is constantly subdivided as it approaches a line, the two will never be completely parallel. Still, it is possible to speak of a parallel point between the two—the tangent. Drawing a parallel to the theological concept is helpful but not perfect. In

1) All men have sinned (Rom. 3:23).
2) Joel Arnold is a man.
3) Joel Arnold has sinned.

Though this conclusion is not on an epistemological parity with biblical data, it can be stated with confidence because the logic that underlies it is almost impossible to doubt—a simple categorical syllogism (not to mention the significant empirical support available). Possible distinctions and resolutions exist for every one of the five paradoxes considered in this study, but these solutions have varying degrees of plausibility. Every assumption or presumed inference leaves the process slightly more open to error or distortion. This is the underlying basis for logical guidelines such as Ockham's razor: between two sufficient explanations, the simpler should always be preferred because it involves fewer opportunities for error.

Another way to state this conclusion is that possible theological solutions for antinomies will always have a lower epistemic status than the original biblical propositions. This follows naturally from the fact that these solutions always have some type of inferential relationship to the biblical data. This is not a legitimate basis for dismissing the solutions out of hand; it is only a recognition of the epistemic status that all theological conclusions actually have and an acknowledgment of the subservient relationship such solutions must have to the text. If the inferential chain extends very far, or if a model depends entirely on inference, it cannot have the same epistemic status as the starting propositions.[22]

Apophatic Inference

One other principle should guide the interpreter's handling of paradoxical data in the biblical text. Throughout the history of the church, theologians have repeatedly suggested that our knowledge of God may be only negative. The argument is that because of God's transcendence, humans can speak of him only in terms of what he is not, rather than making solid affirmations of what he is. Though strict apophatic theology is unwarranted in general, a related concept may have significant utility for paradox.[23] Where theologians face paradoxical propositions, they should affirm what the biblical text states without drawing out the negative inferences. Using the example of the Trinity, for instance, it is proper to say that God is one and that God is three, since the biblical text affirms both of these. However, it is unwarranted to

---

theology, the reason for the near certainty is that the loss of confidence is so small as to be negligible on the practical level. Still, it is worthwhile to recognize that every inferential process involves at least some loss of epistemological confidence, even if that loss is meaninglessly small.

[22] John Feinberg illustrates this principle in *No One Like Him* (Wheaton: Crossway, 2001), 469-70.

[23] This is not apophaticism but an apophatic limitation on inference specifically. When faced with paradox we often discover that limitations on our reasoning are by far the clearest inferential moves we can make, or to say it differently, paradox leaves us more confident of what is not true (avoiding heresy) than how the biblical propositions themselves fit together.

state the negative of each—that God is not three (since he is one), or that God is not one (since he is three).[24] Likewise, it is clearly legitimate to state that Jesus Christ is God and that he is human, but invalid to state that he is not human (because he is God) or not God (because he is human).[25]

The rationale for this limitation is relatively easy to demonstrate. Theological antinomies arise from the epistemological slippage between implicit contradictions, or as James Anderson speaks of it, areas of unarticulated ambiguity. The text makes it clear that in one sense God is three and in another sense he is one, but it never explains the senses in which each is true. As a result, the additional step of drawing negative inferences (such as "God is not one" based on the fact that he is three) only refutes the converse proposition but adds nothing to the understanding of the biblical data. As such, it uses an area of unknown logical ambiguity to deny a statement that is known with certainty. This analysis points back to the basic axiom for evaluating hermeneutical and logical warrant—if an attempted resolution adds more epistemological problems than it actually helps to solve, there is no reason to suggest it. The result is the limited apophaticism suggested here—theologians should state paradoxical propositions positively without also inferring the negative form, even if the negative can be derived logically.

Using a Complementarian Model

Considering the components of this model, it is crucial to integrate them into a coherent model that is practically useful for analyzing paradox. It is equally

---

[24] Of course, this is precisely the type of reasoning that chapter 3 used in the attempt to demonstrate that simple solutions for antinomy are insufficient. This was to demonstrate that significant logical conflicts do exist. In fact, apophatic limitation is one way to describe the difference between the paradox-minimizing view and the complementarity advocated here.

[25] It is interesting that at the specific point where theologians most struggle to integrate the Christological data, Chalcedon is essentially apophatic ("without confusion, change, division, or separation, the property of each nature being in no way annulled by the union ... not as parted or separated into two persons"). Sarah Coakley comments that "Chalcedon is apophatic in the sense that it is intended to eliminate heretical doctrines; not explain all the details or answer all of the questions. The issues it does not resolve are: (1) Chalcedon does not tell us in what the divine and human 'natures' consist: (2) it does not tell us what *hypostasis* means when applied to Christ; (3) it does not tell us how *hypostasis* and *physeis* are related, or how the *physeis* relate to one another (the problem of the *communicatio idiomatum*); (4) it does not tell us how many wills Christ has; (5) it does not tell us that the *hypostasis* is identical with the pre-existent Logos; (6) it does not tell us what happens to the *physeis* at Christ's death and in his resurrection; (7) it does not tell us whether the meaning of *hypostasis* in this Christological context is different, or the same, from the meaning in the trinitarian context; (8) it does not tell us whether the risen Christ is male." See Sarah Coakley "What Does Chalcedon Solve and What Does it Not? Some Reflections on the Status and Meaning of the Chalcedonian Definition," in *The Incarnation: An Interdisciplinary Symposium on the Incarnation of the Son of God* (Oxford: Oxford University Press, 2004), 162-63.

imperative to identify the practical challenges for how the process works out in actual usage.

The five conceptual components of this model have a distinct logical relationship to one another. Inter-propositional ambiguity provides the logical space within which paradox exists and where analysis functions. The methodological spiral provides a framework for progress and implies that the process of identifying paradox is never completely finished, while legitimate and significant progress is still possible. It also serves as a reminder that delimiting paradox is a reciprocal process, moving from the biblical data to logical correlation and back again for reevaluation. Within this framework epistemic warrant is the analytical core of the entire model by separating genuine antinomy from resolvable tensions or absurdity. Diminishing epistemic certainty plays a part in accurately evaluating logical conclusions by qualifying the epistemic warrant in theological constructions that rely heavily on inference.

Once a specific issue has been identified as paradox, the complementarian model also helps to guide analysis. Inter-propositional ambiguity dictates that theologians allow ambiguities to stand as they exist in the data, rather than suggest possible distinctions or paradox-resolving models as though they are demonstrated theological facts. Apophatic inference limits the reasoning that can rest on paradoxical propositions. Epistemic warrant guides the extent to which theologians should proceed in pursuing resolution and limits the explanatory models or attempted resolutions that theologians can reasonably proffer.

Putting this completed model to use guides the theological task in four major ways. The first and most basic is the principle that any construction that violates biblical data clearly has a negative epistemic value. If the veracity of the biblical text is certain, denying it levies absolute epistemic costs that outweigh the benefits of any theological construction out of hand. This is why only the three conservative views of paradox merit serious consideration in this study—because the other views involve assumptions outside the scope of orthodoxy.

A second implication is the importance of evaluating the epistemic significance of biblical antinomy accurately. Naturally enough, most proponents of the paradox-minimizing view label any complementarian paradox as contradiction and argue that it has an overwhelmingly negative epistemic impact. Because of this, proposed resolutions play a critical role in their system, rescuing the apologetic warrant and coherence of the theological program at large. This places high epistemic priority on the value of the resolutions and makes them warrantable positions at almost any cost. But in the case of paradox, theologians should acknowledge that the threat is not full, explicit contradiction but areas of unclarified ambiguity for which there are currently no solutions. The result is that the epistemological threats from paradox are not nearly as critical as the paradox-minimizing view presents them, and the means used to resolve paradox, therefore, should still be evaluated in terms of warrant.

Third, theologians should evaluate the presumptions and assumptions that theological constructions make, recognizing that models that inject logical complexity also inject greater opportunities for problems. This is why the principle of diminishing epistemic certainty is crucial. Theologians should monitor the extent of their inferential reasoning, recognizing that every inferential move increases the possibility of mistakes. A conclusion at the end of a 12-step inferential chain likely does not have the same epistemic basis as a simpler process of reasoning. One of the factors to consider in the process of evaluating any conclusion, therefore, should be the amount of inference that was involved in reaching it.

Finally, theologians should maintain each theological conclusion with a level of dogmatism that matches the warrant for that conclusion. Interpreters intuitively recognize that every exegetical or inferential decision should be evaluated for its plausibility—the extent to which the conclusion has a sufficient informational basis. It is not enough to be aware of the evidence; one must also know the weight of that evidence and the degree to which he can be sure of his conclusions. Some conclusions are so clear as to approach certainty. Others are only possible or likely because of the relative strength or weakness of their logical supports. In theology as well, there is certainly a middle ground between the extremes of knowable and unknown. In certain borderline cases the benefits of a theological construction might be roughly equivalent to the epistemic costs or only slightly lesser or greater. The proper response is to adjust one's level of dogmatism gradually across the continuum of epistemic support. Just as with hermeneutical decisions, the theologian's certainty or dogmatism about such conclusions should correspond to the level of data supporting them. If the total epistemic value is negligible, theologians can speak of these conclusions with only a negligible confidence. As the relative benefit of a correlation or logical resolution increases, so does the confidence with which it can be argued. Once again this highlights the importance of carefully monitoring the level of support each theological proposition has and knowing the difference each theological move makes on the total epistemic value.

Ramifications of a Complementarian Method

As with almost any component of theological prolegomena, the complementarian method for understanding and systemizing antinomy has broad ramifications. Three stand out in particular. The first answers one of the starting problems from the beginning of this study—how to distinguish antinomy from more basic theological problems, or protect it from degenerating into boundless, unaccountable speculation. Second, and even more fundamentally, the complementarian model also addresses the difficult problem of spreading inferential conflicts.

Identifying Antinomy

Based on the foregoing analysis, there is an objective basis for distinguishing antinomies from theological difficulties. An antinomy is simply a set of propositions for which no warranted solution exists.[26] In other words, all

---

[26] While criticizing complementarity, William Hasker, *Providence, Evil and the Openness of God* (New York: Routledge, 2004), 152, inadvertently acknowledges this criterion. "To be sure, if all the available options reveal themselves as hopelessly flawed, we may find

possibilities for resolution require more assumptions or cause more problems than they solve, and the balance of epistemic value is negative for any of the proposals. On the other hand, if a correlation adds some amount of epistemic consistency to the total epistemic equation, it is warranted. Beginning with apparently incommensurable propositions, theologians should investigate the possible resolutions and evaluate each according to the complementarian model. The problem is merely a difficulty if one of the models allows the two data sets to comport while maintaining biblical data in an epistemically warranted way.

On the opposite extreme, this model also provides a way to limit paradox and protect against abuse. Theologians who grant the existence of paradox sometimes find it far too easy to make use of the concept as a kind of *deus ex machina*, saving them from theological difficulties. Critics of paradox have charged that paradox exposes theology to uncontrolled speculation, since logic is no longer an authoritative control on theological conclusions. As Stephen Davis points out, "Once we allow that mysteries can be introduced and believed there is nothing to prevent people from producing any mysterious doctrine they want to produce about anything at all. All kinds of ridiculous and unfalsifiable suggestions can be made."[27]

Here the distinction is with the starting propositions. Within a complementarian model a paradox is much more than two propositions at logical odds. The tension is a paradox because these starting ideas are solidly grounded in biblical data. In order to distinguish between paradox and abuse, theologians should simply evaluate the exegetical merits of the incommensurable data sets. This eliminates wild speculations by the simple fact that they are not biblically supported.

This also allows theology to maintain its heresy-eliminating power. As James Anderson points out, to be meaningful, a positive affirmation must also be able to eliminate contrary statements.[28] But if paradox allows some statements to stand that theologians would otherwise dismiss, how can theological assertions fulfill this role and remain meaningful? The answer is that heretical formulations do not have the confirmation of Scripture for both poles of the tension.

Therefore a set of propositions is authentically paradoxical only if it passes both tests: (1) Both propositions must rest solidly on biblical data. (2) The tension between both propositions must be irresolvable given the information presently available to theologians. In other words, no interpretational reevaluations or attempts at theological clarification can set the tension aside in a warrantable way; every attempt at resolution only raises more epistemic costs than values, at least for the present. Those tensions that fail the first requirement are merely the muddle of

---

ourselves with a tension in our thinking we are unable to resolve. But that unhappy conclusion should at least wait until we have exhausted the non-contradictory options available to us." Of course, Hasker regards open theism as a warrantable solution to the tensions created by the problem of evil.

[27] Stephen T. Davis, *Logic and the Nature of God* (Grand Rapids: Macmillan, 1983), 142.

[28] Anderson, *Paradox in Christian Theology*, 278-81.

theological speculation; those that fail the second are merely resolvable difficulties for which another solution will do.[29]

One of the greatest challenges in implementing the complementarian model is the problem of subjectivity. Ideally, a model for antinomy would be objective, clearly identifying instances of paradox, eliminating abuses, and demarking the limits for legitimate inference.

Is this process completely objective? Clearly not. But this hardly nullifies the value of the model. This is because the core of the complementarian model is evaluating epistemic warrant, but this is also one of the most subjective elements. Theologians will inevitably regard the relative epistemic weight of various lines of reasoning differently. In fact, the difference between their subjective evaluations of warrant is probably the underlying reason for the different views on paradox. If logical congruity and explanatory clarity are non-negotiable, for instance, it only follows that theology should minimize paradox as much as possible.

Still, the model provides a conceptual scaffolding for how to proceed. Once again, the best comparison is with hermeneutics. Any realistic exegete acknowledges that there is no absolutely objective way for determining the best reading of a biblical text. Yet interpreters also acknowledge that there are inferior ways to carry out the process. Even more importantly, there are certain hermeneutical considerations or guiding dictates that every good interpreter must grapple with, many of which can make the hermeneutical process more objective than it would otherwise be. Having a self-consistent conceptual grid never guarantees the right outcome, but it can certainly help the process.

Spreading Conflicts in Biblical Truth

Mystery cannot be confined to one part of a system without also touching every other part. Every individual proposition has a complete network of other implications that can be inferred. But if two propositions are related in a mutually exclusive way, a network of validly derived inferences from one should also contain logical conflicts with propositions derived from the other. The final result would be a deep epistemological cleavage that extends as far as inferences from either proposition can be drawn. Therefore, any workable model must also limit the spread of paradox to keep it from deconstructing epistemology and the theological endeavor as a whole.

---

[29] Discussing this same question, James Anderson, *Paradox in Christian Theology*, 265-66, offers three criteria for distinguishing legitimate and illegitimate claims to paradox: (1) The claims in the proposed paradox must be warranted in special revelation. (2) There must not be available any alternative and non-paradoxical ways to understand the information. (3) There must be metaphysical complexity that involves the nature of God. He then offers three examples of invalid appeal to paradox: (A) "God is identical to the world and God is distinct from the world," falsified by criterion 1. (B) "We are justified by faith alone and we are not justified by faith alone," falsified by criteria 2 and possibly 3. (C) "There was exactly one angel at the tomb and there were exactly two angels at the tomb," falsified by criterion 3.

Returning to the example of Christ's knowledge (Figure 6.5), the implications actually spread to several other points of conflict, some with biblical support and others without it. Theoretically, similar lines of tension could be carried out much further and with even more disastrous results.

Figure 6.5. Inferences Extending from Theological Antinomy

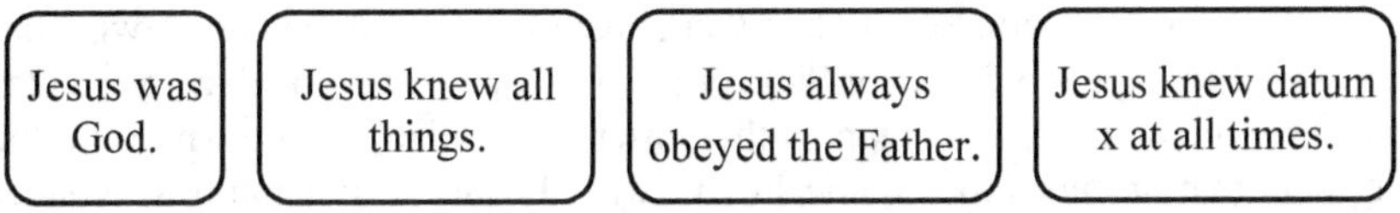

| Jesus was God. | Jesus knew all things. | Jesus always obeyed the Father. | Jesus knew datum x at all times. |

Still, there are limitations that keep this divide from spreading indefinitely. First,

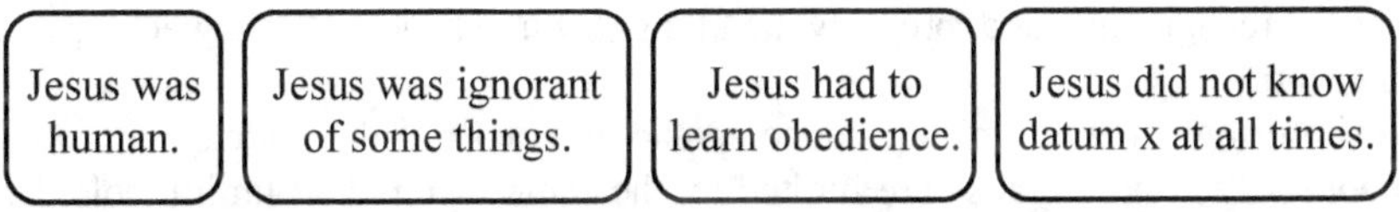

| Jesus was human. | Jesus was ignorant of some things. | Jesus had to learn obedience. | Jesus did not know datum x at all times. |

the field of inferences that can be drawn from a given starting proposition is not infinite. In theory every true proposition is connected to every other true proposition in an endless network of logical relationships. But in reality most of these true propositions are simply unknown, and the sum of human knowledge is only fractional and spotty with broad open gaps.[30] One result of this predicament is that inferential progress is halting and limited. New conclusions require multiple starting premises, and these premises must also fall in a configuration that makes epistemological extrapolations possible.[31]

Another way to describe this limitation is with the concept of diminishing epistemological certainty: paradoxical implications are less and less certain the further they are removed from the starting data. Therefore, spreading implications from paradox have a built-in limitation on the damage they can do to broader epistemology and theology. The epistemological power of implications extends only so far, and without further data these conclusions exhaust themselves in unknowns.

---

[30] This is the tenor of Carson's reference to "the many ambiguous parameters and numerous unknown quantities. The whole tension remains restless in our hands; but it is the restlessness of having a few randomly-selected pieces of a jigsaw puzzle when thousands more are needed to complete the design"—*Divine Sovereignty and Human Responsibility* (Eugene, Oreg.: Wipf and Stock, 1994), 206.

[31] To put this process in the metaphor of physical space, it is less fruitful to draw inferences in a direct line. It is easier to extrapolate new conclusions when data stands in the middle of multiple other propositions that are known. In most cases the data for theological antinomy is isolated and disconnected, like an epistemological island. It is possible to move out from this information only a short distance, since the epistemological context is mostly lacking and other supporting premises are unavailable.

Ambiguity plays an even more direct role in limiting the spread of antinomy. In earlier discussion it became evident that theological antinomies are each implicit contradictions because they involve epistemological space—unclarified ambiguities in which resolution is possible, even if human knowers cannot presently identify what it would be. This ambiguity necessarily limits the implications that can be drawn from both poles of the biblical data. In other words, if theologians cannot presently identify or articulate the precise relationship between two sets of data, extended implications from these data will also have natural limits.

Finally, it is important to recognize that the data sets standing behind antinomies generally have only one point of contact that is paradoxical. Inferences drawn from antinomy extend the logical conflict only if they relate to that particular component.[32] In other words, many other inferences might be drawn from the starting data that are not problematic in any way. In fact, it is natural to wonder whether paradoxical inferences might simply be the original paradox recast in another form. If so, the problem of spreading inferences from antinomies is only a matter of recognizing and properly handling them when they are packaged in another form.

In short, logical antinomies produce spreading cracks in the logical framework of theology, but these cracks are limited by the same factors that limit theological inferences in general. Thus there are certainly broader problems brought upon epistemology by the existence of paradox, but they are isolated and mostly limited to the concepts directly connected to the starting antinomy. If it is actually true that inferential antinomies are only a repackaged form of the original paradox, the problem can almost be set aside altogether.

So how to proceed? How should theologians handle propositions along the extended logical divide an antinomy produces? Inferences are always less certain (albeit to varying degrees) than the biblical data from which they are derived. Recognizing this reality, theologians should regard derived tensions in essentially the same way as the starting antinomies. Moving outward from the biblical data on either side of the divide, theologians can derive legitimate inferences and let them stand in tension with those on the opposite side of the antinomy. To some extent the epistemological cleavage extending from paradox is not a problem but a necessary result of responsible theological analysis. If an inferential move has sufficient epistemic support, it should be made within the limits that the data provides. If the inference requires more epistemic losses than gains, however, it is best to let it remain ambiguous.

The most important guiding principle is also connected to a previously discussed concept: apophatic limitations on paradoxical conclusions. Inferences should never

---

[32] Of course, the principle of explosion is a proven philosophical axiom—that anything can be proven from a contradiction. The critical distinction is that theological antinomies are not ultimately contradictions. Of course, as they stand without further clarification or disambiguation, they take the form of implicit contradictions, but this is simply because the biblical text never explains how the propositions relate. The inferential result from ambiguously related propositions and unknown parameters is not logical explosion, but more ambiguity and unknowns—the principle of apophatic inference.

lead to the denial of another biblically supported proposition.[33] In simpler terms, it is never warranted to cross over the divide inferentially. Both sets of data must exist independently, along with their field of inferentially connected propositions.[34]

Evaluation

This chapter has sought to outline a basic model for identifying and dealing with theological paradox, but several observations should be made about the process itself. First, this approach reduces to a reemphasis on the preeminence of the biblical text. To quote John Frame again, *"The primary goal of exegesis is not logical consistency but faithfulness to the text. . . . If no explicit logical consistency can be obtained without conflict with other biblical teaching, then we must remain satisfied with paradox."*[35] Where the text does not provide correlations, it is certainty tempting to provide them, and at times it is legitimate to do so. But in the scramble to offer explanations it is never forgivable to distort exegesis. Said differently, it is always better to tolerate inconsistencies and tensions than to force the data in order to avoid them.

A practical observation also bears mention: it is interesting and probably significant that none of the antinomies mentioned here directly involve human responses that would leave an individual in a quandary. Scripture never issues commands that face believers with an ambiguous tension.[36] The biblical tensions are more abstruse, involving the underlying structure of reality or the specific interrelationships of theological propositions. As James Anderson describes it, antinomies involve significant metaphysical assumptions about what is possible, the connections between underlying realities, or what is involved in certain

---

[33] Of course, this applies not only to inferences that deny biblical propositions, but also to inferences that deny other legitimate inferences, albeit only to the degree of confidence that both propositions can be demonstrated as true. Some form of apophatism extends along the entire inferential divide that forms out of an antinomy.

[34] This is essentially equivalent to Packer's explanation of the problem. "Be careful, therefore, not to set [antinomous truths] at loggerheads, nor to make deductions from either that would cut across the other.... Use each with the limits of its own sphere of reference (i.e., the area delimited by the evidence from which the principle has been drawn)"—J.I. Packer, *Evangelism and the Sovereignty of God* (Downers Grove: InterVarsity, 2008), 28-29.

[35] John Frame, *Van Til, the Theologian* (Phillipsburg, N.J.: Pilgrim, n.d.), 33, original emphasis.

[36] The nearest example of such an ambiguity is the tension between the believer's security and the doctrine of perseverance. But in fact, the ambiguity is itself part of the point—it is possible to show many of the apparent signs of faith without in fact being regenerated. See R. Bruce Compton, "Persevering and Falling Away: A Reexamination of Hebrews 6:4-6," *DBSJ* 1 (Spring 1996): 135-71. Still, this tension leads to no ambiguity in the responses of believers, since the response is always the same: live in persevering faith that drives genuinely God-honoring behavior. Of course, moral dilemmas do face believers with conflicting perspectives on how to apply the truth, but these are not biblical paradoxes as it has been defined here.

concepts.³⁷ Simply put, the text provides clear guidance on the information that believers need, but it does not answer all questions that they might ask.³⁸ Though it provides sufficient information for philosophical questions, for instance, Scripture is not organized or intended as a philosophical textbook, and it is no surprise that many of the unexplained tensions in Scripture relate to problems that impinge on deeper philosophical concern. Believers can rest assured that the text provides all that they need to know for life and godliness. None of the biblical antinomies lead to quandaries that obscure personal decisions or limit any believer's ability to pursue sanctification.

Finally, it is important to answer the common charge that complementarity faces from the paradox-minimizing view. The approach advocated here allows tensions to stand but without suggesting that they are fundamentally or irresolvably contradictory for God. In his understanding the ambiguities in each tension are perfectly clear, and true propositions always comport in some way.³⁹ Antinomies simply arise from the fact that God has not revealed all truth and that he might sometimes reveal two propositions without also explaining how they relate.⁴⁰

---

[37] Anderson, *Paradox in Christian Theology*, 225-226. There is a logical connection between application and every point of theology, no matter how abstruse. However, the principles of inter-propositional ambiguity and diminishing epistemic certainty limit how far inferential chains can extend. Antinomies are conceptually distant enough from ethics that they do not cause a quandary.

[38] This comports with Scripture's own description of its intended purpose (2 Tim. 3:16-17; 2 Pet. 1:3). This is also the tenor of Calvin's discussion of incomprehensibility in *Institutes of the Christian Religion*, trans. John Allen, 2 vols. (Philadelphia: Presbyterian Board of Publication and Sabbath-School Work, 1921), 1:196-97.

[39] The major writers who have articulated complementarity have clearly maintained this position. To quote R. B. Kuiper, "A paradox is not, as Barth thinks, two truths which are actually contradictory. Truth is not irrational. Nor is a paradox two truths which are difficult to reconcile but can be reconciled before the bar of human reason. That is a seeming paradox. But when two truths, both taught unmistakably in the infallible Word of God, cannot possibly be reconciled before the bar of human reason, then you have a paradox." George Marston, *The Voice of Authority* (Phillipsburg, N.J.: P. & R., 1960), 16.

[40] The fact that two propositions are both revealed does not necessarily include the relationship between the two, even given the doctrine of perspicuity. Revelation never guarantees that a proposition will be known perfectly and completely. In fact, it is impossible to know any single proposition perfectly and completely without also knowing every other proposition and its relationships, and perfect knowledge of any proposition (including all of its relationships with other propositions) is possible for God alone. Our knowledge of any revealed proposition is only provisional and partial, excluding logical relationships with many other propositions. It is nothing out of the ordinary, therefore, for the relationship between two individual propositions to be unrevealed. Of course, it is also worth asking whether two paradoxical propositions in an otherwise contradictory relationship are each still meaningful if the relationship between them is unknown. If God had revealed the relationship between the propositions, it would certainly have added additional meaningful information about both of them. But just as it is possible to have genuine, meaningful knowledge without omniscience (understanding the relationship to every other proposition), it is possible to know both sides of an antinomy genuinely

Conclusion

All attempts to set aside either logic or paradox are ultimately unsuccessful. Orthodoxy requires both, and the question of how they relate is still problematic, no matter how much one or the other is minimized. Since the *sui generis* view must still rely on logic and mystery still appears in the paradox-minimizing view, theologians must answer difficult questions about their relationship, regardless of the view they take. Therefore, theologians are best served by letting the biblical data determine the balance of logic and paradox, rather than distorting this reality in the interests of cloaking a methodological problem. As in the hermeneutical process, decisions are rarely absolute or completely objective, but there are objective standards and measurable controls that can improve the analytic process.

---

without understanding how they relate. It is possible to understand that Jesus is God and that he is also human. The conflict between the two propositions certainly limits human knowers from having a full understanding, but it does not make either proposition meaningless.

CHAPTER 7

General Application

If a plausible alternative interpretation of the biblical data is available, all well and good. But if it becomes clear that any reinterpretation would stretch norms of vocabulary and grammar to breaking point, then resting with paradox and appealing to mystery will be the most rational course.[1]

In theological prolegomena the best way to prove or disprove a method is to test it, and the more that a method is precisely defined and objectively controlled, the easier this is to do. As individual theological questions pass through the sieve of a method, weaknesses in the process become more obvious. In fact, this is exactly the process this study used to falsify the other views on paradox. The *sui generis* view fails by making it possible to derive all kinds of inferences that are clearly unworkable, as well as failing to propose objective and consistent standards for how to limit logic. On the opposite extreme, chapter 4 concluded that the paradox-minimizing view cannot actually fulfill what it sets out to do—successfully resolve conflicts in the biblical data. In each case the clearest way to expose problems in the method is through specific examples.

We are now in a position to test the proposed complementarian approach. Returning to the Trinity, the Incarnation, the problem of evil, sovereignty and free will, and the infinity of God, each problem will be evaluated in terms of epistemic warrant and hermeneutical support. Where qualification adds a positive net value of epistemic clarity it may be possible to eliminate ambiguities, but if full resolution has a negative epistemic value, these tensions must remain as antinomies.

The Trinity

In keeping with previous analysis, the only evidence that stands with complete certainty is the biblical data. In the case of the Trinity, the data indicates both unity and separation, but the passages that speak of each are not equivalent. A number of passages revealing distinctions in the Trinity also record relational interactions or components of personal existence.[2] This seems to support the orthodox description

---

[1] James Anderson, *Paradox in Christian Theology* (Eugene: Wipf and Stock, 2007), 273.

[2] Matthew 3:16 and John 14:26 depict personal interaction among all three members of the Trinity. Of course, it is also possible to argue that Scripture only seems to link distinction with the Trinitarian personalities because personal interaction necessarily highlights distinction. At a minimum, theologians can safely maintain that personality is at least one

of the distinction as persons.³ To be sure, some passages also distinguish the members of the Godhead without explicitly specifying any especially personal components involved, but it is still fully warranted to represent plurality in the Trinity as personal.⁴

Where the data becomes more challenging is identifying the specific sense in which the three members of the Trinity are one. We could suppose that it is not with the personal components and look toward some other, deeper reality such as the metaphysical—God's essence. This assumption is reasonable and certainly possible, but, strictly speaking, there is no solid basis in the exegetical data for this conclusion, and other distinctions that would be equally plausible could easily substitute for it.⁵

All of this is to say that we simply do not know the sense of unity in the Godhead with any significant support from the biblical data. There is legitimate basis for describing the sense in which the three persons are distinct, but without a way of more precisely describing his unity, it is impossible for this distinction to resolve the problem entirely. Even more critically, we have no means at all for

---

area where the Trinity primarily involves distinction rather than unity. What makes deriving distinctions from exegesis even more difficult is that Scripture repeatedly describes God interacting personally, but as a unity (Exod. 19:19; Deut. 1:6; Isa. 45:5-7). In other words, God is fully personal whether spoken of as a unity or as the individuated members of the Trinity. This does not negate the observation that personality and distinction seem to be linked, but it does limit the strength of the argument.

³ R.C. Sproul, *The Mystery of the Holy Spirit* (Wheaton: Tyndale, 1994), 68-73, attributes distinction in the Trinity to personhood because of Hebrews 1:3—"[the Son is] the express image of his person" (AV). "Person" translates u9po/stasij. The argument is that if Christ is the exact representation of God's u9po/stasij, there must be a distinction between the two. But Paul Ellingworth, *The Epistle to the Hebrews* (Grand Rapids: Eerdmans, 2007), 99-100, comments that "the patristic distinction between the three u9po/stasij and the one ou0si/a in God is irrelevant since u9po/stasij is in fact used here with a meaning closer to that which ou0si/a acquired in later christological discussion. All the stress in this passage falls on Christ's unity with God." Citing u9po/stasij as exegetical support for distinction actually has the effect of focusing the passage on the opposite of its intended emphasis.

⁴ As John Murray, *The Collected Writings of John Murray* (Carlisle, Pa.: Banner of Truth, 1982), 4:279, describes it, if the Father and Son can address one another as "Thou," there is sufficient basis for a fully personal distinction. On the other hand, it is equally critical to maintain the truth that the one God (all three persons described without distinction) is also personal. See John Feinberg, *No One Like Him* (Wheaton: Crossway, 2001), 226.

⁵ James Anderson, *Paradox in Christian Theology*, 310, asks concerning this paradox, "Is the paradox-generating imprecision to be attributed to our notion of *identity*, or *numerical unity*, or *being*, or *personhood*, or something else? If such revelational hints are to be discerned, it will require careful exegetical spadework." It is not at all clear that any such revelational hints exist—certainly not in any conclusively significant way. In fact, the biblical data on the Trinity is sufficiently ambiguous as to allow any of these notions for the "paradox-generating imprecision." See, also, Richard Cartwright, "On the Logical Problem of the Trinity," in *Philosophical Essays* (Cambridge, Mass.: The MIT Press, 1987), 193-98.

describing the relationship between the two poles in the biblical data—God's unity and the individual persons.

This is where the doctrine of the Trinity stands based on the biblical data. The question is whether there is epistemological benefit in going beyond the foundational information. We might assume that some type of logical resolution does exist by which both of these propositions can be true and comport, since we have every indication that God is self-consistent. This implies that at least one term of the two propositions must involve an unarticulated distinction in the way the biblical data indicates that the same God is one and three. We could legitimately infer, therefore, that the distinction lies in "one" and "three" and even state this in symbolic form to say that God is one^a and God is three^b, where the superscripts represent two different senses for the predicates, rather than simple numerical identity. We might even assign more familiar labels such as "essence" for the first and "persons" for the second. This reasoning adds real epistemic value to our understanding of the Trinity, especially when it comes to guiding other inferences from the doctrine. Yet the reasoning rests on a solid basis (the fact that God is self-consistent), and the inferential linkage is also very strong. It is not challenging to say that the epistemological benefits are worthy of the costs or to regard this formulation as possessing a relatively strong epistemic status.

The epistemic benefits are much less clear in a positive identification of "one^a" and "three^b" or the confident assumption that it is precisely the distinction by which they comport.[6] What is the evidential basis for these assumptions? Ontology seems to be a logical candidate for unity, but this is a far cry from solid support. The problems in this construction become even more evident in further inference. How do person and essence relate to one another? If distinct persons rest on the foundation of unified ontology, how can theologians avoid inadvertently separating personality from essence? These problems ultimately make full resolution impossible and levy large epistemic costs. On the other hand, it is hard to see the epistemic or analytical benefits of a highly specific identification for person and essence. These additional steps do not seem to add any real information to the construction, and it is even harder to demonstrate solid reasons to support them.[7]

---

[6] This is exactly the position argued by A.P. Martinich, "Identity and Trinity," *JR* 58.2 (April 1978): 169-81, and more popularly by R.C. Sproul, *The Mystery*, 49-52. The problem with using this solution to claim that no genuine tension exists is the rather simple fact that the same analysis would work to resolve any contradiction. This would result in (1) Jesus is God^a and Jesus is not God^b, where the difference between God^a and God^b is unclarified and undesignated. Until there are explicit, meaningful answers about the meaning of God^a and God^b that also allow the two to comport, the conflict between the two remains. The same analysis applies to the doctrine of the Trinity.

[7] The ontological relationships within the Trinity (generation and spiration) are nearly impossible to support with clear biblical data and thus stretch well beyond the requirements of epistemic warrant. Shedd, *Dogmatic Theology* (Nashville: Thomas Nelson, 1980), 245, suggests that "the trinal names *Father, Son,* and *Spirit*, given to God in Scripture, force upon the theologian the ideas of paternity, filiation, spiration, and procession. He cannot reflect upon the implication of these names without forming these

General Application

On balance, therefore, it is best to say that (1) God is one in some sense, but (2) three in another sense, and (3) the two propositions do involve some distinction (known in its fullness only to God) that allows them to comport completely. Some biblical evidence might incline us to connect plurality with personal components, but biblical supports for the concept of essence are essentially nonexistent. In general the formulation with the best balance of epistemic costs and benefits is relatively careful: assign labels to each term of the distinction (such as person and essence), and deal with them as analytic descriptions, without attempting to identify positively the realities behind the terms.

When it comes to inferential conclusions derived from the Trinity, the ambiguity of the distinctions simply follows. The result is a natural limitation to the conclusions that can be derived because the starting propositions provide a limited amount of information. The problem of how God's distinct persons share a single essence, for instance, requires no final answer. The answers to all such questions can remain as ambiguous as the biblical data itself, exactly fulfilling what the principle of inter-propositional ambiguity demands, and best maintaining epistemic warrant.

The Incarnation

The doctrine of the hypostatic person is clear in the biblical data—it is impossible to deny that Jesus Christ was fully God and fully human. The biblical data also supports specific attributes of each nature, supporting both limited human knowledge and divine omniscience, for instance. Conspicuously absent from the biblical data, however, is any discussion about how the two natures relate. This is true both with general statements about the natures and with specific information about individual attributes. The text simply does not comment.

Just as with the Trinity, there is solid biblical support for the fact that Christ was a unified person, and also that he possessed two distinct natures. The problem is with precisely identifying the sense behind each.[8] Here it seems difficult to press

---

ideas." Shedd fails to demonstrate in any way, however, the inferential relationship between the doctrines. There are multiple basic problems with the ontological relationships in the Trinity. (1) Exegetical support is also almost nonexistent. (2) There is no real logical basis for inferring the concept from other doctrines. (3) Worse than the nearly total absence of support for the ontological relationships is the logical problems it causes. Elsewhere Shedd argues that he can resolve the paradox of the Trinity with these relationships. But the ontological relationships distinguish the three persons in terms of their essence. If the Father, Son, and Spirit differ in their essence, what remains for their unity? (4) Theologians have also chronically disagreed about the specific details of the ontological Trinity, with little recourse to any objective means for establishing the proper view. All of this betrays the lack of an objective foundation for discussing the relationships within the ontological Trinity. See Feinberg, *No One Like Him*, 488-92.

[8] Charles Hodge, *Systematic Theology*, 3 vols. (Grand Rapids: Eerdmans, 1973), 387-91, is one of the few conservative theologians who attempts to define precisely the meaning of person and nature. Roland McCune examines some of the complexities involved in this type of analysis in *A Systematic Theology of Biblical Christianity* (Allen Park, Mich.:

much further than using "person" and "nature" as labels for distinct categories. Instead, "person" can simply be used for all of the senses in which Christ was one, and "nature" for the instances in which distinction is necessary. Most attempts to be more specific essentially reduce to guesswork.

Though this understanding stops far short of a full explanation, it provides a basic framework for describing the biblical data. It establishes clear limits for any models that would violate scriptural teaching about the Incarnation.[9] It also helps to simplify the process of reasoning about the Incarnation. Here, just as with the Trinity, inferences derived from theanthropic theology should carry the same ambiguities as the starting propositions.

Of course, derived inferences about the theanthropic person produce another multitude of problems. Theologians have proposed solutions for several of these conflicts, and in some cases these can helpfully mitigate the tension. Because there are multiple attributes and multiple tensions, it is impossible to survey them all. But to take only one example, the problem of Christ's knowledge might be understood with two different levels of conscious awareness. In this construction Christ possessed all information in some sense, but chose to access only some of it consciously. Any lacunae in Christ's knowledge were voluntary self-limitations from the knowledge that he did possess on another level of consciousness.[10]

In this specific case the epistemic benefits are real—the construction does help to satisfy some of the tension. But it also spawns additional questions—such as which level of consciousness was the more ultimate, or how Christ was a unified person if he possessed dual levels of consciousness. More importantly, this construction has no supports other than the fact that it seems to mitigate some of the tension in a difficult logical problem. Ultimately it also relegates some of the tension to another logical level. On the whole, therefore, it seems that a theory like this might warrant consideration, but it should not be granted any certainty above being an interesting possibility that may or may not accurately represent reality.

In a few cases not only is the relationship between attributes unclear, but it is not even simple to describe the nature of the attributes the theanthropic person possessed. With the question of Jesus' peccability, for instance, what exactly was Jesus' relationship towards sin and temptation in the Incarnation?[11] What exactly

---

Detroit Baptist Theological Seminary, 2009), 2:148-49. It is a necessary distinction, but it is unclear how consistent this distinction really is when pressed into more detailed service, and even less clear that a precise definition of the terms can be solidly supported.

[9] Millard J. Erickson, *Christian Theology* (Grand Rapids: Baker, 1998), 746-47.

[10] Donald Macleod, *The Person of Christ* (Downers Grove: InterVarsity, 1998), 168-70, 193.

[11] Of course, the question is not whether Christ actually sinned, but whether it was hypothetically possible that he could have. Hodge suggested that it was possible, McCune, Macleod and others maintain that it was not, and there are a host of mediating positions—Charles Hodge, *Systematic Theology*, 2:457; Roland McCune, *A Systematic Theology*, 2:149-152; Macleod, *The Person of Christ*, 229-30. Joseph G. Sahl offers an overview of the arguments and issues involved in "The Impeccability of Jesus Christ," *Bib Sac* 140 (January 1983): 11-20. Michael McGhee Canham, "Potuit Non Peccare or

was the status of his human nature—fallen as inherited from Adam, innocent as Adam was before the fall, or some other option altogether?[12] The biblical text gives some indication, and some logical extrapolations are helpful, but in the final analysis any conclusions must have a provisional status that falls far short of certainty.[13] The plethora of theories and disparate viewpoints proves this fact admirably.[14]

The Problem of Evil

Probably no other antinomy has received as much discussion and defense as the problem of evil.[15] For instance, some theologians helpfully point out that God has his own purposes for evil. We also know that evil is not always as it might appear; in particular, there is a different standard of good from the one with which we often evaluate reality. Most importantly, much evil is temporary; God will eventually overcome and reverse the suffering brought about by sin and the curse (though the suffering of the damned will never be reversed). Most of these theodicies have some type of direct support from Scripture or strong logical linkage to biblical propositions.[16] These defenses also helpfully clarify the proper limits of the logical problem by restoring a biblical context for the debate.

As helpful as they are, however, the standard theodicies are only partial defenses, and at best they can serve to mitigate only some of the tension in this problem.[17] In reality we lack information about how most instances of evil are

---

Non Potuit Peccare: Evangelicals, Hermeneutics, and the Impeccability Debate," *Master's Seminary Journal* 11.1 (Spring 2000): 93-114, offers an interesting hypothesis, suggesting impeccability for Christ's divine nature and peccability for the human. The relationship between the two is ultimately paradoxical, but in the kenosis, Christ's peccability limited the impeccability of the divine nature. It is not at all clear that this is the best conclusion, but it is an intriguing way of proceeding.

[12] Macleod, *The Person of Christ*, 221-29.

[13] The problem in this case is that Scripture never specifically describes Christ's attributes in this respect. Of course, it is clear that he possessed full human and divine natures, and it is also clear that each of these natures has its natural characteristics toward sin and temptation, but it is still unclear how this worked out together in the theanthropic person. This illustrates that inferential reasoning is actually quite limited in its capacity to answer questions that Scripture never addresses.

[14] Macleod, *The Person of Christ*, 229-30. Lewis Sperry Chafer, *Systematic Theology* (Dallas: Dallas Seminary Press, 1948), 5:74-80.

[15] Daniel B. Clendenin makes an excellent survey of most of the theodicies that have been proffered in "God is Great, God is Good: Questions About Evil," *Ashland Theological Journal* 24 (1992): 35-54.

[16] Scripture mentions God's greater purposes for evil in a number of passages (Exod. 14:17; Rom. 9:17, 22-26). Romans 8:28 is the clearest statement that evil may have surprising outcomes, and Joseph's comment in Genesis 50:20 is the clearest example. Of course, the entire narrative of Scripture records how God will ultimately overcome evil and reverse the effects of the curse (Rev. 21:1-4; 22:1-5).

[17] Thus Daniel B. Clendenin, "God is Great, God is Good," 48, concludes his survey of theodicies with the observation that "in their better moments most theodicists admit that a

actually good. To take one example from previous discussion, some have vigorously maintained that the universe must be the best of all possible worlds, since everything works together to maximize the highest good—God's glory.[18] But this theodicy cannot solve the problem of evil completely. To begin, Scripture itself is not so simple in its definition of good. God is zealous for his own glory, but his goodness also includes an earnest, authentic desire for the best interests of his creatures (Ezek. 18:32; Matt. 23:37-39; 1 Tim. 2:4; 2 Pet. 3:9). To put the question in the hypothetical, if God could be glorified more in a universe of constant misery in which everyone were eventually damned, would it have any implications on the doctrine of his goodness or love? Or if all of God's purposes and desires can be simplified in terms of his own glory, how can Scripture say that he genuinely desires possibilities that are never realized when people reject him, when this will only culminate in glorifying him more?

Even more importantly, Scripture never puts the analysis in terms that are this simple. Rather, the biblical data speaks more generally of God's purposes (Rom. 9:11).[19] One of the most explicit biblical explorations of the problem of evil—the book of Job—concludes without a simple explanation and deliberately confronts the human tendency to seek one-dimensional answers. Rather, God acts according to his own purposes, and men are responsible to accept what he has done (Job 42:2-5).

In essence this view myopically claims more knowledge than it is possible for a human mind to know apart from revelation. Given that human desires and motivations are complex and multi-dimensional, is it credible to monolithically flatten all of God's thoughts and purposes to one concern? Even if he acted strictly in terms of his own glory, he still has the prerogative to showcase one specific aspect of his nature in this particular created universe, such as his love. The simple calculus of declaring that this universe achieves his maximum glory in every respect is a human oversimplification of much more complex questions.

Evaluating the epistemic benefits, this view does bring the center of attention towards God's glory and away from human evaluations of good—the place where many discussions of the problem of evil wrongly leave it. But beyond this the

---

large degree of mystery attaches itself to the problem of evil. That posture does not make ignorance an ally; it only recognizes that theodicy consists of fallible options."

[18] An example of this argument is John Piper, *The Justification of God: an Exegetical and Theological Study of Romans 9:1-23* (Grand Rapids: Baker, 1993), 214-16. Also Jay E. Adams, *The Grand Demonstration: a Biblical Study of the So-Called Problem of Evil* (Santa Barbara, Calif: EastGate, 1991). John Frame, *Apologetics to the Glory of God* (Phillipsburg, N.J.: P&R, 1994), 151-52, criticizes Adams's perspective, arguing for an element of mystery in the problem of evil. There is no reason to evaluate open theism here, since it is the subject of more extended discussion in the next chapter.

[19] Romans 9 certainly grounds God's actions in his desire for his own glory (9:17), but the passage also links God's actions to his purpose to save those whom he has chosen. Other passages describe his desire to save based on his compassion, without specific reference to his glory (Mark 6:34; John 3:16; Ezek. 18:32). Neglecting either of these biblical realities in order to answer the question results in an incomplete theological picture.

theological construction cannot solve the problem of evil. The theologian must still answer why an infinitely loving and gracious God would doom people to certain hell, even if it were in keeping with his glory. In essence the problem is the same—how does the goodness of God integrate with the reality of evil?

If this theological construction makes no further progress toward resolving the problem of evil, it is hard to suggest that its epistemological benefits are worthy of the cost. Since the main benefit of the conclusion is to realign the discussion to a more biblically accurate center, it seems much simpler to qualify the crucial role that God's glory plays and the biblically supportable truth that God does use evil and suffering to his own glory. It does not seem helpful, however, to take the additional step of saying that the created universe is the best of all possible worlds (as it is defined in this construction).[20]

Many of the standard theodicies bring helpful qualifications and clarifications to the debate. In most cases these are warranted because they bring real epistemic value to the discussion without making overwhelming assumptions; in some cases they are as simple as restoring emphases found in the biblical data. What makes the problem of evil a genuine antinomy, however is that the theodicies that are warranted can only mitigate the tension. All of the attempts at full resolution have serious problems and are therefore epistemically unwarranted.

Divine Sovereignty and Human Responsibility

The tension between God's sovereignty and human responsibility involves the problem of causality. Scripture indicates that God controls all things to such an extent that there is no pure contingency in the universe. Yet Scripture always avoids the idea that God is in any way the causal agent behind sin.[21] Rather, the responsibility for sin is always placed firmly on the free agents whom God has created. While he earnestly desires the responses of repentance and righteousness, people sinfully oppose his will and are completely responsible for their actions. The result is significant ambiguity in the biblical data on where the causal agency for sin actually lies.[22] This ambiguity is the epistemological space in which a significant theological tension exists.

Various models propose to clarify this ambiguity and causally separate God from sin. The two most common strategies are libertarian free will and secondary causation. Of the two, libertarian free will creates the more effective causal barrier, but it also involves some problems with the biblical data, which enjoys an absolute epistemic status. No matter how large the epistemic benefits of a logical move, the

---

[20] This is not to state dogmatically that the position cannot be true. It is fully possible that it might accurately describe reality. Based on the presently available information, however, the construction is too difficult to support, and it is therefore equally important not to state dogmatically that the position is true. For the present it must remain unknown.

[21] Wayne Grudem, *Systematic Theology* (Grand Rapids: Zondervan, 1994), 328-29.

[22] The question of how sin first entered the universe most naturally belongs to this antinomy rather than to the problem of evil, since it involves the issue of causal agency.

costs of contradicting biblical data are always too great for it to be warranted, and this makes the libertarian model unworkable.

Secondary causation is more in keeping with the exegetical data. In fact, some of the passages that approach the issue seem to imply a kind of causal separation that vindicates God.[23] Scripture consistently maintains an asymmetry in the way it attributes causal agency.[24] Furthermore, the distinction adds a measure of logical clarity to the problem. To this extent it is probably both helpful and epistemologically warranted. Still, even if God passively allows evil to occur, the obvious question is why he does so.[25] Scripture clearly reveals that God's desires are always for the elimination of evil. Furthermore, even his direct agency in positive things leaves challenging questions. If God desires the repentance of sinners (Ezek. 18:23; 33:11; 1 Tim. 2:4; 2 Pet. 3:9), and if he is causally responsible for anyone's repentance (Acts 13:48; Rom. 8:29-30; 2 Tim. 2:25), why do so many people continue in an unrepentant state?[26] Theologians who cite secondary causation as though it were a completely sufficient answer ignore significant logical problems and expose their reasoning to further confusion. As with each antinomy, there is an abiding logical problem that is not subject to any simple solutions.

The interesting thing about this situation is that the proposed solution actually has significant support in the biblical data. Besides the obvious epistemic strength the model has through its foundation on Scripture, the help it brings to the tension is another epistemic benefit. Clearly, then, it is warranted to see some type of causal

---

[23] A number of passages seem to imply God's causal involvement in people's sin. However, these passages also have a consistent ambiguity to avoid implicating God. Romans 9:22 speaks of vessels that were prepared for demonstrating God's wisdom through his wrath, but it stops short of saying that God is part of the reason for their rebellion. Earlier in the chapter Paul also references the example of Pharaoh's rebellion and speaks of God's hardening whom he wills (Rom. 9:18).

[24] Where the action involved is sinful, Scripture describes God's role more indirectly, using passives (Rom. 11:7), or often with other agents directly involved (Matt. 18:7; Luke 22:22; Acts 2:23; 4:27-28). Even in the strongest statements it appears that God confirmed the obduracy of already rebellious hearts (Exod. 14:4, 17 with 8:15, 32; 9:34; 1 Sam. 6:6; also 1 Sam. 2:25 with 2:12). Other challenging passages speak of individuals rather than actions (Jude 4; 1 Pet. 2:8 [the verb *destined* requires a plural subject]), and the final responsibility for rejecting truth is always on the person who made that choice (John 3:19; 5:40). Where the outcome is faith in God or repentance, Scripture describes a more direct causal link (Acts 13:48; Rom. 8:29-30; 9:11-13; Eph. 1:3-6; 1 Thess. 1:4-5; 2 Thess. 2:13; 1 Pet. 1:1-2). Examples exist for both types of passage—those that record rebellion or that record faith—that indicate either God's involvement or that of human beings, but there is still an observable pattern in the emphases. God is in control of both types of outcomes, but in a secondary way when it comes to sin, avoiding the problem described in James 1:13-14. See Leon Morris, *The Epistle to the Romans* (Grand Rapids: Eerdmans, 1997), 361.

[25] Brenda B. Colijn offers a list of theologians arguing for secondary causation and some of the logical problems this produces in "A Parable of Calvinism," *Ashland Theological Journal* 36 (2004): 107n.10.

[26] Even Shedd, *Systematic Theology*, 1.327, concedes that this problem is intractable in a certain form.

separation between God and sin. The problem is that this model cannot fully resolve the tension. Essentially this solution only delays the paradox of divine sovereignty to a deeper level. The idea that secondary causation fully resolves the problem of divine sovereignty and human responsibility, therefore, is completely unwarranted. God relates to human actions in some type of compatibilistic way, and we simply lack any details on how that relationship works.[27]

Infinity of God

The infinity of God is the most challenging antinomy to discuss, because it is the most ambiguous. The biblical data demonstrates that God relates to his creatures within time and space but that he is also infinitely above time and space, which is to say that he transcends dimensional categories. Some explanations of the tension can be eliminated immediately because they violate biblical data. It is apparent, for instance, that God is not subject to time as we experience it, in either his presence or his knowledge.[28]

Some of the discussions related to God's infinity have also pressed beyond the limits of what is knowable. Discussions concerning God's relationship to time quickly become intensely philosophical, because one of the most critical issues is the nature of time itself.[29] Scripture never investigates these questions about the metaphysical structure of reality, and philosophy is hardly univocal when it comes to theories about time.[30] To make the problem even more complex, this issue

---

[27] See Layton Talbert, *Not by Chance* (Greenville, S.C.: Bob Jones University Press, 2001) for an excellent survey of the biblical data supporting compatibilism.

[28] Proponents of open theism imply that God is limited with respect to time when they suggest that he is "surprised" by the outcome of certain events, a view that Sanders calls "presentism." See John Sanders, "A Tale of Two Providences," *Ashland Theological Journal* 33 (2001): 48. But Scripture explicitly teaches that God has a unique relationship to time in which he has complete knowledge of the future. In fact, God's knowledge of the future is one of the major pillars Isaiah uses to prove that he is the true God (Isa. 41:21-24; 42:9; 43:9; 44:7, 25-28; 45:21; 46:8-11; 48:3-5). Open theism essentially removes this biblical pillar as a legitimate argument. Edward R. Wierenga proposes a philosophical answer to the concept of God within time in "Timelessness out of Mind: On the Alledged Incoherence of Divine Timelessness," in *God and Time: Essays on the Divine Nature*, ed. Gregory E. Ganssle and David M. Woodruff (Oxford: Oxford University Press, 2002), 153-64.

[29] Alan G. Padgett, for instance, presents and argues for his view of God and time without a single reference to specific biblical data—"Eternity as Relative Timelessness," in *God and Time: Four Views*, ed. Gregory E. Ganssle (Downers Grove: InterVarsity, 2001), 92-110.

[30] Richard Gale discusses the philosophical conundrums involved with time. The fact that the concept is problematic even by itself only serves to highlight the challenges when the infinite God becomes one of the considerations. However, this paradox is more than just the theological form of a common philosophical problem. In fact, the converse is probably more accurate—the philosophical conundrums stem from a basic theological paradox, since the problem lies at the crossroads of the finite and infinite and concerns God's relationship to the underlying fabric of dimensionality. Richard M. Gale, "Time,

involves a nexus between theology and philosophy, between the finite and infinite. Theologians and philosophers can never give a biblically sufficient account of time until they can explain the causal link between God's creative act and the underlying metaphysical givens of the created world.

Putting all of these problems together, the truth is that theologians have very little real understanding about God's relationship to time and very few pathways of inquiry by which to proceed.[31] Much of the debate concerning whether God is within or outside of time stems from the failure to recognize these limits. Each side amasses legitimate logical arguments against the other, failing to acknowledge that they are invoking only one side of an antinomy.[32] A discussion of God and time such as that from John Feinberg is simply too detailed to have adequate biblical support.[33] In this case the major supports for his conclusion are inferences derived from other inferences, which are in turn extrapolated from other inferences. Invoking the concept of diminishing epistemic certainty where multiple logical steps are involved, the certainty of the conclusion is not only as strong as the weakest link; it is as weak as all of the supporting weaknesses combined.[34]

The same is true with the problem of omnipresence. The biblical data supports only the fact that no place can be absent of God's presence and that God is present everywhere in the fullness of his being.[35] Obviously we should recognize that God's presence is spiritual and not physical, but this illustrates the problem,

---

Temporality and Paradox," in *The Blackwell Guide to Metaphysics* (Malden, Mass.: Blackwell, 2002), 66-86.

[31] The doctrine of omnipresence proceeds along a very similar line. However, there has been little controversy or debate when it comes to this tension, and there is little reason to evaluate specific examples regarding omnipresence.

[32] Of course, the debate is not strictly a matter of co-opting the two sides of a tension. There are real and consequential issues at stake in some cases, such as a denial of God's omniscience or his eternality. As already stated, these denials are problematic because they violate clear biblical data. Generally it is the views that fall within the biblical data that are guilty of using one side of the tension polemically.

[33] Feinberg, *No One Like Him*, 375-433. This is not to say that philosophical evaluation never has a place in the theological process, but the concept of diminishing epistemic certainty is the key consideration. The more assumptions and inferential moves involved in the process, the less confident we should be of the conclusion. Where philosophers are completely unsettled on questions about time, and theologians realistically know almost nothing of the possible ways God might relate to it, the value of these speculations is negligible to nil. The same is true when it comes to God's relationship to space.

[34] Where multiple lines of argument support a single conclusion independently, the epistemic data might be regarded as roughly additive. In this case five weak supports might be stronger than a single strong support. But where the logical steps are sequential—inferences resting on other inferences—weakness in the argument is multiplicative.

[35] 1 Kings 8:27; Psalm 139:7-12; Proverbs 15:3; Isaiah 66:1; Jeremiah 23:23-24; Amos 9:1-4; Jonah 1:3, 10; Acts 17:27-28; Romans 10:6-8; Colossians 1:17; Matthew 28:19-20 with Acts 1:8. To these could be added the verses and consistent biblical principle that God has no limitations (Job 5:9; 9:10; 11:7-9; Ps. 145:3; 147:5).

because we have no meaningful category for non-physical presence in space. In fact, even the terminology is self-contradictory. Theologians can hypothesize about how God's presence relates to spatial grids, but the simple fact is that no one knows, and the lines of evidence to support analysis are scanty to none.[36]

In cases such as these, theologians must honestly assess the quality of the supports involved and be content to let tensions stand without further clarification. It is better to leave questions unanswered than to offer authoritative conclusions without adequate support.

Since the foundation of the various solutions is philosophical, and since these philosophical conclusions remain highly controversial, any solution to God and time or God and space will necessarily be quite weak. Similarly the choice between various models for God's relationship to time is mostly a matter of choosing between logical drawbacks; there is no established way to resolve either tension, and both viewpoints have problems. From this it is not hard to see that the few epistemic benefits are far short of the significant epistemic challenges. It is best, therefore, to assume the basic propositions of the text and let ambiguities remain without attempting fuller logical resolution.

Conclusion

The process of evaluating epistemic warrant is hardly a purely objective, mechanical task. Still, the attempt to be as aware and self-critical as possible exposes the fact that even a basic rationale is missing in some areas or that in other cases the theological construction is hardly worthy of the assumptions involved in suggesting it. In each case the biblical data is foundational and absolute, and no conclusion can stand that conflicts with the text, however helpful or logical it might seem.

Logical inferences and extensions from the text also play a critical role in the theological process. Propositions extrapolated for the purpose of bridging a logical gap, however, simply do not have the same epistemic status as propositions resting on explicit biblical data. The crucial part of the analysis that many theologians miss is the need for varying degrees of confidence in these conclusions. In every case the confidence invested in a particular conclusion must directly correspond with the amount of support that actually exists for the conclusion. Apart from this epistemic

---

[36] For whatever reason, discussion on this point has been far less than the analysis of God's relationship to time. This may stem from the fact that our provisional assumptions about the metaphysical structure of space are much simpler than the long-standing conundrums with time. If so, the debate about God and time represents more about our ignorance and assumptions than it represents genuine progress towards demonstrable understanding. The more likely cause for the lack of discussion on omnipresence, though, is that God's relationship to time has broad implications for the doctrine of omniscience and even sovereignty. This is certainly the reason that open theism has reexamined God and time. It is not at all clear, on the other hand, what doctrines would be influenced by a reevaluation of God's relationship to space or even what form such a reevaluation would take.

honesty and self-awareness, the theological process inevitably disintegrates into logical scholasticism.

There are also interesting differences in the nature of each paradox. The examples analyzed here are different enough to provide a beginning palette of epistemic problems. The data on the Trinity and Incarnation are the "purest" instances of paradox—both rest on easily supportable propositions with a clear logical conflict. In both cases reflection and historical development produced basic formulae distinguishing the two sides of the tension. The problem is with defining the terms of the distinction—placing meaningful content behind the wording. The best method is to deal with both sides of the tension analytically. Further analysis is little more than sophisticated guesswork.

The paradox of the Incarnation involves several more specific problems. Regarding Christ's dual consciousness, the new questions and problems it generates are greater than the questions it answers, though it is still an interesting possibility. With Christ's peccability the problem is an almost complete lack of information, as though one tried to complete a puzzle without any of the clues. As a result, the paradox of the Incarnation has a greater inferential significance because of the number of related questions it involves. This example illustrates how conflicts can inferentially spread outward from the basic paradox.

The problem of evil illustrates that a single paradox may have a wide variety of possible solutions, each of which must be evaluated independently. In this case a number of helpful qualifications mitigate the tension, and most are quite warranted. Taken together, these considerations play a significant role in reducing this tension but not solving it, and none of the attempts at complete resolution are warranted because they ultimately fail to solve the problem.

The problem of sovereignty and responsibility illustrates the temptation to extend a legitimate biblical truth beyond its original intention. Though Scripture supports secondary causation regarding God's relationship to sin, it also includes propositions that this model cannot fully rectify. As with certain theodicies, this biblical truth is helpful, but not a full solution to the paradox.

Finally, the infinity of God demonstrates that theologians sometimes devolve into speculative philosophy, pontificating what may or may not be meaningfully possible for God's existence. We can say with full confidence only that God relates to time in a way that is completely different from us and that we have little chance of elucidating the concept by extrapolating from our own experience. More than the others, this paradox illustrates a wide field of possible views with little help for how to proceed. What is interesting about this situation is that even with a large number of options, all of the proposed solutions still lead to significant logical problems. As a result the position with the best balance of epistemic costs and benefits is to leave the propositions as they stand with the ambiguities in the biblical data.

In each of these cases, the complementarian model provides helpful guidelines for how far attempts at resolution should go. The process of applying the model to specific examples also demonstrates that complementarity yields diverse outcomes on how to analyze paradox. Some qualifications and distinctions are warranted; others are not. Individual interpreters may disagree on specific conclusions, but at the core of complementarity is a model that evaluates each proposal for its merits. Rejecting suspicion of logic on the one hand and the ambition to resolve logical tensions at any cost on the other, complementarity approaches each problem individually, yet on the basis of controlled, defined criteria. These criteria are even more critical when applied to a complex example for analysis such as open theism.

CHAPTER 8

Specific Application to Open Theism

> After reading some neat theodicies that stress, say, that all suffering is the direct result of sin, or that free will understood as absolute power to contrary nicely exculpates God, I wonder if their authors think Job or Habakkuk were twits. Surely they should have seen that there is no mystery to be explained, and simply gone home and enjoyed a good night's sleep. It is better to let the biblical texts speak in all their power. Many things can then be said about the God who has graciously disclosed himself, but all of them leave God untamed.[1]

Open theism is an ideal choice for further inquiry because it specifically touches on three related antinomies—the problem of evil, divine sovereignty with human responsibility, and the infinity of God (in respect to time). It is also ideal to give special consideration to these three since James Anderson gives extended discussion to the Trinity and the Incarnation.

Open theism proposes elements that are explicitly unbiblical as well as elements that simply fail the complementarian analysis suggested here. As in the previous chapter, each element of the openness model will be evaluated according to the biblical data first and then evaluated as to its epistemic warrant—whether the strength of the supporting arguments outweigh the vulnerabilities, logical problems, and assumptions of the new construction. In both respects the evaluation will serve to demonstrate that the complementarian model for paradox is useful.[2]

---

[1] D.A. Carson, *How Long, O Lord?* (Grand Rapids: Baker, 1990), 225.

[2] Several definitions are in order. First, open theism is a broad movement represented by a range of different viewpoints. For instance, John Sanders, "Be Wary of Ware," *JETS* 45.2 (June 2002): 222-23, unfairly dismisses Bruce Ware for saying that open theism limits God's knowledge, citing several open theists that take a different view. If this is not a characteristic of open theism, the movement is beyond description. When dealing with movements and positions, it is necessary to interact with the major proponents and to generalize. Second, "the traditional view of God" as an antithesis to open theism represents a category even broader and harder to define. For the sake of simplicity, "the traditional view of God" will refer in this chapter to the basic view of God presented in Wayne Grudem, *Systematic Theology* (Grand Rapids: Zondervan, 1994). In most of the openness literature this category excludes traditional arminianism, but many open theists misrepresent compatibilism so that it sounds more like hardened determinism, sometimes resulting in little more than a caricature. D.A. Carson, "God, The Bible And Spiritual Warfare: A Review Article," *JETS* 42.2 (June 1999): 258-60, comments that openness advocates contrasts their view with a distorted traditional theism, implying that there are

A Brief Introduction to Open Theism

Open theism is a contemporary rethinking of God's sovereignty and omniscience.[3] The particular theological propositions that openness proponents have reconfigured may initially seem arbitrary, but one possible common denominator among them all may be the ambition to remove logical tensions in the more traditional Augustinian view of God.[4] Open theism hopes to resolve both the problem of evil and the problem of divine sovereignty and human responsibility by making these adjustments, not to mention answering several of the challenging problems regarding God's relationship to time. Logical coherence is one of the major bases on which open theists suggest that their position is superior.[5]

Open theism can be summarized with several propositions.[6] First, openness teaches that at creation God chose to grant the power of choice to completely free agents. He did so because he desires authentic, reciprocal relationships with human beings, rather than the control that would produce only automatons. Subsequent to that decision God does not generally intervene in a way that would violate free choice.

Second, open theism teaches that because of God's creative choice, he can be surprised, shocked, and grieved by the reality that develops in human decisions. In

---

only two theological options available. The impersonal, megalomaniac God they present as the traditional view is, of course, to be rejected. But as Michael Horton, "Hellenistic or Hebrew," 327, asks, who really believes in this kind of God? Are there actually serious theologians who articulate this model, or is it only the product of open theists' polemical concerns?

[3] Regarding history, open theism developed as a *tertium quid* between evangelical theology and process theism. The earliest published work to promulgate this view in evangelicalism was Richard Rice, *God's Foreknowledge and Man's Free Will* (Minneapolis: Bethany House, 1985), originally published as *The Openness of God: The Relationship of Divine Foreknowledge and Human Free Will*. Clark Pinnock and John Sanders were the primary developers of the system, and Greg Boyd has subsequently popularized it.

[4] This is a stated purpose for one of the key books advocating open theism. Clark Pinnock, "Preface," in *The Openness of God* (Downers Grove: InterVarsity, 1994), 8-9.

[5] Of course, the ambition to remove difficulties is not faulty in itself, as long as they can be removed in a biblically and theologically legitimate way. This is why it is helpful to evaluate openness according to a complementarian model—to test how epistemically sustainable these solutions really are.

[6] Clark Pinnock offers a helpful summary of open theism in "Preface," in *The Openness of God*, 7. Open theists tend to emphasize God's reciprocal interaction in relationships as the core of the system. The supposition is that genuine relationship requires open reciprocity and libertarian free will. However, this assumes from the outset that the more traditional understanding of God makes him less relational and responsive. See Richard Rice, "Biblical Support for a New Perspective," in *The Openness of God*, 15, where he defines open theism with two basic convictions: "Love is the most important quality we attribute to God, and love is more than care and commitment; it involves being sensitive and responsive as well."

fact, because of his immense knowledge and love, God is even more shocked and grieved by tragedy than any of those who experience it.

Of course, this requires an adjustment on the traditional view of God's omniscience. In open theism God still knows everything that can be known. Yet future developments are not yet genuine realities, and there is no way to speak of knowing something that does not yet exist. Therefore, God does not know the future fully and exhaustively. Considering his infinite wisdom and his complete knowledge of all that exists, God does possess extraordinary predictive power, and he can look ahead to extrapolate what events will likely take place. But he does not possess immediate or absolute knowledge of the future because it has not yet passed into reality.[7]

Finally, open theism rethinks God's relationship to time and the traditional view of immutability. In open theism, time is part of the underlying structure of reality, and the traditional view of God outside of or transcending time is nonsensical. Rather, God experiences changing realities in much the same way that people do. In response to people's choices he often adjusts his own purposes or actions. This naturally leads to a reevaluation of the doctrine of immutability. In place of immutability, Clark Pinnock prefers "changeable faithfulness," by which he means that God is unchanging in his character and faithful to his promises, but he dynamically adjusts to changing circumstances and developments in history. According to openness proponents, the idea of a static, unchanging God developed in Greek philosophy and entered Christian theology through early theologians with a philosophical background.[8] An honest evaluation of the biblical texts, they claim, supports the open model. Likewise they argue that God's total control of all events is the megalomaniac, artificial thinking of pagan philosophers, while Scripture actually teaches that God is relational and responsive to human choices.[9]

Open Theism's Aversion to Theological Antinomy

In examining the connection between open theism and theological antinomy, the best starting point is the direct statements of openness theologians on paradox. When it comes to paradox, openness proponents univocally subscribe to the paradox-minimizing view, and openness literature openly criticizes positions that allow for unresolved tensions, such as the *sui generis* or complementarian views. Confident that a workable and logical solution exists, openness theologians mostly regard theological paradox as the logical dead end of a failed theological program.

---

[7] Traditional Arminianism has denied determinism while maintaining that God has a complete knowledge of the future, exposing a serious logical inconsistency. Open theism escapes this dilemma by denying God's exhaustive knowledge altogether. See Clark H. Pinnock, *Most Moved Mover: A Theology of God's Openness* (Grand Rapids: Baker, 2001), 47-53.

[8] John Sanders, "Historical Considerations," in *The Openness of God*, 59-100.

[9] Richard Rice, *The Openness of God* (Nashville: Review & Herald, 1980), 53-54.

In their view the proper response is not to let tensions stand but to resolve them as logical problems, even by rethinking other major doctrines if necessary.[10]

John Sanders dismisses paradox as a legitimate solution to these basic problems, discussing it as one of the two major objections to openness. He rejects the appeal to antinomy for several reasons: (1) the concept of apparent contradiction is problematic, (2) if something is contradictory for us but not for God, there is no way to know it, (3) and contradictions would make all of theology unintelligible.[11]

In fact, all of the major proponents of open theism openly attack either the concept of paradox or the complementarian view.[12] In their view the appeal to paradox is an act of theological desperation, a way of escaping the logical implications of an unworkable theological system.[13] This leads to elaborate logical defenses as open theists attempt to demonstrate that their system ameliorates the logical conflicts inherent in the traditional view of God.

Three Theological Antinomies Open Theism Seeks to Resolve

Open theism is a theological model, but its primary emphasis seems to be apologetic, proposing to answer the antinomies that have plagued theologians. In particular, the problem of evil, divine sovereignty, and the infinity of God are interconnected, so that most attempts to solve one produce problems in one of the

---

[10] William Davis, "Why Open Theism is Flourishing Now," in *Beyond the Bounds*, ed. John Piper, Justin Taylor and Paul Kjoss Helseth (Wheaton: Crossway, 2003), 124-25, 137-38, regards "impatience with mystery" on the popular level and "open theism's offer of mystery-free explanations" as one of the reasons that the model has recently flourished in evangelicalism. Openness advocates do sometimes speak of "mystery," but this apparently refers to informational unknowns rather than the logical issue of paradox. See Pinnock in *Mover*, 36, 61, 179. Elsewhere Pinnock *God of the Possible*, 57, is equally clear in his disavowal of mystery as logical conflict. Similarly Greg Boyd speaks of allowing the mystery of God's repentance to stand, but in the next paragraph argues that the open view leaves little to mystery and that in this understanding "the paradox of how God could experience genuine regret over a decision he made disappears".

[11] John Sanders, *The God Who Risks: A Theology of Providence* (Downers Grove: InterVarsity, 1998), 34-37.

[12] Clark Pinnock, "Systematic Theology," in *The Openness of God*, 114-15. William Hasker, "A Philosophical Perspective," in *The Openness of God*, 143, 197 n.34. David Basinger, "Biblical Paradox: Does Revelation Challenge Logic?" *JETS* 30.2 (June 1987): 205-13. Greg Boyd, *God of the Possible*, 90-92, extends this view to the Trinity and Incarnation, arguing that we can test the plausibility of a theological position based on "whether it is able to reconcile coherently elements of God's Word that otherwise stand in tension with each other." In his view this is why the early church articulated and accepted the orthodox views on the Trinity and Incarnation—because these formulae reconciled the biblical teachings on these subjects that otherwise seemed contradictory.

[13] Michael Horton, "Hellenistic or Hebrew? Open Theism and Reformed Theological Method," *JETS* (June 2002): 335-37, traces the aversion to paradox back to a methodological pre-commitment—pursuing univocal knowledge (as opposed to the analogical knowledge espoused by Van Til), or, said differently, regarding ectypal knowledge as archetypal.

others. Openness suggests such a sweeping program of interpretive and theological reevaluation that it combines solutions for all three problems into an integrated theological model.[14]

Divine Sovereignty and Human Responsibility

The problem of God's sovereignty is ultimately a question of how he is not morally culpable for sin if he controls every event in some way. For open theism the answer is that God is not responsible because he is not causally involved. Sin and evil arise by the free choice of independent agents. God chose to limit himself by creating people who have the ability to choose what is right or to sin, and that fact does not impinge on his sovereignty in any way.

In a deeper way this explanation rests on a specific ontology. Openness is willing to suggest that only certain creative options were available to God. If he created the world so that he had complete control over his creatures, they would be automatons and genuine relationship would be impossible. On the other hand, if he created them with a genuinely free will and the ability to respond to him relationally, he introduced the risk that they would rebel against him. Knowing these realities, God accepted the risk that great evil might come because he valued relationships with his creatures more.

It is true that theologians of various persuasions have acknowledged obvious qualifications to omnipotence. God cannot—or better, God *would* not—make a square circle or create an uncreated world, simply because these entities make no sense. God would not actualize them because there is nothing to actualize.[15] Openness argues that free will operates in the same way—if God desires authentic,

---

[14] Pinnock, *Most Moved Mover*, 2, suggests that atheism may be due to the classical model of God. "Atheism is, in part, an unpaid bill of the church which has too often presented God as an alienating substance, remote and unsympathetic, and who exists at humanity's expense. Many of the difficulties with faith are due to problems inherent in conventional theism. Atheists have not been told about the God of the gospel who loves us freely, wants a relationship with us and wants to empower us, not foster our weakness." Arguing the opposite direction, Larry Pettegrew, "Is There Knowledge In the Most High?," *Master's Seminary Journal* 12.2 (Fall 2001): 145, suggests that the attempt to answer the mysteries of human tragedies might almost be the primary reason for open theism.

[15] It is standard for systematic theologians to qualify God's omnipotence. A good definition of this perfection would be "God is able to do whatever He desires," or "God has the power to perform whatever is in keeping with His nature"—Millard J. Erickson, *Christian Theology* (Grand Rapids: Baker, 1998), 303-304. Also, John Feinberg, *No One Like Him* (Wheaton: Crossway, 2001), 278-89. Thus it is logical that God would not violate human choices if he chose to limit himself in that way. The question is whether there is truly biblical basis for arguing that God limited himself like this. The weakest link in the openness argument is probably the idea that God's nature as a relational being logically requires that he create free agents and therefore limit himself from dictating their choices. To some extent this seems to limit God's ontological ultimacy by declaring ontic requirements that seem to precede creation and even God Himself. Ron Highfield, "The Function Of Divine Self-Limitation In Open Theism: Great Wall Or Picket Fence?" *JETS* 45.2 (June 2002): 279-300.

reciprocal relationships with his creatures, libertarian free will follows by definition.[16]

The openness solution to the paradox follows on this basis. Those who reject God are personally and exclusively responsible for their actions. God is never culpable for sin or rebellion, simply because God is never involved in the choice.[17] The same follows with the passages that indicate God's desire towards sinners—he is authentically disappointed by their rebellion because he does not have a controlling influence in the decision.

Of course, Scripture does speak of people's total depravity—the truth that apart from God's intervention all human beings will necessarily reject him. Other passages speak of God's choosing some people for salvation and his effectual call. Openness understands election as God's choice of certain people for a special role of service. Regarding total depravity, openness advocates use some combination of semi-pelagianism and Wesleyan Arminianism.[18]

John Sanders disparages antinomy when it comes to the problem of responsibility, regarding it as a defense of desperation and an argument of last resort.[19] Greg Boyd suggests that an advantage of open theism is that it "avoids the impenetrable paradox (or, many of us would argue, the contradiction) of asserting

---

[16] David Basinger defines libertarian free will as the idea that when a person has freedom to chose, she "has it in her power to choose to perform A or choose not to perform A. *Both A and not A could actually occur;* which *will* actually occur has *not yet been determined*"—"Middle Knowledge and Classical Christian Thought," *Religious Studies* 22 (1986): 416 (quoted in *God, Time and Knowledge*, 66). David Basinger, *The Case for Freewill Theism: A Philosophical Assessment* (Downers Grove: InterVarsity, 1996), 34-36, lists three reasons that God's nature is inconsistent with his consistent and pervasive intervention against the wills of free agents: (1) It would destroy the reality of meaningful choice. (2) It would present a misleading, deceptive reality (contrary to God's moral character) in which the free choices people assume are only a misleading farce. (3) It would violate God's creative agenda for a world in which people voluntarily choose to relate to him. A better attempt to describe the biblical presentation is "compatibilism"—the belief that genuine human choices align compatibly with God's sovereign control as individuals act completely according to their own desires and choices. See Carson, *Spiritual Warfare,* 262-64, for a short but clear exegetical description of compatibilism.

[17] Of course, the traditional view also denies that God has a part in sinful choices, though the events are determined through some type of secondary causation, or at least known in a way that requires that they will occur. The difference is that open theism regards these choices as completely undetermined and causally disconnected from anything but the libertarian choices of free agents.

[18] It is difficult to state definitively what openness maintains on these points, because there is still wide variety among various writers on this level of theological detail. To take only one example, Clark Pinnock, *Mover,* 166, seems to suggest semi-pelagianism when he comments that sinners "cannot attain salvation but, yes, they can receive the gift of salvation. They are, after all, persons not corpses. . . . I suppose that the divine inspiration is fruitful in us because of an ember still glowing in us."

[19] Sanders, *God Who Risks,* 256.

that self-determining free actions are settled in eternity before free agents make them so".[20] Clark Pinnock is quite explicit on the subject:

> There is no antinomy here. God rules the world in such a way as to allow for creaturely input. There are not two sets of texts—one affirming exhaustive sovereignty and the other affirming human freedom. That would create a contradiction. We are not asked to believe that God exercises all-controlling sovereignty and still holds human beings morally responsible. The Bible is coherent and the contradiction is imaginary. All-controlling sovereignty is not taught in Scripture. There may be mysteries that go beyond human intelligence but this is not one of them. One can hold both to divine sovereignty and human freedom because sovereignty is not all-controlling. The Bible, not rationalism, leads to this solution.[21]

The Problem of Evil

One of the basic tenets of open theism is that at creation God took a risk that terrible evils might develop. In this framework, evil is the fact that this disastrous possibility is exactly what happened. If the problem of evil is stated in the form of Hume's famous three propositions (God is good, God is omnipotent, and evil exists), open theism answers the problem by qualifying God's omnipotence. God is genuinely and deeply grieved by the evil that develops in the created world, but because he voluntarily limited himself by creating free agents God cannot act against evil without contradicting his creative act and his own nature.[22] The only possible solution would be if he rescinded the freedom that he gave human beings at creation—something that God refuses to do because he values authentic relationships with people and the genuine love of choice.

---

[20] Boyd, *God of the Possible*, 91.

[21] Pinnock, *Mover*, 55. Elsewhere Pinnock attacks the idea that divine sovereignty and human freedom are a paradox and uses this as his core argument for openness. "A tension is allowed to stand in the biblical text; a definitive resolution is nowhere attempted. Ought we even to attempt a resolution? Some theologians have concluded we should not. The relationship between sovereignty and freedom is an impenetrable mystery transcending human logic, they say, and therefore one should suppress the imperious demands of reason and submit to the antinomy." Pinnock goes on to give three levels on which he regards this as unworkable. See Clark Pinnock, "God Limits His Knowledge," in *Predestination and Free Will: Four Views of Divine Sovereignty and Human Freedom*, ed. David Basinger and Randall Basinger (Downers Grove: InterVarsity, 1986), 144.

[22] By extension this argument draws a necessary causal chain stretching from God's nature and choice to create to the existence of evil. (1) God is a relational being who desires authentic relationships, and he created agents with libertarian free will. (2) Therefore, God created the world with the necessary possibility of suffering and evil. (3) Therefore, all human suffering is a direct function of the nature and creative choice of God. William Hasker, *The Triumph of God over Evil* (Downers Grove: InterVarsity, 2008), 93, rejects theological determinism and molinism as "world types" that God could have created. He does leave open, however, the logical possibility that God could have chosen not to create at all (pp. 97-100). In this sense, the causal chain begins with God's choice to create something rather than nothing.

What then is the source of evil? Openness advocates suggest that recognizing the great evil that could result from free will, God still chose to create free agents with the power to chose either good or evil. In spite of the risk, God considered a world of automatons to be worse.[23] Evil obtains, therefore, from the flux that a risky universe entails. To put it crudely, in the cosmic gamble of the universe, God's decision turned out badly. As shocking evils unfold, God is also grieved and shocked, and he moves with infinite resourcefulness to minimize this evil for the sake of his creatures. In a few cases God has intervened for the sake of stopping greater evil from developing.

Open theists still view the problem of evil as a significant challenge. Greg Boyd, for instance, is unwilling to "claim that the open view entirely solves the problem of evil," but he does regard openness as the most plausible answer for the problem.[24] The more traditional view is not a genuine solution for him because "the maneuver simply cannot be rendered logically coherent, despite the best efforts of some of the church's best minds to make it so."[25] Similarly, John Sanders comments that "open theists are under no illusions that they have the perfect solution to the problem of evil. Every response to the problem of evil has difficulties."[26] Nevertheless he argues that the openness perspective on evil is better suited to answer the problem than theological determinism because its answer is more logically coherent. William Hasker likewise concedes that the problem of evil "is a topic in which mystery is unavoidable" but goes on to describe theological determinism as promulgating mystery on another level.[27] In his view a deterministic

---

[23] One of the problems is that it is not at all clear how this universe with its evils could be a better option, and even less clear that a universe of automatons would be worse. Granted, those who chose God and have a relationship with him can be thankful for this reciprocity, but what of those who have suffered the most or who would suffer eternally for the sake of a few enjoying reciprocal relationships with God? Of course, this may be part of the reason that a number of open theists have reevaluated the biblical data on eternal, bodily, conscious torment in hell. See Clark Pinnock, "The Destruction of the Finally Impenitent," *Criswell Theological Review* 4.2 (Spring 1990): 243-59; Greg Boyd, *Satan and the Problem of Evil: Construicting a Trinitarian Warfare Theodicy* (Downers Grove: InterVarsity, 2001), 345-57. For the same reason, Sanders, *No Other Name: An Investigation into the the Destiny of the Unevangelized* (Grand Rapids: Eerdmans, 1992), 131-285, denies that salvation requires explicit faith in Jesus Christ alone, opting for a "wider hope" of universally accessible salvation, even for those who have not heard the name of Christ.

[24] Boyd, *God of the Possible*, 99.

[25] Gregory Boyd, *God at War: The Bible and Spiritual Conflict* (Downers Grove: InterVarsity, 1997), 48.

[26] Sanders, *Perspectives on the Doctrine of God*, 213.

[27] Hasker's perspective on mystery is more clear in *Providence, Evil and the Openness of God* (New York: Routledge, 2004). "Can't we simply accept each side of the antinomy in its full force, acknowledge the resulting paradox, and move on to other matters? What is at stake here, of course, is whether logical contradictions must be expunged from theology. There is a considerable tradition that this need not be done; reality is either inherently paradoxical or else so impenetrably mysterious that we can have no reasonable

view creates an "insuperable difficulty" in which "mystery takes over right from the beginning and no light of reason can be thrown into the resulting darkness."[28]

This leads to an interesting situation: open theists attack the traditional perspective of God for its logical problems while conceding that other logical problems inhere in their own model. The difference between the two, presumably is the degree of logical misalignment. Open theists seek to minimize logical conflicts and dismiss the more traditional view of God because of how they evaluate the logical challenges it entails. Still, there is significant inconsistency in how these standards are applied.[29]

The Infinity of God

Just as with omnipotence, theologians have always needed to qualify God's infinity. Clearly he is not infinite in every way possible. He does not possess every possible attribute, for instance (such as evil or hatred). He exists in three persons—not an infinite number.[30] Recognizing this reality, open theism suggests that God relates to the world within time rather than transcending it in some way. God watches events unfold together with human knowers, and God himself even adjusts and responds within time.

Open theists are less clear about the metaphysical basis for this model. Did God create time and then choose to limit himself by existing and acting with it, or does time exist as one of the givens of reality?[31] Generally, open theists go only so far as to say that the traditional view (God's timelessness) is a confused conceptual muddle without any real meaning and badly in need of revision.

Why have open theists not attacked the traditional view of God for relying on mystery in this area? The tension in God's relationship to time is more difficult to state clearly because it involves a large inferential gap. In other words, only an extended chain of reasoning can bridge the propositions and data sets on either side of the tension, and this linkage involves so many unknown parameters that it is nearly impossible to state the tension explicitly. What open theists have used, however, is *reductio ad absurdum* against the traditional view, reasoning from one

---

hope of grasping it in a way that is free from contradictions. I have to say, however, that I am simply unable to adopt this strategy as my own. If logical contradiction does not constitute a sufficient reason for rejecting a position, then I will turn in my philosopher's union card; I no longer know any way of practicing my trade" (152).

[28] Hasker, *Triumph of God*, 93. Richard Rice and others also argue for openness based on its answers to the problem of evil. *The Openness of God* (1980), 39-44.

[29] How can Hasker dismiss the traditional view out of hand as illegitimate and beyond the light of reason, when by his own description the difference is merely at what point in the discussion the mystery enters?

[30] Feinberg, *No One Like Him*, 243-49.

[31] William Hasker provides an extended and quite specific discusion of God and time as one of the major advocates of open theism in *God, Time, and Knowledge* (Ithaca: Cornell University, 1989), 144-85. Paul Helm defends the traditional view in *Eternal God* (Oxford: Clarendon, 1988).

side of the tension to falsify the other. Open theists seek to demonstrate that if God transcends time, he must also be static, incapable of responding to his time-bound creatures in a meaningful way. Theologically this is analogous to deconstructing the hypostatic union by constructing an inferential bridge across the tension: (1) If Jesus was fully divine, (2) He knew all things, and (3) therefore, he never learned any new information. Similarly open theists argue from God's transcendence to falsify chronological immanence, denying the tension that traditional theists willingly maintain, misrepresenting the traditional view in the process.[32]

Openness has not led to a reevaluation of omnipresence, but Michael Horton points out that this is a logical implication of their theological method. If open theists abandon an anthropomorphic understanding of God's interactions and response to people (in favor of taking these expressions literally), should they not also follow this precedent with the biblical data on God's presence?[33] Indeed, Clark Pinnock proposes a more imminent view of God within space together with his view on time.[34] Here as well, the open view may be naturally inclined to deny one side of the tension, emphasizing God's spatial immanence at the expense of his transcendence.

Evaluating Open Theism from a Complementarian Model of Antinomy

The complementarian model offers foundational concepts for understanding paradox, but ultimately the model evaluates possible solutions for paradox, not particular antinomies. The first step in the process is to evaluate the epistemic warrant of the solution. Assessing the epistemic value that open theism adds, complementarity asks how well this model relieves logical tension and adds coherence to the final theological picture. It is true that open theism mitigates the immediate poignancy of several tensions and also clear that these benefits are real and significant. At the same time, open theism does not solve the problem entirely. The biblical evidence is quite clear that God has intervened decisively against the will of his creatures, and even most open theists acknowledge that God can intervene and has intervened unilaterally under certain circumstances.[35] But this is tantamount to a full surrender, since this concession exposes the model to the same

---

[32] Clark H. Pinnock, "There is Room for Us: A Reply to Bruce Ware," *JETS* 45.2 (June 2002): 215-18; Boyd, *God of the Possible*, 131-32.

[33] Horton, "Hellenistic or Hebrew," 335.

[34] Pinnock, *Mover*, 32. Pinnock does acknowledge the real danger of further development on this point (61).

[35] Basinger, in *The Openness of God*, 156. Pinnock, *Mover*, 50; Boyd, *God of the Possible*, 34; David Basinger, "Practical Considerations," in *The Openness of God*, 158. Attempting to answer why God does not exercise this ability more often, Basinger, *Divine Power in Process Theism: A Philosophical Critique* (Albany: State University of New York Press, 1988), 63, answers that perhaps he is already working to the maximum extent he is willing to contravene human freedom. Also, John Sanders, "Divine Providence and the Openness of God," in *Perspectives on the Doctrine of God* (Nashville: Broadman & Holman, 2008), 211-13.

questions in traditional theism. In the final analysis, therefore, open theism mitigates several difficult conundrums and could theoretically offer epistemic benefits, but ultimately fails to resolve the antinomies.

The other side of the equation is to evaluate epistemic costs—the degree to which open theism causes logical or theological problems. The basic and most glaring epistemic cost in open theism is certainly the many aspects at which it contradicts biblical data. On this point examples are myriad. John Sanders comments that the openness model proposes that "God sovereignly decides not to control each and every event, and some things go contrary to what God intends and may not turn out completely as God desires."[36] In contrast he criticizes the traditional model for maintaining that "the divine will is never thwarted in any respect."[37] Yet this almost perfectly parallels the biblical statement that "He does according to his wish in the host of heaven and among the inhabitants of earth; and no one can push off his hand or say to him, 'What have You done?'" (Dan. 4:35). Likewise Greg Boyd believes that "the hope that the New Testament offers is not the hope that God has a higher, all-encompassing plan that secretly governs every event, including the evil intentions of malicious angelic and human beings, and that somehow renders these evil wills 'good' at a higher level."[38] But this almost exactly contradicts Paul's confidence that "[God] is working all things together for good, for the ones who are loving God" (Rom. 8:28).[39]

Open theists do not entirely dismiss the biblical evidence; on the contrary they are quite committed to arguing for their position exegetically.[40] Still, the model's

---

[36] Sanders, *God Who Risks*, 10-11.

[37] Ibid., 10.

[38] Boyd, *God at War*, 292-93.

[39] The context of this statement is Boyd's extended argument that evil is partly attributable to the ongoing conflict between God and diabolical forces opposed to him. But Paul refers to diabolical forces only ten verses later ("angels" and "principalities," Rom. 8:38), together with the confidence that believers are completely secure from these threats. Exegetically, there is nothing to suggest qualification to "all things"—Douglas Moo, *The Epistle to the Romans* (Grand Rapids: Eerdmans, 1996), 529. Boyd goes on to root his theodicy in eschatology: God will eventually reverse evil and right many of the injustices of earthly life in eternity. This still does not explain Boyd's careless statements. At a minimum the way he expressed his view is quite misleading. More likely it simply violates clear Scripture.

[40] Extended examples of exegetical content can be found in Pinnock, *God of the Possible*, 33-51, or Sanders, *The God Who Risks*, 39-137. When it comes to omniscience Clark Pinnock argues that Psalm 139 does not teach deterministic knowledge but God's immense, comprehensive knowledge of present realities and predictive clairvoyance. He regards Jeremiah 1:5 as conditional on Jeremiah's accepting the call. For him many prophecies are also conditional (Exod. 32:14; Jer. 18:9-10). Others are imprecise forecasts based on the present and may not be precisely fulfilled. In other cases the fulfillment of a prophecy may be significantly different from what the prophet expected. Finally, Pinnock, *Mover*, 49-51, acknowledges that some prophecies may point to realities that have been determined. Serious consideration of these texts demonstrates significant problems in his exegesis. This only illustrates much deeper, serious flaws in the

problems are evident in the weakness of their exegesis. Open theists illegitimately bracket the passages teaching God's knowledge, immutability, or sovereignty to a degree that would yield very wooden readings if applied elsewhere.[41] One cannot help feeling that open theists heavily skew the balance of exegetical attention toward passages that sound supportive of openness and minimize the weight of passages against the model or ignore them altogether.[42] What makes this situation worse is that the passages cited in support of openness do not conclusively support the model, and conservative exegetes have already articulated answers for these problems. One of the largest groups of exegetical data, for example, is the passages that talk about God repenting, which open theists regard as changing his mind.[43]

---

hermeneutical approach some or even most open theists have taken. Without denying the Divine authorship of Scripture, Pinnock, *Most Moved Mover*, 21, nevertheless comments, "The Bible does not speak with a single voice; there is dialogue between the different voices. The writings contain a long and complex search for the mind of God and in this struggle various points of view compete and interact. In constructing a doctrinal model, therefore, it is important to remember that the Bible is a complex work by many authors whose view may vary and that the text is open to various plausible interpretations." Also, David Basinger and Randall Basinger, "Inerrancy, Dictation, and the Free Will Defense," *EQ* 55 (July 1983): 177-80, and Stephen J. Wellum, "Divine Sovereignty-Omniscience, Inerrancy, and Open Theism: An Evaluation," *JETS* 45.2 (June 2002): 257-78.

[41] For instance, Sanders on Isaiah 55:8-9, Numbers 23:19, and 1 Samuel 15:29 in *God Who Risks*, 22.

[42] Clark Pinnock, *Mover*, 54-55, lists seven passages that teach sovereignty and answers with his own readings, but the passages he chooses hardly provide the strongest biblical data on the subject (omitting Dan. 4:35 as only one example), not to mention the fact that dismissing seven passages hardly constitutes an answer to this broad biblical strand of data. Critiquing Gregory Boyd's *God At War: The Bible and Spiritual Conflict*, D.A. Carson points out that he emphasizes the strand of biblical evidence that seems to support God's responsiveness but never adduces or significantly discusses the extensive data on God's omniscience—Carson, *Spiritual Warfare*, 260-63.

[43] Pinnock, *God of the Possible*, 75-87. On the one hand, a number of these passages seem to indicate that God can regret or change his mind about something (Gen. 6:6; Exod. 32:14; 1 Sam. 15:11, 35; 2 Sam. 24:16; 1 Chr. 21:15; Isa. 38:1-5; Jer. 15:6; 18:8; 26:3, 13, 19; 42:10; Amos 7:3, 6; Jonah 3:10). On the other hand, a group of passages emphatically teaches that God does not change his mind (Num. 23:19; 1 Sam. 15:29; Ezek. 24:14; Mal. 3:6; 2 Tim. 2:13; Jas. 1:17). The simplest solution (the one with the least epistemic disturbance) is to evaluate the exegetical information more carefully. Conservative commentators have always acknowledged that God changes his stance in response to human actions, such as when he answers prayers or relents in response to repentance. The primary term involved (~x;n") can refer either to an emotion or to capriciously changing one's mind or purposes. See Ronald F. Youngblood, "1, 2 Samuel," in *The Expositor's Bible Commentary*, ed. Tremper Longman III and David E. Garland (Grand Rapids: Zondervan, 2009), 156-57, 160. H. Van Dyke Parunak discusses the translational challenges involved in ~x;n" in "A Semantic Survey of NHiM," *Biblica* 56.4 (1975): 512-32. It is evident that this is the distinction in view in 1 Samuel 15, where both senses appear within a few paragraphs of one another (emotion in v. 11, 35; change of mind in v. 29). If there were not a deeper linguistic phenomenon happening here, even a careless author would have been aware of this obvious discrepancy. The other passages on God's repentance can be resolved in the same or similar ways. This issue also

They regard this line of evidence as sufficient basis to reconstruct theology proper after the openness model. But it is simpler to recognize that God responds differently to changing circumstances—a truth that traditional theists have long acknowledged. God's intentions were authentic before Moses and Hezekiah prayed (Exod. 32:14; 2 Kgs. 20:1-6), and his responses fit the changed circumstance afterwards. Nothing in these passages indicates that he was surprised or caught off guard by the development.[44]

In other cases open theists make remarkable exegetical gaffes or suggest highly improbable readings.[45] As Michael Horton observes, "Open theism has still not provided a serious exegetical account of the passages that clearly indicate that God does not change, does not repent, does not depend on the world for his happiness, and passages that do affirm God's knowledge of and sovereignty over all contingencies of history to the last detail."[46]

Therefore, according to the complementarian model the exegetical problems in open theism have an almost lethal effect on the model's epistemic warrant. To the extent that openness violates biblical propositions, it levies the highest costs, and these problems render it an unsuitable model. With only moderate benefits and extraordinarily high costs, open theism is not a warrantable solution for the antinomies it seeks to resolve.

---

helpfully demonstrates that paradox is not always the best way to understand a conflict, even within complementarity. In this case the issue is probably much simpler—an exegetical difficulty rather than a logical tension. To put this in more analytical terms, the exegetical solution is epistemically warranted because it requires a fairly low epistemic cost while providing a very helpful way to understand the biblical data. This also means that it does not fit the definition of a paradox according to the complementarian model. Whatever the resolution, this exegetical tension is one that even open theists must face, and it will not work to simply ignore one side or the other of the exegetical data. None of these passages requires a reassessment of theology proper according to the openness model, since conservative theologians already recognize that God responds to changing circumstances.

[44] Elsewhere, open theists explain prophetic passages by suggesting that God knows people's character and can predict their responses—even to the specificity of Peter's denial. If this is so, it seems that God should have been able to anticipate instances of horrendous evil and stop them as well. If Jesus could predict that Peter would deny him three times and not only two, it should have been obvious, for instance, the kind of person Hitler would prove to be.

[45] Clark Pinnock, *Mover*, 51, views John 2:19-22 ("Destroy this temple and in three days I will raise it up") as the fulfillment of Ezekiel's temple (Ezek. 40-48). Greg Boyd maintains that Jesus anticipated Peter's denial based on what He knew of Peter's character. He fails to explain, however, how Christ anticipated the three-fold denial or that it would be closely synchronized with the rooster crowing (Mark 14:68-72). Pinnock, *God of the Possible*, 35-37. For Ephesians 1:4 Boyd inserts the qualification that "*whoever chooses* to be 'in Christ' is predestined" (emphasis original), when there is simply no indication of this idea in the passage at all. And yet discussing a different passage on the next page, he comments, "We must be careful not to read into the verse more than is there." Ibid., 47-48.

[46] Horton, "Hellenistic or Hebrew," 330.

If open theism is so epistemically bankrupt, why then has it received credible consideration or even adoption by scholars who acknowledge the authority of Scripture? Quite simply, open theists evaluate the epistemic costs of their model lower and the epistemic benefits higher. Logical resolution (avoiding the appeal to paradox) has an exceedingly high epistemic value—even a critical role in maintaining the coherence of the theological endeavor. Likewise, open theists minimize the exegetical problems in their view and suggest that their readings are superior. The result, then, is that they naturally regard their view as better warranted by increasing the benefits and minimizing the costs.

Yet another epistemic cost is in the practical ramifications that impoverish legitimate theological answers for suffering. Rather than a God who simply allows suffering, open theism argues that he is grieved and shocked by what transpires so that sufferers can look to a God who suffers with them and empathizes with their struggle. But it is hard to see how this is a practical or existential advantage over the more traditional model. To a believer facing catastrophe is it not much of an advantage to think that God took a risk on creating the universe and that there is little he can do to prevent or ameliorate human suffering.[47] Similarly, it nullifies the biblical truth that God designs trials to challenge, shape, and strengthen believers if these circumstances may simply result from God's decision to let free agents exercise their own will. While removing some of the logical sting from the problem of evil, it also removes the meaning and greater purpose of suffering. Most critically, a shocked and hurting God may seem to provide more emotional empathy, but this is not a God that anyone would want to run to for help.[48]

---

[47] Arguing for the openness answer to evil as a practical benefit, Greg Boyd cites the example of a girl who wanted to serve God in Taiwan with her husband. After apparent confirmation from multiple sources, Suzanne married a godly man she met at a Christian college who later turned out to be immoral and abusive. Boyd counseled her that "God felt as much regret over the confirmation he had given Suzanne as he did about his decision to make Saul king of Israel. . . . Not that it was a bad decision—at the time, her ex-husband was a good man with a godly character. The prospects that he and Suzanne would have a happy marriage and fruitful ministry were, at the time, very good. Indeed, I strongly suspect that [God] had influenced Suzanne and her ex-husband toward this college with the marriage in mind." With time, however, the man had exercised his choice as a free agent until he "had become a very different person from the man God had confirmed to Suzanne to be a good candidate for marriage." Pinnock, *God of the Possible*, 106. This may have the appearance of helpful, empathetic counsel, but who would want to trust a God that failed so conspicuously? Should I be comforted that God takes huge risks with my life and often loses his gamble? There is much clearer biblical counsel in the example of Hosea—God sometimes knowingly ordains marriages that will end in conspicuous failure but that will also accomplish greater eternal purposes. This is not an easy answer, but it is both biblically grounded and as a result more practically profitable.

[48] When it comes to God's suffering and grieving empathetically with his creatures, there is no reason that the traditional view of God cannot countenance this. God personally suffered the greatest evil of all time when he bore the sins of the world in the person of his Son. It is hardly necessary to adopt open theism in order for believers to know God's empathetic concern for their suffering.

This is significant because it demonstrates that there are practical reasons to maintain theological paradox. Complementarity fully acknowledges the complex duality between the ultimate reality—full determination in the sovereignty of God—and the phenomenological experience of the creature—real and significant choices that make life and relational interaction meaningful. Though solutions that seem to relieve some logical tension initially seem like an advantage, there is a practical benefit in allowing paradox to have its full biblical proportions. Suffering believers are not to turn to dubious, problematic comforts for their solace; Scripture calls them to humbly rest in the inscrutable wisdom of God.

Conclusion

The literature critically interacting with open theism is already myriad, and like any theological model it can be assessed from a variety of starting points. The preceding discussion seeks to demonstrate that (1) antinomy plays a critical role in open theism, (2) the complementarian model is a helpful analytical grid for evaluating it, and (3) those who accept the existence of paradox and disagree with the exegetical bases of open theism can regard that model as an unwarranted solution.

If theologizing were simply the process of building a self-consistent and serviceable model for thought, open theism might be an elegant solution to some of the most vexing problems theologians face. But theology has an inflexible control—the biblical data, and there can be no more fundamental pre-commitment than to grant that data an absolute epistemic status. The critical fault of the model, therefore, is that it fails to satisfy the demands of exegesis. Using a complementarian method for evaluating support, any such model automatically and immediately fails by contradicting an epistemological standard higher than any other.

Open theism also fails to achieve the goals it is intended to accomplish because it still does not fully resolve the problem of sovereignty and responsibility and the problem of evil. The fact that these biblical tensions cannot be resolved, even within a model as broadly innovative as open theism, testifies to the fact that these problems really are quite intractable. In each of these respects complementarity provides a simpler and more warranted position by limiting the attempts theologians should make at resolution.

Finally, it is critical to acknowledge that open theism illustrates the critical role of paradox for maintaining the traditional view of God and avoiding heretical conclusions. Greg Boyd's argument, for example, seems logically tight and rhetorically powerful when he suggests that

> The only way to deny risks is to maintain that *everything* that occurs in world history is *exactly* what God *wanted* to occur. If anything is other than what God wanted, to that extent he obviously risked not getting what he wanted when he created the world.

So, if God is truly "above" taking risks, then we must accept that things such as sin, child mutilations, and people going to hell are all in accordance with God's will.[49]

The apparent result is that the traditional understanding of God stands on the horns of a difficult dilemma: either God is responsible for evil or he is not in control of everything.[50] But by drawing out the most troublesome possible implications for sovereignty, Boyd has ignored a *tertium quid*: God is in control of every event; he is also not culpable for sin; most importantly, he is not obligated to explain how these two realities relate. Apart from paradox it might appear that we must either deny God's goodness or accept a truncated form of omnipotence and deny clear passages of Scripture in the process. Paradox allows both biblical truths to stand and protects biblical accuracy from the pressures of apparently rationale arguments. As with other doctrinal aberrations in historical theology, open theism illustrates that a *bona fide* theology of paradox is also one of the best protections for biblical orthodoxy.

---

[49] Pinnock, *God of the Possible*, 58.

[50] This over-simplistic reduction is also rather misleading, since the same problem afflicts open theism to the extent that God still has any ability to intervene in earthly events—a concession that Boyd himself makes.

CONCLUSION

The infinite transcendence of God and His consequent incomprehensibility should always constrain us in the profound sense of mystery, awe, and reverence. It is at the highest reaches of our apprehension, understanding, and contemplation that we are most deeply, gratefully, and adoringly aware of the transcendent and incomprehensible glory of God. It is then that we are most truly conscious that God dwells in light unapproachable and full of glory, and we are constrained to exclaim, "Great is the Lord, and greatly to be praised; and his greatness is unsearchable."[1]

This study has spanned a broad spectrum of theological discussions to analyze paradox. It may be helpful to retrace the entire analysis for the sake of clarity. The discussion began by distinguishing three orthodox perspectives on paradox: the *sui generis* view, complementarity, and the paradox-minimizing view, all of which have existed in some form throughout church history. In an attempt to evaluate them, this study also considered biblical and exegetical statements about God's knowledge, concluding that biblical data supports a disjunction between divine and human thoughts. Examples of mystery in systematic theology provide more pertinent data, of which this study considered five: the Trinity, the Incarnation, the problem of evil, divine sovereignty with human responsibility, and the infinity of God. In each case basic biblical data supports propositions leading syllogistically to contradictions. Theologians have proposed various distinctions and clarifications for these conflicts, many of which are quite helpful and legitimate, but they cannot completely solve the problem. Rather, they either move the problem to a different level or they represent it in analytic terms that are as unhelpful as they are undefined.

Recognizing the fact that human knowledge is only a partial representation of the divine, the simplest understanding of the problem is that paradoxical propositions are ultimately coherent in God's understanding. Apparent contradictions arise because foundational propositions involve equivocations that theologians cannot distinguish without further information.

Naturally this leaves an unanswered issue: how can theological reasoning proceed without violating the logical limits of paradox? Theologians must be aware of five basic principles:

- inter-propositional ambiguity,

---

[1] *Minutes of the Fifteenth General Assembly of the Orthodox Presbyterian Church* (Philadelphia: OPC, 1948), 17 (appendix).

- the methodological spiral,
- hermeneutical support and epistemic warrant,
- diminishing epistemic certainty, and
- apophatic inference.

The sufficiency of Scripture offers the confidence that theologians have everything necessary for an honest and sufficient understanding of the truth; the transcendence of God and the noetic limitations of all human knowers insure that human understanding will never be perfect or complete.

Finally, these conclusions have a natural pertinence to open theism. In fact, open theism serves as an excellent case study in the biblical and exegetical failures of a system that fails to clearly analyze the problem of paradox. Open theism is clearly incommensurable with a complementarian model for paradox, both in openness's pre-commitment to mitigate theological tensions wherever possible and in the high epistemic costs it must pay to do so.

Picturing Antinomy

The discussion and conclusions of this study have been almost entirely abstract. Yet there are several visual illustrations for paradox that are quite helpful even though they are imperfect. Edwin Abbot's classic novel, *Flatland*, describes a world of two-dimensional characters.[2] The squares, triangles, and circles living in this plane are utterly incapable of imagining any existence other than the one they have always known, and they reject the idea of three dimensions on this basis. Similarly, several writers have pointed out that two geometric figures might be completely incommensurable in two dimensions.[3] For instance, there is no way to conceive of one figure in two dimensions that is both a triangle and a square. Yet it is entirely possible to combine these or many other shapes when thinking in three dimensions, such as the shape represented in Figure 8.1 (see next page).

Of course, the angle of the viewer dictates the shape he sees, but a flatlander could never explain or comprehend how the two shapes are part of one figure.[4] This illustration also represents the soft epistemic dualism connected with paradox. The flatlander fails to comprehend precisely because his sphere of experience does not allow for the fuller reality.

---

[2] Edwin Abbott, *Flatland* (London: Penguin, 1998).

[3] Christian Cryder, "Reymond's Rejection of Paradox," *TJ* (2001): 105; James Anderson, *Paradox in Christian Theology* (Eugene: Wipf and Stock, 2007), 230-31; C.S. Lewis, *Mere Christianity* (New York: Harper Collins, 2001), 161-63; Hugh Ross, *Beyond the Cosmos* (Colorado Springs: NavPress, 1996), 56.

[4] Putting this in a syllogistic format, this situation exactly parallels the arrangement of theological antinomy. Given the proposition (in the view of a flatlander) that a square is not a triangle, we may reason,
MP: Figure 8.1 is a square.
mp: A square is not a triangle.

Conclusion: Figure 8.1 is not a square and (MP) Figure 8.1 is a square.

Figure 8.1. Geometric Figures in Three Dimensions

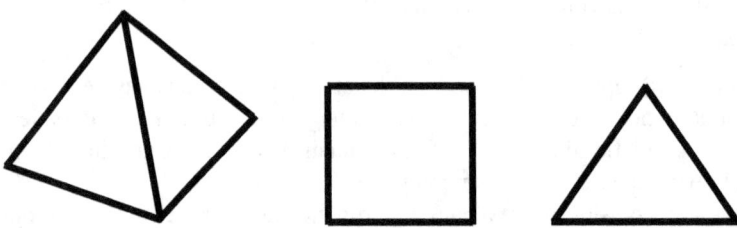

But anyone familiar with three dimensions not only understands that they comport but sees no difficulties with the relationship. Similarly, Scripture describes our present human experience as inchoate and merely provisional compared with the fullness of God's knowledge (Deut. 29:29; Job 11:7-9; 26:14; Rom. 11:33-34).[5] It should be no surprise that theologians cannot integrate certain theological data sets or explain how they relate, but this does not mean they are incommensurable in God's understanding. When Scripture teaches believers to expect that God's knowledge transcends our own, theologians cannot legitimately insist that all theological propositions either fit within their present epistemic frame of reference or they are completely unwarranted on *a priori* bases. One can hardly fault a flatlander for assuming that reality is limited to the frame of reference he knows, but he is culpable for rejecting the clear, verified testimony of someone who transcends his experience. If revelation cannot indicate that two truths are beyond current understanding or comprehension, what will?

Another comparison is more whimsical. A goldfish on someone's desk experiences only what occurs within the cubic space of its aquarium. If a fish could reason, one might imagine it perceiving the outlines of an existence beyond its own. Knowing no other experience by which to evaluate reality, the fish extrapolates from what it knows of the aquarium, making a number of critical assumptions. The fish might reason, for instance, that the universe is cubical, bounded on four sides by a transparent container, or it might infer that all food comes from above, delivered by a massive hand. Whatever the result, the fish will reach a number of absurd conclusions by extrapolating from what it knows to what exists outside of its experience.

Because of revelation, human knowers have warranted basis for realities outside of their experience. But when it comes to questions beyond that revelation, human minds simply do not know what exists. It is possible and tempting to make extrapolations. One might link assumptions together with extended inferential chains in order to derive answers that seem probable. But these answers are as

---

[5] The concept of a fuller epistemic reality—something analogous to a third dimension—does adequately represent how antinomous propositions might relate. But in fact the complementarian model does not even require this concept to be workable. The concept of unarticulated ambiguity works just as readily in the simple epistemic reality we currently experience.

subject to error as the goldfish's extrapolations. Within this comparison the confident declaration that all biblical data must cohere within a specified logical framework seems sophomoric or even arrogant. If human knowers cannot extrapolate with any absolute certainty to answer unknowns, how much more so with data sets that appear to be at odds, given our present limited knowledge?

Practical Implications

A theology of paradox is critical to the theological process and helps to guide what conclusions theologians should infer. But the theology of paradox is hardly limited to the abstract; it also has significant practical consequences. One obvious ramification is epistemological humility. Whether a theologian recognizes it or not, his knowledge of theological realities is only partial. Even the apostle could claim only to "see in a mirror by reflection" (1 Cor. 13:12), and in light of the foolishness of the cross, God declares, "I will destroy the wisdom of the wise, and the discernment of the discerning I will nullify" (1 Cor. 1:19), so that the "the one who boasts, let him boast in the Lord" (1 Cor. 1:31).[6] The clearest and most emphasized conclusion in the exegetical data on paradox is the fact that God's knowledge transcends our understanding. There is a candid epistemological humility in recognizing that the most penetrating theological observations are only vague outlines of the overwhelming reality.[7] As with apologetics, Scripture provides sufficiently warranted answers to questions, but it never stoops to submit to the demands of human minds. Rather, unexplained biblical tensions force the mind to accept truth on the basis of revelation. With each biblical antinomy believers have no choice but to humbly submit to biblical authority and accept biblical propositions as they stand. Theological investigation should always leave the student marveling at the immensity of God's incomprehensible truth and deeply aware of the limits of our knowledge.

---

[6] Of course, this is written in opposition to the prevailing pressures against the gospel—Jewish requirements for confirmatory wonders, and the Greek evaluation according to earthly wisdom (v. 12). The gospel is intentionally counter-cultural in this respect, not bowing to the epistemic requirements of its hearers, compelling them instead to bow humbly before the cross of Christ alone. In a post-enlightenment context, might it be equally counter-cultural that God's truth refuses to bow before the demand for exhaustive explanations? Indeed, it counters the universal human tendency of self-sufficient and autonomous epistemology that God's words demand humble submission to his truth without his answering every question or problem that human knowers might raise. Gordon Fee, *The First Epistle to the Corinthians* (Grand Rapids: Eerdmans, 1987), 75, comments that the cross and specifically "Christ crucified is a contradiction in terms, of the same category as 'fried ice.' One may have a Messiah, or one may have a crucifixion; but one may not have both—at least not from the perspective of merely human understanding."

[7] Job confesses this truth in Job 26:14, based on the immensity and power of God's works in creation. Even with the observational power of modern astronomy, humankind has yet to reach the end of the created universe. Perhaps this immensity is intended as a massive, physically embodied illustration of how far God transcends human fractional knowledge.

Second, this kind of intellectual humility also serves as a guard against error. Academicians in general and theologians in particular chronically allow their confidence to outstretch their knowledge. It is far too tempting to answer questions on scanty or nearly non-existent evidence rather than admit that we simply do not know. In fact, the limits of our knowledge should serve as a protection against aberrant theology. Nicaea and Chalcedon reaffirmed the foundational exegetical data but never fully integrated the propositions, proposing a partial apophatism to limit further speculation.[8] In contrast, most of the Trinitarian and Christological heresies arose from the unguarded attempt at logically explaining how foundational theological propositions relate.[9] Pelagianism, likewise, violated biblical data in the attempt to integrate logically the problem of sovereignty and responsibility. Hyper-calvinistic models intimating that God may not be completely grieved by evil fail for the same reason. Most recently open theism is an aberrant theological model that goes awry by trying to explain too much.

Third, the theology of paradox also functions as a reminder about the nature of biblical faith. Though biblical truth is not fideistically grounded, faith ultimately rests on God's authority and not on any human epistemological criteria. Revelation moves on God's agenda, not ours. Biblical faith, therefore, necessarily includes a component of silent trust—the willingness to accept revealed truth as it stands and believe without demanding a complete explanation. In the words of Solomon, "God is in heaven and you are on earth; therefore let your words be few" (Ecc. 5:2).

Fourth, it is also crucial to recognize that God's wisdom in revelation pertains to what is not revealed as well as what is. God has not revealed or explained every truth or logical relationship. Theologians ought to seek greater understanding and propose models where it is tenable to do so, but it is illegitimate to hypothesize and then confidently assert logical models that are neither revealed nor epistemologically warranted. Like the information that God told John not to record in Revelation 10:4, the logical lacunae in antinomy perform a critical role: they remind the attentive reader of his epistemic limits and ignorance in the face of God's immensity.

Finally, one of the practical ramifications with the most exegetical support is the theology of silence. Scripture sometimes raises difficult theological questions for which the only response is silence. This response appears in a number of contexts. Job struggled to understand the evil that befell him. While it is over-simplistic to characterize the book as a discussion of the problem of evil, it is certainly central to the book. Specifically, Job struggles with why God sends evil upon righteous people. On the converse side of the struggle, Job is keenly aware that wicked people often avoid suffering (Job 21:7-21). Simply put, Job seeks for the reason or purpose behind suffering and struggles because it seems morally unfair.[10]

---

[8] Millard J. Erickson, *Christian Theology* (Grand Rapids: Baker, 1998), 746-47.

[9] E.L. Mascall, *Via Media* (Greenwich: Seabury Press, 1957), 79-90.

[10] The central issue of the book is the over-simplistic retributionist theology of Job's friends, and to some extent, Job himself. God corrects Job's faulty assumption that blessings or catastrophes from God are directly linked to human actions. Even though this issue is

Conclusion

There are biblical truths that God could have given to Job. The New Testament truth that God uses suffering to refine believers is a partial answer to Job's problem.[11] Much simpler, God could have clued Job in to the drama that had unfolded in heaven between Satan's challenges and God's confidence in Job's character. In essence, this would have been a situation-specific form of a common theodicy—God has purposes that transcend our suffering. But shockingly, there is no indication that Job ever knew that the interchange happened. The reader finishes the book understanding a critical detail about Job's suffering that he himself never received.[12]

In place of turning Job's understanding to either of these basic truths, the book ends with God's demand that Job simply trust. The ultimate answer to Job's struggle is that God completely transcends human understanding. In Job 38-41 God replies that Job does not even understand the things God has created, much less the Creator himself. Accepting God's rebuke, Job humbly acknowledges that he cannot comprehend God or his ways. In the process Job illustrates the appropriate response to God's transcendence: humble, worshipping silence. Job confesses that in demanding that God give him answers, he has tried to stretch beyond what is right for him to ask, and there is a component of arrogance in his demands (Job 40:3-5; 42:1-6). The central tenet of the book, therefore, is that God is beyond human comprehension and that he is not required to answer every human question. For such theological issues the only right response is the silence of faith.

---

different from the problem of evil, the basic answer is the same: God's purposes transcend any simple solutions. The factor that made this problem significant for Job was probably the degree of his suffering. Had he suffered a smaller catastrophe he might have assumed that God had sent retribution for some personal failure or even that it was merely an inevitable disappointment. But the overwhelming combination of so many catastrophes perfectly choreographed together forced Job to recognize that God had singled him out for some reason (observe the repetition of "while he was still speaking" in Job 1:13-19). This is similar to the problem of evil, where the challenges are much greater with gratuitous evil. It is easier to see divine purposes served by minimal evil but harder to perceive any good in the senseless suffering or deaths of thousands in world catastrophes. Still, both moderate and extreme cases of suffering are subject to the same analysis and the same basic conclusion.

[11] It is critical to the story that Job's catastrophe did not primarily arise because of his failures—D.A. Carson, *How Long, O Lord?* (Grand Rapids: Baker, 1990) 158-59. The central issue in the narrative is the honor of God before the slander of Satan—Layton Talbert, *Beyond Suffering* (Greenville, S.C.: Bob Jones University Press, 2007), 28-34, 35-47. It is completely invalid to understand Job 23:10 as Job, being purified through trial (137-41). Of course, it is also true that the trial drove Job to a fuller, richer understanding of God.

[12] One cannot but wonder about Job's response to another common defense. If God had simply explained that by creating free actors he had given up full control of every event, would Job have been comforted and drawn to greater dependence on the Almighty? On the contrary the book depicts God as utterly controlling every part of Job's suffering, permitting Satan to send only the afflictions that God ordains. It is significant that the book that most discusses the problem of suffering also emphasizes God's complete control of every detail in the process.

Habakkuk asked similar questions when God revealed the impending destruction of Judah. Like Job, Habakkuk demands an answer as to how God can spare the wicked while punishing a people more righteous than they (Hab. 1:13; 2:1).[13] The final answer to his questions, however, is silence (Hab. 2:30; 3:16). Those who are aware of God's nature and realize the marvel of his dwelling with humanity can only respond in quiet awe.[14]

While teaching God's sovereignty in salvation, Paul acknowledges the problem of how God can hold people responsible for saving faith if his own agency is integrally involved (Rom. 9:19-21).[15] While God's right of ownership as creator is part of the answer, Paul also reminds the reader that God is not obligated to answer every question and bases this conclusion on divine transcendence.[16]

A number of other texts also commend or even enjoin a response of silence (Eccl. 5:2; Ps. 46:10; 131:1-3). In each of these examples, difficult theological questions arise for which the biblical text ultimately enjoins the response of trusting faith. A similar group of passages forbid asking unanswerable questions. The Pastoral Epistles contain a thematic strand demanding that there are certain questions that should not be asked or issues that should not be investigated (1 Tim. 1:4; 4:6; 6:3, 20; 2 Tim. 3:14-16; 4:2; Titus 1:9, 13). The point is quite clear that Timothy and Titus should be wary of distorting the truth by focusing on unknown concerns. Instead the Pastoral Epistles command preoccupation with those truths that have been revealed (1 Tim. 1:4; 4:6; 6:4, 20; 2 Tim. 2:14; 3:7; 4:4; Titus 1:14;

---

[13] Habakkuk's struggle is not with the existence of suffering per se, but the moral problem of how God can be causally linked to sin by using a wicked nation to punish his people.

[14] It is no accident that in chapter 3 Habakkuk turns to extolling the majesty of God (3:2-15), nor that the final answer is to find contentment in the satisfying sufficiency of God's person (3:17-19).

[15] It is true that Paul goes on to answer part of the question: God creates according to his own purposes for the sake of his own glory. But, in fact, Paul never answers the question his hypothetical opponent raises which is actually regarding the moral justice of God's dealings—how God can hold people responsible (v. 19). Instead of providing a theodicy on this point, Paul's response is to rebuke the insinuation that questions God's moral character. See Leon Morris, *The Epistle to the Romans* (Grand Rapids: Eerdmans, 1997), 364-66; Douglas Moo, *The Epistle to the Romans* (Grand Rapids: Eerdmans, 1996), 601-602.

[16] It is interesting and probably significant that the examples discussed here all involve the problem of evil in some way. In general the problem of suffering is the paradox that believers struggle with the most, because it has the greatest emotional potency. Romans 9 may be the only exception, since while involving the problem of evil, it is mostly concerned with the moral problem of divine sovereignty and human responsibility. When believers face tragedy or disappointment, most naturally ask why God allowed their challenging circumstances. The best biblical answer for these questions is that we simply do not know. The biblical solution frees sufferers to set their questions aside and turn to the person that is greater than the questions that suffering brings. See Carson, *How Long, O Lord?*, 243-46.

Conclusion

3:9). The implication is that theological investigation should accept its own limits, and investigation beyond these limits is simply presumption.[17]

All of this data could be summarized in several propositions:

> (1) Silence is an appropriate and meaningful response to some theological problems because it affirms that not everything can be known or understood.
>
> (2) Not every question should be asked, because some problems must remain unresolved.
>
> (3) Full logical explanation or even complete logical resolution is not required as a prerequisite for faith. In fact, God sometimes gives only certain propositions and demands that we accept them without a full explanation. This kind of trusting faith is not merely pietistic fideism; it has a solid basis in clear exegesis.

Theologians must also recognize that not every question should be asked. Even clearer, not every question has a simple answer, nor should theologians always seek for one. Whatever conclusions a theologian might draw, he has not adequately grappled with all of the data until he is willing to remain silent on some questions. Scripture and genuine faith require us to limit our own theologizing. As a result, systematic theology must be self-limiting in order to take into account all of the exegetical data on silence.

Considerations for Further Study

As with almost any extended study, the process of investigating only reveals more questions worthy of further investigation. There are several areas that are particularly worthy of further detailed thought. First, this discussion has provided only a basic, general evaluation of the five examples of paradox. Future studies could extend and test the model proposed here with each specific issue. This is particularly true of the exegetical basis for each, though more work can be done with historical analysis as well.[18] It is even possible that other examples of paradox exist that have not been considered here.[19]

---

[17] In keeping with the Pastoral Epistles' emphasis on doctrine that produces right living, these passages warn against empty disputes because they distract from the truth or from the commands that should dictate believers' lives. In 1 Timothy 6:4, 20, false teachers ask needless questions so that they can obscure what is genuinely true. In all of these ways, the warnings in the Pastoral Epistles parallel the concerns of Deuteronomy 29:29.

[18] James Anderson, *Paradox in Christian Theology*, 11-106, has already given extended discussion to paradox in the Trinity and Incarnation, but his concern is largely with the historical orthodox formulations and the historical support they have enjoyed. As he suggests, further exegetical analysis with these two examples might demonstrate an even clearer pattern for where distinction and unity lie. The other three antinomies require further discussion both in exegesis and in historical theology.

[19] One possible example is creation *ex nihilo*—how it is possible that God brought everything out of nothing when this is a complete impossibility from the standpoint of mathematics and physics. See Cryder, "Reymond's Rejection of Paradox," 105-106. This is an imperfect example because only one side of the tension is clear in Scripture. It is quite possible that it could be subsumed under the same category as omnipresence and

This also points to an especially pertinent contemporary issue: open theism. As was pointed out, the problem of evil and the tension of sovereignty and free will combine into a tightly interrelated apologetic problem. Open theism has sought to unravel the problem by aggressively redefining or even negating God's sovereignty. The present study made some critical assessments of open theism, but the innovations openness makes on the biblical view are much more involved and are also ongoing. An entire thesis could effectively focus on the problems with how open theism has handled paradox.[20]

Third, this study suggested not only a process for identifying paradox but also guidelines for drawing valid inferences from paradoxical propositions. Future studies could extend and evaluate this model in light of historical and philosophical theology. For the former, studies might investigate what inferences the church has historically drawn from antinomies and evaluate them according to the complementarian model. Carrying out further evaluation in philosophical theology, this model might be further integrated with Plantinga's theory of warrant and assessed in its broader implications for theological prolegomena.[21] This investigation might also assess the degree to which inferentially derived antinomous pairs of propositions are genuinely distinct tensions, or whether they are merely the same antinomy stated in a different form.

Finally, the survey of church history offered here is only cursory, and an extended analysis could profitably trace the concept of paradox through each period of church history. Though an extended discussion of the Trinity and the Incarnation already exists, the problem of evil or the tension of divine sovereignty and human responsibility are two areas that could be quite fruitful.

God's relationship with time, but it is still a possibility worth considering. Another possibility is the tension between believers' positional standing in salvation and their experiential responsibility in sanctification. This might be easily subsumed under the tension between sovereignty and responsibility, but it is still distinct enough with a unique set of propositions that it could merit significant study from a complementarian standpoint. John Frame suggests Adam and Eve's innocent holiness with the fact that they somehow chose to sin, but this fits best under the problem and origin of evil. See John M. Frame, "Logic," in *Dictionary for Theological Interpretation of Scripture*, ed. Kevin J. Vanhoozer (Grand Rapids: Baker, 2005), 464.

[20] Jon Tal Murphree critically assesses open theism from the standpoint of paradox in *Divine Paradoxes: A Finite View of an Infinite God* (Camp Hill, Pa.: Christian Publications, 1998). Nevertheless, his work does not at all fulfill this need. First, Murphree defines paradox as "sets of concepts that initially seem to be contradictory but upon closer scrutiny will be understood as complementary. In no way am I referring to antinomies or contradictions" (13). Second, Murphree is quite sympathetic to openness. This work essentially reaches the same conclusions as open theism but attempts to support it on bases that are less theologically revisionist.

[21] James Anderson comments that his apologetic model for paradox builds on the foundations laid by both Van Til and Plantinga. James Anderson, interview by Camden Bucey, *Paradox in Christian Theology*, http://reformedforum.org/ctc132/, July 23, 2010.

Conclusion

The Relationship of Paradox and Revelation

It is critical to acknowledge that the central issue of theological prolegomena is not paradox but revelation. This is evident in a number of respects. Unknowns are a reality; they are a necessary and unavoidable part of the theological process. But they occupy a very small role in light of the immense truth that believers have been given—revelation that is utterly sufficient for all that is necessary in their Christian experience. Christianity is a religion of propositional truth revealed from God, not a fideistic mash of contradictions offered as dialectic theology. Any view of paradox that mitigates the authority of revealed truth is aberrant and definitively unwarranted.[22]

The fact that revelation far exceeds paradox in the theological process is no reason to ignore paradox, however, because in a number of specific ways, paradox and revelation have a mutually reinforcing, compatible relationship. First, the ambition to delineate epistemic limits does not encroach on revealed knowledge; it only specifies more clearly what can and cannot be known. A better awareness of these epistemic limits, in fact, protects theology from illegitimate conclusions.

Second, paradox rests on the sufficiency of Scripture—believers have been given everything they need for salvation and relationship with God. While this doctrine exalts what has been revealed, one corollary is that unanswered questions cannot be critical to the Christian experience. Wayne Grudem writes, "The sufficiency of Scripture also tells us that God does not require us to believe anything about himself or his redemptive work that is not found in Scripture."[23] On this basis it is not acceptable to elevate correlating models and distinctions as nonnegotiable requirements for theological intelligibility.

Third, a high view of revelation actually requires theologians to acknowledge the limitations of their models, since Scripture itself testifies to the limitedness of human knowledge and alludes to the fact that God has not revealed all truth. Biblical revelation is ultimately the foundation behind every instance of paradox; the complementarian definition requires two propositional data sets supported in Scripture. In such a case, a high view of Scripture allows theologians to assert both sides of the tension confidently without excessive concern for their interrelationship. Complementarity, then, is a reminder that biblical authority stands above any other. If Scripture teaches two truths that are in logical tension with each other, there is no recourse but to accept both sides of the tension as they stand, even without a clear logical correlation.

In each of these ways paradox ultimately points the believer not to unknowns but to revealed theological realities. Complementarity does not have to collapse into

---

[22] Carl F.H. Henry, *God, Revelation and Authority* (Waco: Word, 1976), 2:47-57.

[23] As Wayne Grudem, *Systematic Theology* (Grand Rapids: Zondervan, 1994), 127, defines it, "The sufficiency of Scripture means that Scripture contained all the words of God he intended his people to have at each stage of redemptive history, and that it now contains all the words of God we need for salvation, for trusting him perfectly, and for obeying him perfectly." He goes on to provide helpful qualifications for how we understand the doctrine.

negative theology or fideism. Rather, by candidly acknowledging the limits of knowledge, it drives us back to the truths that are revealed and calls us to submit to them. The alternative is to place so much importance on finding logical resolution that the focus shifts away from the biblical text to extra-biblical distinctions and "necessary" qualifications to the biblical data.[24] By simply accepting the tensions as unknowns, complementarity allows the emphasis to remain on the truth that is revealed. This is apparently the exact contextual concern of Deuteronomy 29:29—"The hidden things belong to Yahweh our God, but the revealed things to us and to our sons forever, in order for us to do all the words of this law."

Conclusion

The question of paradox in Christian theology has broad and critical implications that extend throughout theological prolegomena. But the fact that human minds cannot penetrate beyond the surface of theological understanding should also guide the thinking of every believer. The questions that Scripture chooses not to answer are part of the divine intentions of revelation alongside of the truths that Scripture does explain. There are times in the experience of every believer when confusion and questioning must bow before the majestic transcendence of God. In the final analysis the only proper response is silent faith, trusting that God alone can account for the unanswered questions of theology. Bowing before his majesty, we can only marvel at the beauty too great to know or comprehend.

> Can you solve the mysteries of God?
> Can you venture as far as the limits of the Almighty?
>
> They are higher than the heavens—what can you do?
> They are deeper than Sheol—what can you know?
>
> They measure longer than the earth
> and broader than the sea.
>
> Job 11:7-9

---

[24] Naturally most thinkers regard their solutions to biblical paradoxes as warranted because they are clear and necessary inferences from the biblical data. But one does wonder why there should be so much ambiguity or outright difference of opinion on how to resolve each paradoxical proposition if the inferential relationship is in fact so clear.

BIBLIOGRAPHY

Abbott, Edwin. *Flatland.* London: Penguin Classics, 1998.

Abelard, Peter. *Historia Calamitatum.* Translated by Henry Adams Bellows. New York: William Edwin Rudge, 1922.

Adams, Jay E. *The Grand Demonstration: a Biblical Study of the So-Called Problem of Evil.* Santa Barbara: EastGate, 1991.

Anderson, James. Interview by Camden Bucey. *Paradox in Christian Theology* http://reformedforum.org/ctc132/. July 23, 2010.

———. *Paradox in Christian Theology.* Waynesboro, Ga.: Paternoster, 2007.

Aquinas, Thomas. *Summa Theologica.* Translated by Fathers of the English Dominican Province. 3 vols. New York: Benziger Bros., 1947-1948.

Augustine, St. *The Confessions of St. Augustine.* Translated by J. G. Pilkington. Edinburgh: T & T Clark, 1876.

Austin, William H. "Complementarity and Theological Paradox." *Zygon*, December 1967: 365-381.

———. *Waves, Particles, and Paradoxes.* Houston: William Marsh Rice University, 1967.

Basinger, David. "Biblical Paradox: Does Revelation Challenge Logic?" *JETS* 30, no. 2 (June 1987): 205-213.

———. *Divine Power in Process Theism: A Philosophical Critique.* Albany: State University of New York Press, 1988.

———. "Practical Considerations." In *The Openness of God*, 155-176. Downers Grove: InterVarsity, 1994.

Basinger, David. *The Case for Freewill Theism: A Philosophical Assessment.* Downers Grove: InterVarsity, 1996.

Basinger, David, and Randall Basinger. "Inerrancy, Dictation, and the Free Will Defense." *EQ* 55 (1983): 177-180.

Bauder, Kevin T., "Shall We Reason Together? Part Seven: Probability and the Limits of Logic." In the Nick of Time, Central Seminary. October 27, 2006.

———. "In the Nick of Time." *Central Seminary.* November 3, 2006. http://www.centralseminary.edu/publications/20061103.pdf (accessed March 19, 2010).

Bavinck, Herman. *Reformed Dogmatics.* Edited by John Bolt. Translated by John Vriend. Vol. 2. Grand Rapids: Baker, 2004.

Beale, B.K and Benjamin Glad, *Hidden But Now Revealed*. Downers Grove: Intervarsity, 2014.

Beeley, Christopher A. *Gregory of Nazianzus on the Trinity and the Knowledge of God.* New York: Oxford University Press, 2008.

Berkhof, Louis. *Systematic Theology.* Edinburgh: Banner of Truth, 2000.

Boa, Kenneth. *God, I Don't Understand.* Colorado Springs: Victor, 2007.

Bock, Darrell L. "Covenants in Progressive Dispensationalism." In *Three Central Issues in Contemporary Dispensationalism*, edited by Herbert W. Bateman, 169-203. Grand Rapids: Kregel, 1999.

———. *Luke.* Vol. 2 in Baker Exegetical Commentaries. Grand Rapids: Baker, 1996.

Boyd, Gregory A. *God at War: The Bible and Spiritual Conflict.* Downers Grove: InterVarsity, 1997.

———. *God of the Possible.* Grand Rapids: Baker, 2000.

———. *Satan and the Problem of Evil: Constriucting a Trinitarian Warfare Theodicy.* Downers Grove: InterVarsity, 2001.

Boyer, Stephen D., and Christopher A. Hall, *The Mystery of God* (Grand Rapids: Baker Academic, 2012)

Brümmer, Vincent. *The Model of Love.* Cambridge: Cambridge University Press, 1993.

Broadie, Alexander. "Duns Scotus and William Ockam." In *The Medieval Theologians*, edited by G. R. Evans, 250-265. Malden, Mass.: Blackwell, 2001.

Broadus, John A. *Commentary on Matthew.* Grand Rapids: Kregel, 1990.

Calvin, John *Institutes of the Christian Religion.* Translated by John Allen. Vol. 1. 2 vols. Philadelphia: Presbyterian Board of Publication and Sabbath-School Work, 1921.

Canham, Michael McGhee. "Potuit Non Peccare or Non Potuit Peccare: Evangelicals, Hermeneutics, and the Impeccability Debate." *Master's Seminary Journal* 11, no. 1 (Spring 2000): 93-114.

Carson, D. A. "A Sketch of the Factors Determining Current Hermeneutical Debate in Cross-Cultural Contexts ." In *Biblical Interpretation and the Church: Text and Context*, edited by D. A. Carson, 11-29. Grand Rapids: Baker, 1984.

———. *Divine Sovereignty and Human Responsibility.* Eugene, Oreg.: Wipf and Stock, 1994.

———. "God, The Bible And Spiritual Warfare: A Review Article." *JETS* 42, no. 2 (June 1999): 251-270.

———. "How Can We Reconcile the Love and the Transcendent Sovereignty of God?" In *God Under Fire: Modern Scholarship*

Reinvents God, by Douglas S. Huffman and Eric L. Johnson, 279-312. Grand Rapids: Zondervan, 2002.

———. *How Long, O Lord?* Grand Rapids: Baker, 1990.

———. "Unity and Diversity in the New Testament: The Possibility of Systematic Theology." In *Scripture and Truth*, edited by D. A. Carson and John D. Woodbridge, 65-95. Grand Rapids: Baker, 1992.

Cartwright, Richard. "On the Logical Problem of the Trinity." In *Philosophical Essays*, 187-200. Cambridge, Mass.: The MIT Press, 1987.

Chafer, Lewis Sperry. *Systematic Theology.* Dallas: Dallas Seminary Press, 1948.

Chesterton, G. K. *Introduction to the Book of Job.* London: S. Wellwood, 1907.

Clairvaux, Saint Bernard of. *Life and Works of Saint Bernard.* Edited by John Mabillon. Translated by Samuel J. Eales. Vol. 2. New York: Burns and Oates Limited, 1889.

Clark, Gordon H. "The Bible As Truth." *Bibliotheca Sacra*, April 1957: 157-170.

———. "Determinism and Responsibility." *EQ*, Jan 1932: 13-23.

———. *God and Evil: The Problem Solved.* Unicoi, Tenn.: Trinity Foundation, 2004.

———. *The Incarnation.* Jefferson, Md.: The Trinity Foundation, 1988.

———. *Language and Theology.* Phillipsburg, N.J.: P&R, 1980.

———. *Logic.* Unicoi, Tenn.: The Trinity Foundation, 1998.

———. *Religion, Reason and Revelation.* Philadelphia: P&R, 1961.

———. "Reply to Ronald H. Nash." In *The Philosophy of Gordon H. Clark: A Festschrift*, edited by Ronald H. Nash, 403-419. Philadelphia: P&R, 1968.

———. *The Trinity*. Jefferson, Mass.: The Trinity Foundation, 1985.

Clark, R. Scott. "Janus, the Well-Meant Offer of the Gospel, and Westminster Theology." In *The Pattern of Sound Doctrine: Systematic Theology at the Westminster Serminaries*, edited by David Van Drunen. Phillipsburg, N.J.: P&R, 2004.

Clarke, William Newton. *An Outline of Christian Theology*. New York: Charles Scribner's Sons, 1900.

Clendenin, Daniel B. "God is Great, God is Good: Questions About Evil." *Ashland Theological Journal* 24 (1992): 35-54.

Coakley, Sarah. "What Does Chalcedon Solve and What Does it Not? Some Reflections on the Status and Meaning of the Chalcedonian Definition." In *The Incarnation: An Interdisciplinary Symposium on the Incarnation of the Son of God*, by Stephen T. Davis, Daniel Kendall and Gerald O'Collins, 143-163. Oxford: Oxford University Press, 2004.

Colijn, Brenda B. "A Parable of Calvinism." *Ashland Theological Journal* 36 (2004): 101-108.

Collins, Brian. "Scripture, Hermeneutics, and Theology: Evaluating Theological Interpretation of Scripture." Ph.D. dissertation, Bob Jones University, 2011.

Compton, R. Bruce. "Persevering and Falling Away: A Reexamination of Hebrews 6:4-6." *Detroit Baptist Seminary Journal* 1 (Spring 1996): 135-170.

Craig, William Lane. "Hugh Ross's Extra-Dimensional Deity: A Review Article." *JETS*, June 1999: 293-304.

———. *The Existence of God and the Beginning of the Universe*. San Bernardino: Here's Life Publishers, 1979.

Crawford, Thomas J. *The Mysteries of Christianity.* London: William Blackwood and Sons, 1874.

Cross, Richard. *Duns Scotus.* New York: Oxford University Press, 1999.

Cryder, Christian. "Reymond's Rejection of Paradox." *Trinity Journal* 22 (2001): 99-112.

Dabney, Robert Lewis. *Systematic Theology.* Edinburgh: Banner of Truth Trust, 1985.

Dahms, John V. "A Trinitarian Epistemology Defended: A Rejoinder to Norman Geisler." *JETS* 22 (June 1979): 133-148.

———. "How Reliable is Logic?" *JETS* 21, no. 4 (December 1978): 369-380.

Davis, Stephen T. "John Hick on Incarnation and Trinity." In *The Trinity*, edited by Stephen T. Davis, Daniel Kendall and Gerald O'Collins, 251-272. Oxford: Oxford University Press, 1999.

———. *Logic and the Nature of God.* Grand Rapids: Eerdmans, 1983.

Davis, William C. "Why Open Theism is Flourishing Now." In *Beyond the Bounds*, edited by John Piper, Justin Taylor and Paul Kjoss Helseth. Wheaton: Crossway, 2003.

Dowey, Edward A., Jr. *The Knowledge of God in Calvin's Theology.* Grand Rapids: Eerdmans, 1994.

Dupré, Louis K. *Religious Mystery and Rational Reflection.* Grand Rapids: Eerdmans, 1998.

Ebner, James H. *God Present As Mystery: A Search for Personal Meaning in Contemporary Theology.* Winona, Minn.: St. Mary's College, 1976.

Ellingworth, Paul. *The Epistle to the Hebrews.* Grand Rapids: Eerdmans, 2007.

Elmer, Daniel. "Critique of John Sanders and Clark Pinnock on the Prophetic Necessity and Certainty of the Crucifixion." Th.M. thesis, Capital Bible Seminary, 2007.

Elwell, Walter A. *Baker Theological Dictionary of the Bible.* Grand Rapids: Baker, 1996.

Erickson, Millard J. *Christian Theology.* Grand Rapids: Baker, 1998.

Evans, C. Stephen. *Faith Beyond Reason.* Grand Rapids: Eerdmans, 1998.

———. *Why Believe?* Grand Rapids: Eerdmans, 1996.

Evans, G. R. *The Language and Logic of the Bible: The Earlier Middle Ages.* New York: Cambridge University Press, 1984.

Farrelly, M. John. *The Trinity: Rediscovering the Central Christian Mystery.* New York: Sheed & Ward, 2005.

Fee, Gordon. *The First Epistle to the Corinthians* in NICNT. Grand Rapids: Eerdmans, 1987.

Feinberg, John. *No One Like Him.* Wheaton: Crossway, 2001.

———. *The Many Faces of Evil: Theological Systems and the Problems of Evil.* Wheaton: Crossway, 2004.

Foh, Susan T. *Women and the Word of God: A Response to Biblical Feminism.* Philadelphia: P&R, 1979.

Frame, John M. *Apologetics to the Glory of God.* Phillipsburg, N.J.: P&R, 1994.

———. *Cornelius Van Til: An Analysis of His Thought.* Phillipsburg, N.J.: P&R, 1995.

Frame, John M. *The Doctrine of God.* Phillipsburg, N.J.: P&R, 2002.

———. *The Doctrine of the Knowledge of God.* Phillipsburg, N.J.: P&R, 1987.

———. "Logic." In *Dictionary for Theological Interpretation of Scripture*, edited by Kevin J. Vanhoozer, 462-464. Grand Rapids: Baker, 2005.

———. "Muller on Theology." *Westminster Theological Journal* 56, no. 1 (Spring 1994): 133-152.

———. *No Other God: A Response to Open Theism.* Phillipsburg, N.J.: P&R, 2001.

———. "The Problem of Evil." In *Suffering and the Goodness of God*, edited by Christopher W. Morgan and Robert A. Peterson, 141-164. Wheaton: Crossway, 2008.

———. *Van Til, the Theologian.* Phillipsburg, N.J.: Pilgrim Publishing, n.d.

France, R. T. *The Gospel of Mark.* Grand Rapids: Eerdmans, 2002.

Fretheim, Terence E. !yb. Vol. 1, in *New International Dictionary of Old Testament Theology and Exegesis*, edited by Willem A. VanGemeren, 652-653. Grand Rapids: Zondervan, 1997.

Gale, Richard M. "Time, Temporality and Paradox." In *The Blackwell Guide to Metaphysics*, 66-86. Malden, Mass.: Blackwell, 2002.

Geisler, Norman. "Avoid All Contradictions: A Surrejoinder to John Dahms." *JETS* 22, no. 2 (June 1979): 149-159.

———. "'Avoid... Contradictions' (1 Timothy 6:20): A Reply to John Dahms." *JETS* 22, no. 1 (March 1979): 55-65.

Geisler, Norman. "The Incarnation and Logic: Their Compatibility Defended." *Trinity Journal* 6, no. 2 (Fall 1985): 185-197.

———. *Systematic Theology.* Vol. 2. Minneapolis: Bethany House, 2003.

Good, Kenneth H. *Are Baptists Reformed?* Lorain, Ohio: Regular Baptist Heritage Fellowship, 1986.

Goulder, Michael. "Paradox and Mystification." In *Is the Doctrine of the Incarnation Logically Coherent?*, edited by Michael Goulder, 51-59. Grand Rapids: Eerdmans, 1979.

Grounds, Vernon C. "The Postulate of Paradox." *BETS* 7 (1964): 3-21.

Grudem, Wayne. *Systematic Theology*. Grand Rapids: Zondervan, 1994.

Halsey, Jim. "A Preliminary Critique of Van Til: The Theologian—A Review Article." *Westminster Theological Journal*, Fall 1976: 120-137.

Hamlyn, D. W. *Analytic and Synthetic Statements*. Vol. 1, in *The Encyclopedia of Philosophy*, edited by Paul Edwards, 105-109. New York: Macmillan, 1967.

Harris, Murray J. *The Second Epistle to the Coprinthians*. Grand Rapids: Eerdmans, 2005.

Hart, D. G., and John Muether. *Fighting the Good Fight*. Philadelphia: Orthodox Presbyterian Church, 1995.

Hartley, John E. *The Book of Job*. Grand Rapids: Eerdmans, 1988.

Hartshorne, Charles. *The Divine Relativity*. New Haven: Yale University Press, 1982.

Hasker, William. "A Philosophical Perspective." In *The Openness of God*, 126-154. Downers Grove: InterVarsity, 1994.

———. *God, Time, and Knowledge*. Ithaca: Cornell University, 1989.

———. *Providence, Evil and the Openness of God*. New York: Routledge, 2004.

———. *The Triumph of God over Evil*. Downers Grove: InterVarsity, 2008.

Heim, Karl. *Jesus the World's Perfecter.* Philadelphia: Muhlenberg, 1961.

Helm, Paul. *Eternal God.* Oxford: Clarendon, 1988.

———. *The Providence of God.* Downers Grove: InterVarsity, 1994.

Helseth, Paul K. "On Divine Ambivalence: Open Theism And The Problem Of Particular Evils ." *JETS* (September 2001): 493-512.

Helseth, Paul K. "Neo-Molinism: A Traditional-Openness Rapprochement?" *Southern Baptist Journal of Theology* 7, no. 3 (Fall 2003): 56-73.

Henebury, Paul. "Robert Reymond's Systematic Theology: A Dispensational Appraisal." *Conservative Theological Journal* (August 2004): 245-272.

Henry, Carl F.H. *God, Revelation and Authority.* Vol. 2. 6 vols. Waco: Word, 1976.

———. *God, Revelation and Authority.* Vol. 5. Waco: Word, 1982.

Hepburn, Ronald W. *Christianity and Paradox: Critical Studies in Twentieth-Century Theology.* New York: Pegasus, 1968.

Hick, John. "Jesus and the World Religions." In *The Myth of God Incarnate*, edited by John Hick, 167-185. Philadelphia: Westminster Press, 1977.

Highfield, Ron. "The Function Of Divine Self-Limitation In Open Theism: Great Wall Or Picket Fence?" *JETS* 45, no. 2 (June 2002): 279-300.

Hodge, A. A. *A Commentary on the Confession of Faith.* Philadelphia: Presbyterian Board of Publication and Sabbath-School Work, 1869.

Hodge, Charles. *Systematic Theology.* 3 vols. Grand Rapids: Eerdmans, 1973.

Hoeksema, Herman. *The Clark-Van Til Controversy.* Unicoi, Tenn.: The Trinity Foundation, 1995.

Horton, Michael S. *Covenant and Eschatology: The Divine Drama.* Louisville: Westminster John Knox Press, 2002.

———. "Hellenistic or Hebrew? Open Theism and Reformed Theological Method." *JETS* (June 2002): 317-342.

Jenkins, John I. *Knowledge and Faith in Thomas Aquinas.* Cambridge: Cambridge University Press, 1997.

Jones, W. T. *A History of Western Philosophy.* New York: Harcourt, Brace and Company, 1952.

Klooster, Fred H. *The Incomprehensibility of God in the Orthodox Presbyterian Conflict.* Franeker, Netherlands: T. Wever, 1951.

Ko, Young Woon. *The Beauty of Balance: A Theological Inquiry into Paradox.* New York: University Press of America, 2010.

Lane, William L. *The Gospel of Mark.* Grand Rapids: Eerdmans, 1974.

Lewis, C.S. *Mere Christianity.* New York: Harper Collins, 2001.

Lewis, Gordon R. "God, Attributes of." In *Evangelical Dictionary of Theology*, edited by Walter A. Elwell, 451-459. Grand Rapids: Baker, 1984.

Lundin, Roger. "Beyond the Orphaned First Person." In *The Promise of Hermeneutics*, by Clarence Walhout and Anthony C. Thiselton, 1-62. Grand Rapids: Eerdmans, 1999.

Luther, Martin. *Luther's Works.* Edited by Jaroslav Pelikan and Helmut T. Lehmann. 55 volumes vols. Philadelphia: Muhlenberg Press, 1959.

Mackenzie, Donald. *Christianity—The Paradox of God.* New York: Revell, 1933.

Mackie, J. L. "Evil and Omnipotence." In *The Philosophy of Religion*, edited by Basil Mitchell, 92-104. New York: Oxford University Press, 1971.

Macleod, Donald. *The Person of Christ.* Downers Grove: InterVarsity Press, 1998.

Malherbe, Abraham J. "Mh Genoito in the Diatribe and Paul." *The Harvard Theological Review* 73 (April 1980): 231-240.

Marcel, Gabriel. *Being and Having.* Westminster, UK: Dacre, 1949.

Marston, George. *The Voice of Authority.* Phillipsburg, N.J.: P & R, 1960.

Martinich, A.P. "Identity and Trinity." *The Journal of Religion* 58, no. 2 (April 1978): 169-181.

Mascall, E. L. *Via Media.* Greenwich, Conn.: Seabury Press, 1957.

McCune, Roland. *A Systematic Theology of Biblical Christianity.* Allen Park, Mich.: Detroit Baptist Theological Seminary, 2009.

Minutes of the Fifteenth General Assembly of the Orthodox Presbyterian Church. Philadelphia: OPC, 1948.

Moo, Douglas. *The Epistle to the Romans* in NICNT. Grand Rapids: Eerdmans, 1996.

Moreland, J. P. *Scaling the Secular City: A Defense of Christianity.* Grand Rapids: Baker, 1987.

Morris, Leon. *The Epistle to the Romans* in Pillar. Grand Rapids: Eerdmans, 1997.

Morris, Thomas V. *The Logic of God Incarnate.* Ithaca: Cornell University Press, 1986.

Muether, John R. *Cornelius Van Til: Reformed Apologist and Churchman.* Phillipsburg, N.J.: P&R, 2008.

Muller, Richard A. *Post-Reformation Reformed Dogmatics.* 2 vols. Grand Rapids: Baker, 1987.

———. *The Study of Theology.* Grand Rapids: Zondervan, 1991.

———. "The Study of Theology Revisited: A Response to John Frame." *Westminster Theological Journal* 56, no. 2 (Fall 1994): 409-417.

Murphree, Jon Tal. *Divine Paradoxes: A Finite View of an Infinite God.* Camp Hill, Pa.: Christian Publications, 1998.

Murray, John. *The Collected Writings of John Murray.* Carlisle, Pa.: Banner of Truth, 1982.

Newman, Barklay M., and Eugene A. Nida. *A Translator's Handbook on Paul's Letter to the Romans.* New York: United Bible Societies, 1973.

Oberman, Heiko A. *The Harvest of Medieval Theology.* Grand Rapids: Baker, 1963.

O'Collins, Gerald. "The Holy Trinity: The State of the Question." In *The Trinity*, edited by Stephen T. Davis, Daniel Kendall and Gerald O'Collins, 1-25. Oxford: Oxford University Press, 1999.

———. *The Tripersonal God.* New York: Paulist Press, 1999.

Oren, Michael B. *Six Days of War.* New York: Presidio Press, 2003.

Osborne, Grant. *The Hermeneutical Spiral.* 2nd edition. Downers Grove: InterVarsity, 2006.

Packer, J. I. *Evangelism and the Sovereignty of God.* Downers Grove: InterVarsity, 2008.

Padgett, Alan G. "Eternity as Relative Timelessness." In *God and Time: Four Views*, edited by Gregory E. Ganssle, 92-110. Downers Grove: InterVarsity, 2001.

Parker, Francis H. "Traditional Reason and Modern Reason." In *Faith and Philosophy*, edited by Alvin Plantinga, 37-50. Grand Rapids: Eerdmans, 1964.

Bibliography

Parunak, H. Van Dyke. "A Semantic Survey of NHM." *Biblica* 56, no. 4 (1975): 512-532.

Peterson, David G. *The Acts of the Apostles.* Grand Rapids: Eerdmans, 2009.

Peterson, Robert A. and Michael Williams. *Why I Am Not an Arminian.* Downers Grove: InterVarsity, 2004.

Pettegrew, Larry D. "Is There Knowledge In the Most High?" *Master's Seminary Journal* 12, no. 2 (Fall 2001): 133-148.

Pinnock, Clark H. *Most Moved Mover: A Theology of God's Openness.* Grand Rapids: Baker, 2001.

———. "Systematic Theology." In *The Openness of God*, 101-125. Downers Grove: InterVarsity, 1994.

Pinnock, Clark H. "The Destruction of the Finally Impenitent." *Criswell Theological Review* 4, no. 2 (Spring 1990): 243-259.

———. "There is Room For Us: A Reply to Bruce Ware." *JETS* 45, no. 2 (June 2002): 213-220.

Piper, John. *The Justification of God: an Exegetical and Theological Study of Romans 9:1-23.* Grand Rapids: Baker, 1993.

Plantinga, Alvin C. *God, Freedom, and Evil.* Grand Rapids: Eerdmans, 1974.

———. *Warranted Christian Belief.* New York: Oxford, 2000.

Plummer, Alfred. *A Critical and Exegetical Commentary on the Gospel According to St. Luke.* Edinburgh: T. & T. Clark, 1901.

Poole, Reginald Lane. *Illustrations of the History of Medieval Thought.* London: Williams and Norgate, 1884.

Rakestraw, Robert V. "James 2:14-26: Does James Contradict the Pauline Soteriology?" *Criswell Theological Review* 1 (Fall 1986): 31-50.

Ramsey, Ian T. *Models and Mystery.* New York: Oxford University Press, 1964.

Rescher, Nicholas. *Paradoxes: Their Roots, Range, and Resolution.* Chicago: Open Court, 2001.

Reymond, Robert. *A New Systematic Theology of the Christian Faith.* Nashville: Thomas Nelson, 1998.

Rice, Richard. "Biblical Support for a New Perspective." In *The Openness of God*, 11-58. Downers Grove: InterVarsity, 1994.

———. *The Openness of God.* Nashville: Review and Herald Publishing Association, 1980.

Richards, Jay Wesley. "Is the Doctrine of the Incarnation Coherent?" In *Unapologetic Apologetics*, edited by William A. Demski and Jay Wesley Richards, 131-143. Downers Grove: InterVarsity, 2001.

Ross, Hugh. *Beyond the Cosmos.* Colorado Springs: NavPress, 1996.

Sahl, Joseph G. "The Impeccability of Jesus Christ." *Bibliotheca Sacra* 140 (January 1983): 11-20.

Sainsbury, R. M. *Paradoxes.* New York: Cambridge, 2009.

Sanders, John. "Be Wary of Ware." *JETS* 45, no. 2 (June 2002): 221-232.

———. "A Tale of Two Providences." *Ashland Theological Journal* 33 (2001): 41-57.

Sanders, John. "Divine Providence and the Openness of God." In *Perspectives on the Doctrine of God*, 196-240. Nashville: Broadman & Holman, 2008.

———. *The God Who Risks: A Theology of Providence.* Downers Grove: InterVarsity, 1998.

———. "Historical Considerations." In *The Openness of God*, 59-100. Downers Grove: InterVarsity, 1994.

———. *No Other Name: An Investigation into the the Destiny of the Unevangelized.* Grand Rapids: Eerdmans, 1992.

Schaff, Philip, and Henry Wace, *A Select Library of Nicene and Post-Nicene Fathers of the Christian Church.* Translated by Charles Lett Feltoe. Vol. 12. Grand Rapids: Eerdmans, 1956.

Scheeben, Matthias Joseph. *The Mysteries of Christianity.* Translated by Cyril Vollert. St. Louis: B. Herder, 1946.

Schreiner, Thomas R. *Romans* in Baker Exegetical Commentaries. Grand Rapids: Baker, 1998.

Shedd, William G. T. *Dogmatic Theology.* Nashville: Thomas Nelson, 1980.

Silva, Moisés. *Biblical Words and Their Meaning.* Grand Rapids: Zondervan, 1994.

Simeon, Charles. *Horae homileticae.* Vol. 15. London: Holdsworth and Ball, 1833.

Simpson, J. A., and E. S. C. Weiner. *The Oxford English Dictionary.* Vol. 1. Oxford: Clarendon, 1989.

Snoberger, Mark A. "Engaging the Enemy ... But on Whose Terms? An Assessment of Responses to the Charge of Anti-Intellectualism." *DBSJ* 8 (Fall 2003): 69-84.

Sproul, R. C. *Chosen by God.* Wheaton: Tyndale, 1986.

———. *The Mystery of the Holy Spirit.* Wheaton: Tyndale, 1994.

Sproul, R. C., Jr. *Almighty Over All.* Grand Rapids: Baker, 1999.

Studer, Basilio. *Mystery.* Vol. 1, in *Encyclopedia of the Early Church*, edited by Angelo Di Berardino, translated by Adrian Walford, no page number. New York: Oxford University Press, 1992.

Surin, Kenneth. "Evil, problem of." In *The Blackwell Encyclopedia of Modern Christian Thought*, by Alister E. McGrath, 192-199. Oxford: Basil Blackwell, 1995.

Swinburne, Richard. *The Coherence of Theism*. Oxford: Clarendon, 1977.

Talbert, Layton. *Beyond Suffering*. Greenville, S.C.: BJU Press, 2007.

———. *Not by Chance*. Greenville, S.C.: BJU Press, 2001.

Thiselton, Anthony C. "The Bible and Today's Readers: 'The Two Horizons' and 'Pre-Understanding.'" In *Thiselton on Hermeneutics*, 441-461. Grand Rapids: Eerdmans, 2006.

———. *The Two Horizons*. Grand Rapids: Eerdmans, 1980.

Turner, Nigel. *A Grammar of New Testament Greek: Syntax*. Vol. 3. Edinburgh: T. & T. Clark, 1963.

Van Til, Cornelius. *A Christian Theory of Knowledge*. Grand Rapids: Baker, 1969.

———. *In Defense of the Faith*. Vol. 5. Philadelphia: P&R, 1978.

———. *Junior Systematics*. Philadelphia: Theological Seminary of the Reformed Episcopal Church, 1940.

Van Til, Cornelius. *Letter of Dr. Cornelius Van Til to Dr. Gordon H. Clark*. December 5, 1938. http://www.pcahistory.org/findingaids/clark/cvtletter.html (accessed April 29, 2010).

Vanhoozer, Kevin J. *Is There a Meaning in This Text?* Grand Rapids: Zondervan, 1998.

Walls, Jerry L. and Joseph R. Dongell. *Why I Am Not a Calvinist*. Downers Grove: InterVarsity, 2004.

Ware, Bruce A. *God's Lesser Glory*. Wheaton: Crossway, 2000.

Warfield, Benjamin B. *The Power of God Unto Salvation.* Philadelphia: Presbyterian Board of Publication and Sabbath-School Work, 1903.

———. *The Right of Systematic Theology.* Edinburgh: T. & T. Clark, 1897.

Watson, JoAnn Ford. "Contemporary Views on the Problem of Evil." *Ashland Theological Journal*, 1992: 27-34.

Wellum, Stephen J. "Divine Sovereignty-Omniscience, Inerrancy, And Open Theism: An Evaluation." *JETS* 45, no. 2 (June 2002): 257-278.

———. "The Importance of the Nature of Divine Sovereignty for Our View of Scripture." *Southern Baptist Journal of Theology*, Summer 2000: 76-91.

Wierenga, Edward R. "Timelessness out of Mind: On the Alledged Incoherence of Divine Timelessness." In *God and Time: Essays on the Divine Nature*, edited by Gregory E. Ganssle and David M. Woodruff, 153-164. Oxford: Oxford University Press, 2002.

Youngblood, Ronald F. "1, 2 Samuel." In *The Expositor's Bible Commentary*, edited by Tremper Longman III and David E. Garland, 21-614. Grand Rapids: Zondervan, 2009.

The 'Theological Legacy of Lesslie Newbigin' chapter is taken from the book *Ecumenical and Eclectic: Studies in Honour of Alan P.F. Sell* published by Paternoster.

Paternoster is the theological imprint of Authentic Media, and publishes books across a wide range of disciplines including biblical studies, theology, mission, church leadership and pastoral issues.

You can sign up to the Paternoster newsletter to hear about new releases by scanning below:

Online:
authenticmedia.co.uk/paternoster

Follow us:

www.ingramcontent.com/pod-product-compliance
Lightning Source LLC
Chambersburg PA
CBHW052059230426
43662CB00036B/1696